JAMESTOWN EDUCATION

SIGNATURE READING

LEVEL
K

Mc Graw Hill **Glencoe**

New York, New York   Columbus, Ohio   Chicago, Illinois   Peoria, Illinois   Woodland Hills, California

JAMESTOWN EDUCATION

Reviewers

Marsha Miller, Ed.D
Reading Specialist
Elgin High School
1200 Maroon Drive
Elgin, IL 60120

Kati Pearson
Orange County Public Schools
Literacy Coordinator
Carver Middle School
4500 West Columbia Street
Orlando, FL 32811

Lynda Pearson
Assistant Principal
Reading Specialist
Lied Middle School
5350 Tropical Parkway
Las Vegas, NV 89130

Suzanne Zweig
Reading Specialist/Consultant
Sullivan High School
6631 N. Bosworth
Chicago, IL 60626

Cover Image: Donald E. Carroll/Getty Images

Glencoe

The **McGraw·Hill** Companies

ISBN: 0-07-861730-8 (Pupil's Edition)
ISBN: 0-07-861731-6 (Annotated Teacher's Edition)

Send all queries to:
Glencoe/McGraw-Hill
8787 Orion Place
Columbus, OH 43240-4027

5 6 7 8 9 113 09 08

Contents

How to Use This Book

Working Through the Lessons

The following descriptions will help you work your way through the lessons in this book.

Building Background will help you get ready to read. In this section you might begin a chart, discuss a question, or learn more about the topic of the selection.

Vocabulary Builder will help you start thinking about—and using—the selection vocabulary. You might draw a diagram and label it with vocabulary words, make a word map, match vocabulary words to their synonyms or antonyms, or use the words to predict what might happen in the selection.

Strategy Builder will introduce you to the strategy that you will use to read the selection. First you will read a definition of the strategy. Then you will see an example of how to use it. Often, you will be given ways to better organize or visualize what you will be reading.

Strategy Break will appear within the reading selection. It will show you how to apply the strategy you just learned to the first part of the selection.

Strategy Follow-up will ask you to apply the same strategy to the second part of the selection. Most of the time, you will work on your own to complete this section. Sometimes, however, you might work with a partner or a group of classmates.

Personal Checklist questions will ask you to rate how well you did in the lesson. When you finish totaling your score, you will enter it on the graphs on page 215.

Vocabulary Check will follow up on the work you did in the Vocabulary Builder. After you total your score, you will enter it on page 215.

Strategy Check will follow up on the strategy work that you did in the lesson. After you total your score, you will enter it on page 215.

Comprehension Check will check your understanding of the selection. After you total your score, you will enter it on page 215.

Extending will give ideas for activities that are related to the selection. Some activities will help you learn more about the topic of the selection. Others might ask you to respond to the selection by dramatizing, writing, or drawing something.

Resources such as books, recordings, videos, and Web sites will help you complete the Extending activities.

Graphing Your Progress

The information and graphs on pages 214–215 will help you track your progress as you work through this book. **Graph 1** will help you record your scores for the Personal Checklist and the Vocabulary, Strategy, and Comprehension Checks. **Graph 2** will help you track your overall progress across the book. You'll be able to see your areas of strength, as well as any areas that could use improvement. You and your teacher can discuss ways to work on those areas.

LESSON ⓵ Solo Flight (Part 1)

Building Background

There is an old saying that states, "There's a first time for everything." Parents often use this saying when talking to a child who is facing a new situation or challenge. We all do things that are new in our lives. For example, the first day of school is a hurdle everyone faces, as is riding a bicycle for the first time. Think back to the first time you faced a new situation or task on your own. Choose an experience that was particularly memorable. Was it the first time you cooked dinner by yourself? The first time you took a bus, train, or plane without someone to help you? The first time you gave a speech? Write about your experience on the lines below. Be sure to explain the reason for and events leading up to the experience, as well as your feelings before, during, and after the experience.

_____

_____

_____

_____

_____

_____

decelerated

fuselage

hangared

rudder

sensation

solo

tethered

Vocabulary Builder

1. The words in the margin are from Part 1 of "Solo Flight." Study the words, and then use them to complete the sentences below. If you don't know the meaning of a word, find it in the story and try to use context to figure it out. If using context doesn't help, look up the word in a dictionary.

2. Save your work. You will refer to it again in the Vocabulary Check.

   a. The plane was _____ in a huge building at the airport.

   b. I didn't have a date for the dance, so I decided to go _____.

   c. When I slammed on the brakes, the car _____ quickly.

   d. Passengers and cargo are carried in the _____, or body, of an airplane.

e. In boats and planes, the pilot uses the _____ to steer.

f. We _____ our pony to the fence with a strong rope so it wouldn't get away.

g. In my dream, I felt the thrilling _____ of flying through the air.

Strategy Builder

Summarizing a Story

- Every story has three major elements: characters, setting, and plot. The **characters** are the people or animals who perform the story's action. The **setting** is where and when the story takes place. The **plot** is the series of events that move the action forward.

- Often, a story's plot revolves a problem that the main character or characters must solve. Throughout the story, they try different solutions until they come up with the one that works—the end result. Once the problem is solved, the story usually draws to its **conclusion**, or ending.

- Every story is told from a particular point of view. The **point of view** reveals the thoughts and feelings of the **narrator**—the one who is telling the story. When the narrator is a character in the story, that story is told from a **first-person point of view**. In "Solo Flight," for example, the first-person narrator is a character named Keisha. She uses the words *I, me, my,* and *mine* to describe what is happening in the story.

- Since "Solo Flight" is a longer story, you will read Part 1 in this lesson and Part 2 in Lesson 2. Sometimes when you read a longer story, it helps to stop once in a while and summarize what you've read. When you **summarize**, you briefly describe who is in the story, where it takes place, and what has happened so far.

- Summarizing helps you keep track of the most important details in a story. It also helps you predict what might happen next. In this lesson, you will read a sample summary in the Strategy Break. In the Strategy Follow-up, you will have a chance to write a summary of your own. Then in Lesson 2, you will use your summaries to predict what might happen in Part 2 of "Solo Flight."

Solo Flight (Part 1)

by Allen B. Ury

As you read Part 1 of "Solo Flight," think about how you might summarize it. Underline details that describe the setting and main characters. Also underline the main events of the plot. When you get to the Strategy Break, you will have a chance to compare what you've underlined to the sample summary provided.

Ever dream that you're flying like a superhero? That's what riding in a sailplane feels like. It's just you and the wind, soaring through the sky free and easy like some huge, magnificent eagle. It's a **sensation** most kids can only dream about.

I'm one of the lucky ones. My dad has taken me up in sailplanes since I was old enough to wear a crash helmet. I've probably logged more hours in the air than most kids have logged on their bicycles. If I could, I'd spend my whole life riding the air currents . . . and I almost did.

It was the end of June. The big Fourth of July weekend was coming up, and it was also going to be my birthday. Mom and Dad had a special present in store for me. They were going to let me take my first **solo** flight. Although I'd flown our sailplane countless times with Dad in the cockpit, this would be the first time I'd be going up all by myself.

"Are you sure I'm old enough?" I asked anxiously when they told me of their plans.

"It's not a question of age, Keisha, but experience," my father replied calmly. "Anyone can fly a sailplane if they have the right training. Personally, I'd rather have *you* at the controls than half the adult pilots I know!"

"You'll do fine, Keisha," my mother assured me. Mom was quite a glider pilot herself. In fact, my parents met while soaring past each other at five thousand feet! "Of course, if you don't want to . . ."

"No, I do!" I quickly cut in. "It's just that this kind of caught me by surprise, that's all."

"I remember the first time I soloed," my dad said, his eyes suddenly taking on that weird, faraway look parents have when they start talking about the past. "I wasn't much older than you. It made me feel stronger and freer than I ever had in my life. It's a feeling you're not going to forget for as long as you live."

As it turned out, my dad was absolutely right.

"Ready to go, Keisha?" my mother called from the foot of the stairs.

"In a second!" I yelled back. I was in my bedroom getting myself prepared both physically and mentally for my big day. I'd already spent an entire hour putting together my wardrobe, and now I was standing in front of the full-length mirror on my bedroom door, checking myself out. I was wearing my lucky green shirt, my lucky jeans with the holes in the knees, my lucky leather belt with the silver belt buckle, my lucky red socks I'd worn when I pitched my one and only no-hitter, and, of course, my lucky running shoes with barely any tread left on them. There was only one thing missing.

Going over to my dresser, I opened the small jewelry box on top of it. Inside, nestled among the various pins, commemorative coins, and other assorted odds and ends I'd collected over the years, was a set of silver pilot's wings. They had belonged to my grandfather—my dad's dad—who died before I was even born. My grandfather had been an Air Force fighter pilot during the Vietnam War. In 1966, at the age of thirty-five, he was shot down and killed by a North Vietnamese antiaircraft missile. My dad, who was only ten years old at the time, was given these wings at his father's funeral. For some reason, the wings had not been pinned to his dad's uniform when he was buried. My father never wore these wings himself, but thought I might want to when I became a real pilot. This seemed like the perfect time.

I lifted the small metal wings from the box and carefully pinned them to my left breast pocket. Then I checked myself out again in the mirror. The wings hung straight and true, just like I'm sure my grandfather had always flown. I gave myself a crisp salute, then turned and headed out the door.

"So what are we waiting for?" I shouted as I thundered down the stairs. "Let's fly!"

Our sailplane was **hangared** at the Sky Harbor airport, which is about fifteen minutes north of town. It was

a small private airfield used mostly by recreational fliers on weekends and holidays. This being the Fourth of July weekend, it was as busy as a toy store on Christmas Eve.

The weather was perfect for gliding. The sky was clear and the air temperature was in the mid-eighties. There was a steady ten-mile-per-hour wind blowing in from the west, and the humidity was right around sixty percent. I couldn't have asked for better conditions.

Mom and Dad had already arranged for the plane to be ready for us when we arrived. Climbing out of our car, I saw our glider, the *Sky Dancer,* sitting on the grass **tethered** to the single-engined tow plane that would lift it into the sky.

For those of you who've never seen a sailplane, they're incredibly beautiful, graceful creations. The *Sky Dancer,* for instance, had a narrow, bullet-shaped cockpit, much like a teardrop. Behind that, her **fuselage** extended back thirty-five feet, tapering into a thin, almost fragile-looking tail. Her wings spanned nearly forty feet, giving her the lift and stability she needed to stay aloft even without the benefit of a motor. Not designed for combat, transportation, carrying cargo, or any other practical concern, the *Sky Dancer* had one purpose and one purpose only: fun.

"Ready to go, Birthday Girl?" my father asked, giving me a warm pat on the shoulder.

"Let's do it," I said, fitting my helmet, which was painted metallic blue and covered with orange and red stars, over my head.

Five minutes later, I was belted into our sailplane's pilot seat. I gave my father a firm "thumbs-up," and he lowered the bubble-shaped cockpit hatch into place. My heart beating wildly, I watched my parents enter the tow plane parked about thirty feet in front of me. Then my helmet radio crackled into life.

"You reading me, Keisha?" my father asked.

"Loud and clear, Dad," I replied into my helmet's tiny microphone. "Let's get this baby in the air!"

Launching a sailplane is a relatively easy task. The tow plane does ninety percent of the work. As the glider pilot, all I had to do was release my brakes and let Dad and Mom use their rented plane to tow me onto the runway and up into the wild blue yonder. My only challenge was keeping my **rudder** straight.

A few minutes later, we were at almost 5,000 feet and traveling at about 100 miles per hour—slow for an airplane, but fast for a glider.

"Ready to solo, Birthday Girl?" Mom asked over the radio. "I'll bet you're excited!"

My hands were shaking and my throat suddenly felt dry. I took a deep breath, then answered back. "That's a big ten-four. Ready to release."

Releasing the towline was my job. Taking a deep breath, I reached forward and pulled the lever that disconnected my aircraft from the nylon umbilical cord connecting me to my parents' plane. I heard a clunk as the hook let go, then was thrown forward in my chair as the sailplane instantly **decelerated** by about twenty miles per hour. Looking straight ahead, I saw Mom and Dad's plane quickly pull away as it suddenly found itself free of its five-hundred-pound load.

 Stop here for the Strategy Break.

Strategy Break

As you read, did you underline the information that you would include in a summary? If you did, see if your information matches this:

This story takes place over the Fourth of July weekend. It's Keisha's birth-day, and as a special present, her parents are going to let her take her first solo flight in a sailplane. Keisha is nervous, but she's also excited. As she dresses for the flight, she puts on her lucky shirt, jeans, belt, socks, and shoes. She also puts on the pilot's wings that belonged to her grandfather, an Air Force pilot who was shot down and killed in Vietnam.

At the Sky Harbor airport, Keisha gets into **Sky Dancer**, her parents get into their tow plane, and they all take off. When they are about 5,000 feet up, Keisha is ready to go solo. She releases the towline, and her parents' plane pulls away.

As you continue reading, keep paying attention to the events in this story. When you get to the Strategy Follow-up, you will summarize what has happened so far.

➡️ **Go on reading to see what happens.**

Now I have to tell you there are many differences between riding in a sailplane as opposed to a regular, engine-powered aircraft. The first thing you notice right away is the sound. There isn't any. In a commercial jet—the kind most people fly in—there's always the dull roar of the engines in the background and a constant vibration you can feel in every bone in your body. In small, private planes, like the tow plane my mom and dad were in, the engines are so loud they're almost deafening, and the vibrations can be so bad they make your teeth chatter.

But sailplanes aren't like that. When you're in a glider, the silence is unreal. There's no roar of jets. No buzz of internal combustion engines. No vibrations to remind you that the only thing keeping you from tumbling to earth is this big, complicated machine with hundreds of parts, any one of which could fail.

This incredible silence was exactly what I was hearing as the tow plane circled back toward the airport and I was left to fly all on my own. For several moments, I just sat back and enjoyed the absolute nothingness of it all. This, I imagined, is what hawks must feel as they circle the skies in search of prey. It's as if you, the sky, and the entire universe are one and the same.

Sitting up, I turned my control wheel to the right, causing my sailplane to bank slightly in that direction. As it turned and I tilted sideways, I scanned the ground for likely thermals, columns of warm air rising off the earth. It's these natural updrafts that allow glider pilots to keep themselves aloft for long periods of time even in gentle winds. Because darker areas—like parking lots—absorb sunlight and therefore heat the air around them, you always want to look for dark or paved patches of earth when flying a sailplane. Fly over one of these, and you can gain a few hundred feet without even trying.

As I mentioned earlier, this was a very bright, sunny day, so I had no problem finding all the thermals I needed. In fact, even after a full hour of circling the Sky Harbor area, I was still managing to keep the *Sky Dancer* at between 4,000 and 4,500 feet above sea level. Heck, the way things were going, I could probably stay aloft all the way till sundown if I wanted to. After that, the air would cool and I'd naturally find myself drifting back to earth.

However, my parents had no intention of letting me stay in the air that long. In fact, exactly one hour after the towline was released, my helmet radio came to life with the familiar sound of my father's voice.

"All right, Birthday Girl, it's time to bring *Sky Dancer* home," he said.

"Aw, Dad, do I have to?" I protested. I was having so much fun, I really didn't want to quit.

"We're going over to the Jacksons for a Fourth of July barbecue. Don't you remember?" he countered. "We're supposed to be there in an hour."

"Ten-four," I groaned in disappointment.

I adjusted my wing flaps to direct the sailplane earthward and at the same time began looking for bright patches of earth around which I'd find downdrafts to help bring me down.

Keeping a close eye on my altimeter, I suddenly noticed the oddest thing. No matter what I did to lower my altitude, the sailplane refused to descend below 4,000 feet!

"Come on, Keisha," my father said with some irritation. "I know you like it up there, but you can't stay there forever."

"I'm trying!" I radioed back. "But I seem to be caught in some kind of big thermal. I can't seem to lose altitude."

"Try to turn yourself out of it," my mother advised. "Look for bright patches of earth."

"That's what I'm doing!" I insisted.

Indeed, for the next fifteen minutes, I used every trick I knew to bring myself down, but nothing worked. In fact, I actually ended up gaining more than 200 feet! ●

Strategy Follow-up

Now it's your turn to summarize. Review the second part of this selection if necessary, and then summarize it below. (Or use a separate sheet of paper if you need more room to write.) Include only the most important events, and skip unnecessary details.

_____

_____

_____

_____

_____

_____

_____

_____

_____

_____

_____

_____

_____

_____

_____

_____

✓Personal Checklist

Read each question and put a check (✓) in the correct box.

1. How well do you understand what has happened in this story so far?
   - ☐ 3 (extremely well)
   - ☐ 2 (fairly well)
   - ☐ 1 (not well)

2. How well do you understand the problem that Keisha faces?
   - ☐ 3 (extremely well)
   - ☐ 2 (fairly well)
   - ☐ 1 (not well)

3. How well were you able to use what you wrote in Building Background to understand Keisha's feelings about her solo flight?
   - ☐ 3 (extremely well)
   - ☐ 2 (fairly well)
   - ☐ 1 (not well)

4. How well were you able to complete the sentences in the Vocabulary Builder?
   - ☐ 3 (extremely well)
   - ☐ 2 (fairly well)
   - ☐ 1 (not well)

5. In the Strategy Follow-up, how well were you able to summarize the second part of this selection?
   - ☐ 3 (extremely well)
   - ☐ 2 (fairly well)
   - ☐ 1 (not well)

Vocabulary Check

Look back at the work you did in the Vocabulary Builder. Then answer each question by circling the correct letter.

1. What does it mean when you do something solo?
   a. You do it with another person.
   b. You do it for the first time.
   c. You do it by yourself.

2. Which vocabulary word describes a plane that is stored in a building?
   a. hangared
   b. tethered
   c. decelerated

3. Which word has the same meaning as *sensation*?
   a. feeling
   b. numbness
   c. unconsciousness

4. To which part of a plane are the wings attached?
   a. the cockpit
   b. the fuselage
   c. the rudder

5. What is the opposite of *sped up?*
   a. accelerated
   b. quickened
   c. decelerated

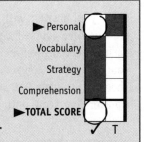

Add the numbers that you just checked to get your total score. (For example, if you checked 3, 2, 3, 2, and 1, your total score would be 11.) Fill in your score here. Then turn to page 215 and transfer your score onto Graph 1.

- ► Personal
- Vocabulary
- Strategy
- Comprehension
- ►TOTAL SCORE

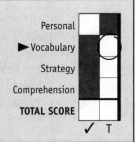

Check your answers with your teacher. Give yourself 1 point for each correct answer, and fill in your Vocabulary score here. Then turn to page 215 and transfer your score onto Graph 1.

- Personal
- ►Vocabulary
- Strategy
- Comprehension
- TOTAL SCORE

Strategy Check

Review the summary that you wrote in the Strategy Follow-up. Also review the selection if necessary. Then answer these questions:

1. Which phrase best describes the setting of the second part of this selection?
    a. the Sky Harbor airport on a warm, sunny day
    b. the cockpit of *Sky Dancer* on a warm, sunny day
    c. up in the air on a warm, sunny day

2. For the first hour that she's in the air, what does Keisha look for?
    a. columns of cool air rising off the earth
    b. columns of warm air rising off the earth
    c. parking lots to land in

3. Why does Keisha's father tell her that she needs to bring *Sky Dancer* home?
    a. Her fuel supply is running low.
    b. He only paid for an hour of air time.
    c. They have a barbecue to attend in an hour.

4. When Keisha tells her parents that she can't lose altitude, what does her mother tell her to do?
    a. put her foot on the brake and decelerate
    b. turn herself out of it and look for bright patches of earth
    c. let some air out of the fuselage

5. What happens as a result of Keisha's attempts to lose altitude?
    a. She ends up gaining 200 feet.
    b. She doesn't lose any altitude at all.
    c. She ends up losing 200 feet.

Comprehension Check

Review the selection if necessary. Then answer these questions:

1. For what occasion do Keisha's parents decide that she should fly solo?
    a. her birthday
    b. the Fourth of July
    c. the anniversary of her grandfather's death

2. What does Keisha put on before leaving her bedroom?
    a. her lucky necklace
    b. a pin from her mother
    c. her grandfather's pilot's wings

3. How is Keisha's sailplane lifted into the air?
    a. The owner of the hangar tows it up with a large plane.
    b. Her parents tow it up with a rented plane.
    c. She uses the sailplane's small engine to launch it.

4. Why are thermals important to sailplane pilots?
    a. They can be used to lower the sailplane.
    b. They make the sailplane very warm.
    c. They are used to keep the sailplane aloft.

5. What is Keisha's problem at the end of Part 1?
    a. The weather is becoming stormy.
    b. She has engine trouble.
    c. She can't get any lower, only higher.

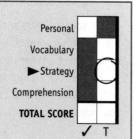

Check your answers with your teacher. Give yourself 1 point for each correct answer, and fill in your Strategy score here. Then turn to page 215 and transfer your score onto Graph 1.

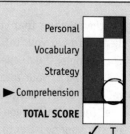

Check your answers with your teacher. Give yourself 1 point for each correct answer, and fill in your Comprehension score here. Then turn to page 215 and transfer your score onto Graph 1.

Extending

Choose one or more of these activities:

WRITE A JOURNAL ENTRY

Imagine that you are flying a sailplane yourself. What would be on your mind? What emotions would you be feeling? Write a journal entry for the day on which you fly a sailplane for the first time. Write from the first-person point of view. Describe your experiences and your reactions to them.

FIND OUT MORE ABOUT SAILPLANES

Using the resources listed on this page or ones you find yourself, learn more about sailplanes and how to fly them. Or, for another resource, look under *Aircraft Instruction* in your local telephone directory and see if there is a flight school in your area. If you can, interview a flight instructor and find out as much as possible about sailplanes and the necessary requirements for flying them. (For example, what are the age and height requirements?) Report your findings in an oral presentation. If possible, include an audio- or videotaped interview with the flight instructor.

Resources

Books

Lambie, Jack. *Building and Flying Sailplanes and Gliders.* Tab Books, 1980.

Morrow, Linda, and Ray Morrow. *Go Fly a Sailplane: An Introduction to Soaring.* Macmillian, 1981.

Wander, Robert. *Learning to Fly Gliders: A Flight-Training Manual and Syllabus.* Soaring Books, 1993.

Whelan, Robert F. *Cloud Dancing: Your Introduction to Gliding and Motorless Flight.* Rainbow Books, 1996.

Web Sites

http://travel.howstuffworks.com/glider.htm
This site offers an explanation of how gliders, or sailplanes, work.

http://www.sailplanes.com/
This Web site provides information and links related to sailplanes.

Video/DVD

Cleared to Land! Westmoreland Productions, 1994.

Solo Flight (Part 2)

Building Background

from "Solo Flight" (Part 1):

"All right, Birthday Girl, it's time to bring Sky Dancer *home," he said.*

"Aw, Dad, do I have to?" I protested. I was having so much fun, I really didn't want to quit.

"We're going over to the Jacksons for a Fourth of July barbecue. Don't you remember?" he countered. "We're supposed to be there in an hour."

"Ten-four," I groaned in disappointment.

I adjusted my wing flaps to direct the sailplane earthward and at the same time began looking for bright patches of earth around which I'd find downdrafts to help bring me down.

Keeping a close eye on my altimeter, I suddenly noticed the oddest thing. No matter what I did to lower my altitude, the sailplane refused to descend below 4,000 feet!

"Come on, Keisha," my father said with some irritation. "I know you like it up there, but you can't stay there forever."

"I'm trying!" I radioed back. "But I seem to be caught in some kind of big thermal. I can't seem to lose altitude."

"Try to turn yourself out of it," my mother advised. "Look for bright patches of earth."

"That's what I'm doing!" I insisted.

Indeed, for the next fifteen minutes, I used every trick I knew to bring myself down, but nothing worked. In fact, I actually ended up gaining more than 200 feet!

Will Keisha bring *Sky Dancer* home successfully? Read on to find out what happens. Keep summarizing as you read. Your summaries will help you predict what might happen next.

chilled

disconnected

isolation

joyous

panicky

proudly

smiling

terrified

Vocabulary Builder

1. Each word in the margin has a base word, or root word. A **root word** is a complete word by itself. However, you can add other words or word parts to a root word to make new words. For example, *build* is a root word. You can add *re-, -er,* and *-ing* to *build* to make *rebuild, builder,* and *building.* Identifying the root word of an unfamiliar word can sometimes help you figure out the word's meaning.

2. After each boldfaced word on page 19, write its meaning. Then write its root word. (You may have to add or change a letter to make some of the root words.)

3. If you have trouble with any of the meanings or root words, find them in the story and use context to figure them out. If context doesn't help, use a dictionary. The first word has been done for you.

chilled	meaning:	frozen with fear
	root word:	chill
disconnected	meaning:	_____
	root word:	_____
isolation	meaning:	_____
	root word:	_____
joyous	meaning:	_____
	root word:	_____
panicky	meaning:	_____
	root word:	_____
proudly	meaning:	_____
	root word:	_____
terrified	meaning:	_____
	root word:	_____

4. Save your work. You will refer to it again in the Vocabulary Check.

Strategy Builder

Using Summaries to Make Predictions

- In Lesson 1, you summarized Part 1 of "Solo Flight." **Summarizing** helped you keep track of what was happening in the story.

- In this lesson, you will use your summaries to help you make predictions. As you know, a **prediction** is a kind of guess. You can guess what will happen in Part 2 of "Solo Flight" by thinking about what happened in Part 1. Go back and reread the summary that you wrote in Part 1. Then, on the lines below, predict what might happen in Part 2. If you can, include some or all of the vocabulary words in your prediction.

- Don't worry if your prediction doesn't match what actually happens. You'll have chances to make new predictions at the Strategy Breaks.

I predict that in Part 2 of "Solo Flight," _____

_____

_____

_____

Solo Flight (Part 2)

by Allen B. Ury

As you read, look for clues to help you predict what might happen next. Also keep track of the main events. When you get to the Strategy Follow-up, you will use them to summarize Part 2 of "Solo Flight."

Now I was getting scared. All around me I could see other sailplanes rising and falling with no problem at all. At one point, Dad had a friend of his, who was also flying a glider, get in front of me and try to lead me home. Although *his* plane dropped without a problem, the *Sky Dancer* stayed exactly where she was.

"Dad, I don't know what to do," I radioed, my voice choked with panic. "What if I can't come down ever? What if I'm stuck up here for the rest of my life?"

"That's not going to happen," my father assured me. "There must be something wrong with your controls. If nothing else, we can wait till sunset."

And that's exactly what we had to do. For five full hours I circled around and around the Sky Harbor airport, becoming increasingly **panicky** with each passing minute. Hungry, thirsty, and desperately needing to go to the bathroom, I watched from my aerial perch as the sun sank with painful slowness below the western horizon, then finally vanished from sight. All the other gliders had long ago returned to the ground. I was now completely and utterly alone.

"The temperature's dropping really fast," my mother radioed. "It's already fallen ten degrees in the last hour. You should be down in no time."

Hearing this, I banked the *Sky Dancer* as tightly as I could and tried my hardest to put the sailplane into a spiraling dive. But, just as before, the craft absolutely refused to drop below 4,000 feet.

I'm going to be up here forever! I thought, **terrified** out of my mind. *A hundred years from now, I'll finally come down, and all they'll find in the cockpit is an old rotting skeleton!*

An hour later, the sky around me was a sea of stars set against a backdrop of inky blackness. I'd never been in a sailplane at night before—this kind of flying usually wasn't done— and the sense of complete **isolation** could easily drive a person insane. At least in an airplane you always had the noise of the engines to keep your senses stimulated. But up here in a sailplane, with no noise, no light, and virtually no sense of movement, you could quickly begin to feel totally **disconnected** from any sense of reality.

In fact, I was certain I was going stark raving mad when, gazing out through the bubble cockpit, I saw two eyes staring back at me. **Chilled** to the bone, I first told myself that I was either looking at my own reflection in the Plexiglas, or that I was seeing some distorted reflection of the full moon. The problem was, there *was* no moon shining this night, and the eyes were part of a face that was definitely not my own.

As I continued to examine the face gazing back at me, I saw that it belonged to a man in his mid-thirties. His hair was cut in the style of a military crewcut, and his uniform collar bore the bronze oak leaves of an Air Force major.

 Stop here for Strategy Break #1.

Strategy Break #1

1. What do you predict will happen next?_____

_____

_____

2. Why do you think so?_____

_____

_____

3. What clues from the story helped you make your prediction(s)?

_____

_____

Go on reading to see what happens.

It took me a moment or two to realize that I'd seen this face before. In fact, it looked out from several framed photographs back home. It was the face of my very own grandfather.

"What are you doing here?" I asked the ghostly image floating before me. "What do you want from me?"

But rather than respond, the transparent face just continued to hang in the air outside my cockpit. It seemed to be looking through me, just as I was looking through it, and for a brief moment, I wondered which of us was truly the ghost.

Unable to stare at this frightening visage any longer, I glanced down at my controls and saw that I was still holding level at 4,000 feet. And then, as if waking up from a dream, I realized what was happening. My grand-father's spirit was holding me aloft. Maybe it thought it was helping me, or maybe it wanted me to join it in the vast beyond, there was no way to tell. I only knew that I had to get it to release me or I could indeed be stuck up here for the rest of my life.

"Grandfather, it's your grand-daughter, Keisha," I said, struggling to remain calm. "You have to let me go. I want to go home. I want to see my mom and dad. They're worried sick about me. I don't want to die up here. Please, Grandfather, release me."

But the image just continued staring at me, and my altimeter refused to budge. What more could I do?

And then I noticed something about the spirit's uniform. There was something odd about it. Something was missing. The pilot's wings!

 Stop here for Strategy Break #2.

Strategy Break #2

1. What do you predict will happen next?_____

_____

_____

2. Why do you think so?_____

_____

_____

3. What clues from the story helped you make your prediction(s)?

_____

_____

Go on reading to see what happens.

I immediately looked down at the wings pinned to my shirt. Could these be what my grandfather wanted? Could these be why he was keeping me aloft?

Hands shaking, I carefully removed the wings from my shirt. There was no response from the plane. I set the wings down on the floor. Still no change. Finally, I checked my seat belt to make sure the buckle was secure, then unlatched the cockpit canopy and opened it just a crack.

Instantly, a burst of freezing-cold wind hit me in the face, and the shock almost caused me to lose my grip. But I held fast and, with my free hand, scooped the pin off the floor and—sad as I was to lose this one solid reminder of my grandfather's greatness—I tossed the wings out into the night. I saw them glisten in the starlight for a few brief seconds. Then they vanished from sight.

I released the cockpit canopy and let it fall back into place. Then I locked it securely and made sure it wasn't about to come loose. Finally, I glanced back at the front of the cockpit bubble . . . and saw that my grandfather's face had vanished!

Excited, I glanced at my altimeter and saw that the needle was starting to drop—4,000 feet . . . 3,950 feet . . . 3,900 feet . . .

"Sky Harbor control, this is *Sky Dancer!*" I said into my radio. "I'm coming home."

Just then the sky around me lit up with a blinding flash. A ball of fire seemed to be heading right for me . . . then seconds later, it disappeared. Stunned, I wondered if I'd just seen my grandfather's angry ghost.

And then it hit me.

"Fireworks," I said to myself with relief. "It's the Fourth of July fireworks!"

The sky around me continued to explode with **joyous** celebration as I continued my rapid descent. And then, as I turned on my final approach to the Sky Harbor runway, I saw, for the briefest instant, my grandfather's image within the glow of the display's grand finale. His pilot's wings were now pinned **proudly** to his chest. For the first time, he seemed to be **smiling**. As I smiled back, the glow from the fireworks faded out, and my grandfather's ghost disappeared forever. ●

Strategy Follow-up

First go back and look at the predictions that you wrote in this lesson. Do any of them match what actually happened in this selection? Why or why not?

Next, write a brief summary of Part 2 of "Solo Flight." Include only the most important characters, settings, and events.

_____

_____

_____

_____

_____

_____

_____

_____

_____

_____

_____

_____

_____

_____

_____

_____

_____

_____

_____

✓Personal Checklist

Read each question and put a check (✓) in the correct box.

1. How well do you understand how Keisha solves her problem?
   - ☐ 3 (extremely well)
   - ☐ 2 (fairly well)
   - ☐ 1 (not well)

2. How well were you able to use your summary of Part 1 to predict what might happen in Part 2?
   - ☐ 3 (extremely well)
   - ☐ 2 (fairly well)
   - ☐ 1 (not well)

3. How well were you able to complete the activity in the Vocabulary Builder?
   - ☐ 3 (extremely well)
   - ☐ 2 (fairly well)
   - ☐ 1 (not well)

4. How well were you able to summarize Part 2 of "Solo Flight"?
   - ☐ 3 (extremely well)
   - ☐ 2 (fairly well)
   - ☐ 1 (not well)

5. How well do you understand why the image of Keisha's grandfather appears to be smiling at the end of the story?
   - ☐ 3 (extremely well)
   - ☐ 2 (fairly well)
   - ☐ 1 (not well)

Vocabulary Check

Look back at the work you did in the Vocabulary Builder. Then answer each question by circling the correct letter.

1. Which vocabulary word describes how most people feel when they lose control of a situation?
   - a. joyous
   - b. proudly
   - c. panicky

2. Which of these is an example of a joyous occasion?
   - a. a wedding
   - b. a stormy day
   - c. a funeral

3. Keisha feels a sense of isolation in the quiet plane. Which word or phrase best describes isolation?
   - a. aloneness
   - b. happy
   - c. with satisfaction

4. Which meaning of the word *chilled* is used in this story?
   - a. made cold
   - b. frozen with fear
   - c. felt unfriendly

5. What would cause a person to feel disconnected from others?
   - a. a sense of panic
   - b. a sense of isolation
   - c. a sense of pride

Add the numbers that you just checked to get your Personal Checklist score. Fill in your score here. Then turn to page 215 and transfer your score onto Graph 1.

Check your answers with your teacher. Give yourself 1 point for each correct answer, and fill in your Vocabulary score here. Then turn to page 215 and transfer your score onto Graph 1.

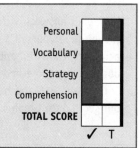

Strategy Check

Review the predictions that you wrote and the summary for Part 2 of "Solo Flight." Then answer these questions:

1. Which clue supported your prediction that Keisha was seeing her grandfather?

   a. I was either looking at my own reflection . . . or a distorted reflection of the full moon.

   b. There was no moon, . . . and the eyes were part of a face that was definitely not my own.

   c. His collar bore the bronze oak leaves of an Air Force major.

2. Which clue would *not* have supported your prediction that Keisha would convince her grandfather to release her?

   a. "I want to see my mom and dad. They're worried sick about me."

   b. The image just continued staring at me, and my altimeter refused to budge.

   c. And then I noticed something . . . was missing. . . . The pilot's wings!

3. After Keisha threw out the wings, she saw a blinding flash. Which clue from the story could have helped you predict what it was?

   a. The air was full of sailplanes.

   b. It was the Fourth of July weekend.

   c. Keisha's dad's friend crashed his glider.

4. When you wrote your summary of Part 2 of "Solo Flight," which new character did you add?

   a. the spirit of Keisha's grandfather

   b. Keisha's mother

   c. Keisha's father

5. Which sentence best summarizes what Keisha's grandfather's spirit wanted?

   a. The spirit wanted to help her stay aloft.

   b. The spirit wanted her to join him in the sky.

   c. The spirit wanted his pilot's wings.

Comprehension Check

Review the selection if necessary. Then answer these questions:

1. Why does Keisha's mother believe that the falling temperatures will help the sailplane come down?

   a. Ice will form on the wings and force the sailplane down.

   b. The plane will run out of fuel.

   c. There will be no more thermals to keep the sailplane aloft.

2. Why would you feel more disconnected in a sailplane at night than in an airplane at night?

   a. A sailplane is smaller than an airplane.

   b. A sailplane has no engine noise and no lights.

   c. A sailplane is lighter than an airplane.

3. Where has Keisha seen the face outside the cockpit before?

   a. in framed photos at home

   b. in the newspaper

   c. at the museum

4. Why do you think Keisha puts the pilot's wings on the floor?

   a. She might think her grandfather's spirit is angry with her for wearing them.

   b. She might think that wearing a pair of wings is keeping her aloft.

   c. She might think that her grandfather's spirit will come and get them.

5. Why does Keisha check her seat belt before she opens the cockpit canopy?

   a. She wants it fastened in case she crashes into her grandfather's spirit.

   b. She doesn't want her grandfather's spirit to snatch her out of the cockpit.

   c. She doesn't want to risk falling out of the cockpit.

Check your answers with your teacher. Give yourself 1 point for each correct answer, and fill in your Strategy score here. Then turn to page 215 and transfer your score onto Graph 1.

Personal
Vocabulary
Strategy
Comprehension
TOTAL SCORE
✓ T

Check your answers with your teacher. Give yourself 1 point for each correct answer, and fill in your Comprehension score here. Then turn to page 215 and transfer your score onto Graph 1.

Personal
Vocabulary
Strategy
Comprehension
TOTAL SCORE

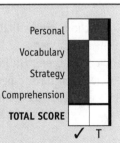

Extending

Choose one or both of these activities:

WRITE YOUR OWN GHOST STORY

Many people enjoy listening to a good ghost story. To write one, you need to let your imagination run wild. Write a ghost story in which a ghost tries to get your attention so you can help him or her. First write some notes about the characters in the story and where it will take place. Then jot down some ideas about what the ghost wants from you. Finally, combine your ideas in either a scary or a funny ghost story. If you'd like, tape record yourself reading the story, and then play it for a group of younger students.

RESEARCH THE VIETNAM WAR

Keisha's grandfather died in air combat during the Vietnam War. That conflict was one of the most controversial wars in U.S. history. Do some research about its causes and outcomes. Use the resources listed on this page if you need a place to start. If you know anyone who served in Vietnam, you might ask for a short interview to get a firsthand account of his or her experiences. Report to the class on what you discover.

Resources

Books

Ashabranner, Brent. *Their Names to Live: What the Vietnam Veterans Memorial Means to America.* Twenty-First Century Books, 1998.

Dorr, Robert F. *Vietnam: The Air War 1965–1975.* Osprey Colour Series. Osprey, 1991.

Gurney, Gene. *Vietnam, the War in the Air: A Pictorial History of the U.S. Air Forces in the Vietnam War—Air Force, Army, Navy, and Marines.* Crown, 1985.

Web Sites

http://www.illyria.com/vnwomen.html
Women who served in the U.S. military during the Vietnam War are the focus of this Web site.

http://www.pbs.org/wgbh/amex/vietnam/index.html
This is the companion Web site to the PBS television series *Vietnam: A Television History.*

http://www.vietvet.org/
The purpose of this Web site is "to honor Vietnam veterans, living and dead, who served their country on either side of the conflict."

CD-ROM

Beyond the Wall: Stories Behind the Vietnam Wall. Twentieth Century Fox Home Entertainment, 1995.

The First Gliders

Building Background

Airplanes have been around much longer than you've been alive. So it's difficult to imagine a time when it took weeks to reach Europe from New York City, or China from San Francisco. Before planes, the only way to make those journeys was by ocean liner. Packages couldn't be delivered overnight to faraway cities, no matter how important they were. Cities and countries felt much farther apart than they do in today's fast-paced world.

How much do you know about the history of flight? Before you begin reading "The First Gliders," work with a partner to complete the chart below. In the first column, list three things that you know about the history of aviation and airplanes. In the second column, list three questions about the history of flight that you hope the selection will answer. When you finish "The First Gliders," you will fill in the last column of the chart.

The History of Flight

K (What I **K**now)	W (What I **W**ant to Know)	L (What I **L**earned)
1. 2. 3.	1. 2. 3.	1. 2. 3.

drag

engineer

gasoline engines

glider

gravity

lift

ornithopter

pilot

variometer

Vocabulary Builder

1. The words in the margin are all related to the topic of flight. Words that are all related to a particular topic are called **specialized vocabulary** words. Knowing what these words mean before you read the selection will help you understand it better.

2. Match each specialized vocabulary word in Column 1 to its definition in Column 2. Use a dictionary if you need help.

drag	person who plans and builds aircraft
engineer	force that pulls objects toward Earth
glider	force that holds an aircraft back
gravity	instrument that measures the rate at which gliders climb or sink
lift	person who flies an aircraft
pilot	force that moves an aircraft upward
variometer	motorless aircraft

3. Save your work. You will refer to it again in the Vocabulary Check.

Strategy Builder

Following Sequence While You Read

- **Nonfiction** is writing that gives facts and information about a particular subject, or topic. The **topic** is what a piece of writing is all about. The topic is usually given in the **title** of a selection, as it is in "The First Gliders."

- When writing nonfiction, authors usually have a specific purpose in mind. For example, when authors write to give facts and information about a particular topic, their purpose is to **inform**. If authors write to give their opinion about something, and try convince others to share that opinion, their purpose is to **persuade**. If they write to describe how they feel about an experience—such as attending a sporting event or watching a sunrise—their purpose is to **express**. If they want to make readers smile, laugh, or be surprised, their purpose is to **entertain**. As you will see, the author's purpose for writing "The First Gliders" is to inform.

- Every piece of nonfiction follows a particular pattern of organization. The most common patterns are listed in the margin. In order to describe the first flying machines in the order in which they were developed, the author of "The First Gliders" uses the pattern of **sequence**, or chronological order. To help you keep track of that sequence, she uses **signal words** such as *then, finally,* and *on December 17, 1903.*

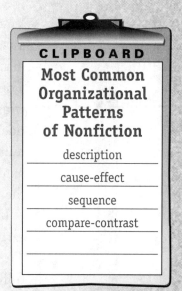

CLIPBOARD

Most Common Organizational Patterns of Nonfiction

| description |
| cause-effect |
| sequence |
| compare-contrast |
| |

- In order to track a selection's sequence of events more clearly, you can use a **time line**. For example, the time line below tracks the development of the bicycle. Notice how the major events are arranged from left to right.

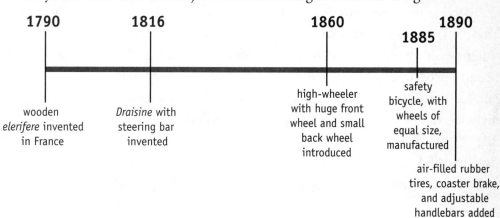

1790   **1816**   **1860**   **1890**
                                         1885

wooden *elerifere* invented in France

Draisine with steering bar invented

high-wheeler with huge front wheel and small back wheel introduced

safety bicycle, with wheels of equal size, manufactured

air-filled rubber tires, coaster brake, and adjustable handlebars added

The First Gliders

by Phyllis J. Perry

As you read the first part of this selection, apply some of the strategies that you just learned. Keep track of the major events that led to the modern glider. You may want to underline any signal words that you find.

From earliest times, people have yearned to fly. There are many stories about attempts at flight using wings made out of feathers. One of the most famous legends is that of Daedalus and his son, Icarus, who were held captive on the Greek island of Crete. In this legend, as they try to escape on their handcrafted wings, the hot sun melts the wax holding the feathers in Icarus's wings, and he falls into the sea.

Another famous story tells of an English monk named Oliver of Malmesbury. The monk is said to have jumped from a tower using homemade wings in 1020. His attempt to fly, however, failed.

Artist and inventor Leonardo da Vinci, who lived from 1452 to 1519, included among his inventions a machine that he called an **ornithopter**. This air machine resembled a bird's wings in shape and was powered by the rider's leg and arm muscles. But humans were unable to pedal and flap hard enough to lift both themselves and the heavy flying machine into the sky.

It's not surprising that so many early flight experiments were clumsy. These early experimenters did not fully understand the forces that affect the flight of an aircraft: **gravity**, **drag**, and **lift**.

It was in 1804, while experimenting with kites, that a British scientist, Sir George Cayley, discovered that air must be forced over a wing to create lift. With this new understanding, Cayley attached a kite to a long stick, added a movable tail, and put a small balancing weight at the front. Cayley's kite was the first **glider**.

The first full-sized glider was built in 1809. The first manned glider flight, however, did not take place until 1853, and the glider crashed after a brief flight.

One famous early glider was flown by a Frenchman named Jean-Marie Le Bris in 1856. Le Bris built the winged contraption, hired a driver with a cart and horse, and stood in his machine on the cart. When the horse was moving at a good clip, Le Bris changed the inclination of his machine's wing and took off. Unfortunately, not only did Le Bris fly but so did the cart driver, who got tangled in the rope.

In 1865, Louis Pierre Mouillard went 138 feet (42 m) using a glider built in Algeria. In these early attempts, people tried to fly by jumping from cliffs and running down hills while attached to their "wings." Their flights were very haphazard. It was not until 1891 that gliders that could be controlled by the **pilot** were built.

 Stop here for the Strategy Break.

Strategy Break

If you were to make a time line for the main events in this selection so far, it might look like this:

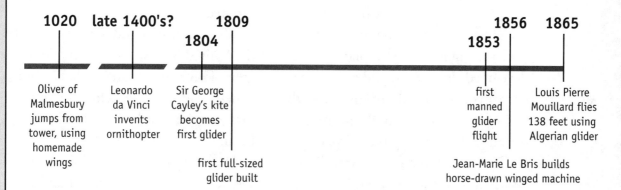

| 1020 | late 1400's? | 1804 | 1809 | | 1853 | 1856 | 1865 |

Oliver of Malmesbury jumps from tower, using homemade wings

Leonardo da Vinci invents ornithopter

Sir George Cayley's kite becomes first glider

first full-sized glider built

first manned glider flight

Jean-Marie Le Bris builds horse-drawn winged machine

Louis Pierre Mouillard flies 138 feet using Algerian glider

As you continue reading, keep looking for the main events in the development of the glider. At the end of this selection, you will complete the time line.

 Go on reading.

In the 1890s, German **engineer** Otto Lilienthal conducted many glider experiments during his efforts to build an airplane. He studied bird flight and tested fixed-wing hang gliders made of wood and fabric. After gathering information from thousands of his hang glider flights, he wrote essays and a book that proved of great help to other experimenters, including the Wright brothers. To fly, Lilienthal would run down a knoll and launch himself into the wind. He was able to glide about ¼ mile (400 m). In 1894, Lilienthal built a single-wing glider that became very popular.

In 1903, Matthew Bacon Sellers built a Lilienthal model glider. He found it hard to balance, so he came up with a new design. Experimenting in Warren County, Georgia, he built a staggered quadruplane hang glider in 1905. Each wing was staggered behind and 2 feet (61 cm) below the one above. These machines were called "step gliders."

People continued trying unsuccessfully to find ways to power a flying machine. While early steam engines provided power for movement, they were too heavy and too big to fly. Not until the late 1800s, when **gasoline engines** were developed, was it finally possible to build a powered flying machine.

The most famous of the early airplane builders were Wilbur and Orville Wright. Their motorized plane, the *Flyer*, flew for twelve seconds on December 17, 1903, at Kitty Hawk in

North Carolina. Before building the *Flyer*, however, the Wright brothers built and flew many gliders. They attached control wires to the wingtips so that they could turn their glider. They also added a tail with a vertical fin and a fuselage, or body.

Once engine-powered planes were developed, interest in gliders decreased, but it did not die. After the end of World War I in 1918, the victorious Allies, fearing that airplanes might be used in a future war, did not allow Germans to build and fly motorized aircraft. So an estimated 200,000 Germans learned to fly gliders during the 1920s and 1930s.

A breakthrough in soaring occurred in 1929 when two Germans, Alexander Lippisch and Robert Kronfeld, invented the **variometer**. This instrument allowed a pilot to know the rate at which the glider was climbing or sinking. Such readings enabled pilots to locate and circle in thermals.

When German glider pilots visited the United States, interest in gliders grew. Three American brothers, Paul, Ernest, and William Schweizer, built many of the first U.S. gliders in Elmira, New York, in 1930.

After the end of World War II in 1945, gliders, or sailplanes, rapidly gained popularity. Some people bought war-surplus training gliders, and before long, factories in America and elsewhere began building sailplanes to fill the demand. ●

Strategy Follow-up

First, work with your partner to complete the K-W-L chart that you began in Building Background. Fill in the column with at least three facts or ideas that you learned about the history of flight.

Next, complete the following time line for the second part of this selection. Use another sheet of paper if you need more room to write. Be careful—some of the events in the selection are described out of order.

1891 1894   1905   1918   1930   1945
              1903| 1929|

✓Personal Checklist

Read each question and put a check (✓) in the correct box.

1. How well were you able to complete the K-W-L chart in Building Background?
    - ☐ 3 (extremely well)
    - ☐ 2 (fairly well)
    - ☐ 1 (not well)

2. In the Vocabulary Builder, how well were you able to match the specialized vocabulary words with their definitions?
    - ☐ 3 (extremely well)
    - ☐ 2 (fairly well)
    - ☐ 1 (not well)

3. How well were you able to complete the time line in the Strategy Follow-up?
    - ☐ 3 (extremely well)
    - ☐ 2 (fairly well)
    - ☐ 1 (not well)

4. How well were you able to find the events in the selection that were out of sequence?
    - ☐ 3 (extremely well)
    - ☐ 2 (fairly well)
    - ☐ 1 (not well)

5. How well do you understand why Germans weren't allowed to build and fly motorized aircraft right after World War I?
    - ☐ 3 (extremely well)
    - ☐ 2 (fairly well)
    - ☐ 1 (not well)

Vocabulary Check

Look back at the work you did in the Vocabulary Builder. Then answer each question by circling the correct letter.

1. What is the function of a variometer?
    a. It gives the rate at which a glider is climbing or sinking.
    b. It tells how many miles per hour a glider is traveling.
    c. It gives the direction in which a glider is traveling.

2. Which word describes a person who plans and builds aircraft?
    a. pilot
    b. engineer
    c. glider

3. Which is the force that pulls objects toward the center of the earth?
    a. gravity
    b. drag
    c. lift

4. Which is the force that holds aircraft down or back?
    a. gravity
    b. drag
    c. lift

5. Which vocabulary word can name either a person's occupation or an object associated with flight?
    a. inventor
    b. ornithopter
    c. glider

Add the numbers that you just checked to get your Personal Checklist score. Fill in your score here. Then turn to page 215 and transfer your score onto Graph 1.

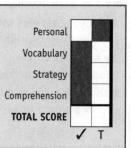

Check your answers with your teacher. Give yourself 1 point for each correct answer, and fill in your Vocabulary score here. Then turn to page 215 and transfer your score onto Graph 1.

Strategy Check

Review the time line that you created in the Strategy Follow-up. Also review the rest of the selection if necessary. Then answer these questions:

1. Which of these events happened first?
   a. Lippisch and Kronfeld invented the variometer.
   b. The Schweizer brothers built many of the first U.S. gliders.
   c. Matthew Bacon Sellers built the staggered quadruplane glider.

2. Which of these events happened in 1903?
   a. The Wright brothers' motorized plane flew for 12 seconds.
   b. Otto Lilienthal built his popular single-wing glider.
   c. Alexander Lippisch and Robert Kronfeld invented the variometer.

3. In what year were the first pilot-controlled gliders built?
   a. 1891
   b. 1894
   c. 1905

4. How many years passed between the Wright brothers' flight at Kitty Hawk and the invention of the variometer?
   a. about 15 years
   b. about 26 years
   c. about 42 years

5. Which of these is *not* an example of signal words?
   a. after the end of World War I in 1918
   b. a breakthrough in soaring occurred
   c. not until the late 1800s

Comprehension Check

Review the selection if necessary. Then answer these questions:

1. According to the legend, how did Daedalus and Icarus try to escape the island of Crete?
   a. They grew wings and flew away.
   b. Large birds carried them away.
   c. They used wings made of wax and feathers.

2. What concept did Sir George Cayley learn while experimenting with kites?
   a. Air must be forced over a wing to create lift.
   b. Gravity pulls aircraft toward the earth.
   c. Aircraft must travel at great speeds to stay up.

3. How was the Wright brothers' aircraft different from gliders?
   a. It had a pilot.
   b. It was built in the United States.
   c. It had a motor.

4. According to the selection, which of these inventors wrote a book about his findings?
   a. Jean-Marie Le Bris
   b. Otto Lilienthal
   c. Oliver of Malmesbury

5. What invention allowed people to build powered flying machines?
   a. the variometer
   b. the gasoline engine
   c. the steam engine

Check your answers with your teacher. Give yourself 1 point for each correct answer, and fill in your Strategy score here. Then turn to page 215 and transfer your score onto Graph 1.

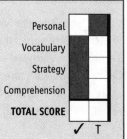

Check your answers with your teacher. Give yourself 1 point for each correct answer, and fill in your Comprehension score here. Then turn to page 215 and transfer your score onto Graph 1.

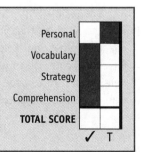

Extending

Choose one or both of these activities:

MAKE A MURAL

With one or two other classmates, plan and create a mural about the history of flight. You can use some of the resources on this page to find information. Decide which inventions you want to include, and create a time line to help you put the inventions in chronological order. Then, using your time line as a guide, create a mural that depicts the inventions and gives a brief history of each one. Include such information as what the invention is called, who invented it, and how it improved upon what came before it.

SEARCH THE INTERNET

Gliding is currently a popular sport. Many companies that sell gliders have sites on the Internet. Using a search engine on the Internet, look up gliders or sailgliders and find out how much a glider—or a glider rental—would cost. If you discover any other interesting information about gliders, share it with the rest of the class. You might want to post a list of Internet sites that you find related to gliding.

Resources

Books

Berliner, Don. *Before the Wright Brothers.* Space and Aviation. Lerner Publications, 1990.

Dale, Henry. *Early Flying Machines.* Discoveries and Inventions. Oxford University Press, 1994.

Dixon, Malcolm. *Flight.* Technology Projects. Bookwright Press, 1991.

Moser, Barry. *Fly! A Brief History of Flight Illustrated.* HarperCollins Juvenile Books, 1993.

Web Sites

http://www.myglider.com/aircraft/cat.asp?cat=3
You can research gliders for sale on this Web site.

http://www.sciencemuseum.org.uk/on-line/flight/flight/history.asp
Check out this time line of the history of flight. Click on various time periods for brief articles and photographs.

http://www.scoh.org/
This is the Web site of a club of sailplane pilots in Texas.

CD-ROM

Daring to Fly! From Icarus to the Red Baron. Arnowitz Studios, 1994.

Video/DVD

Smithsonian: Dreams of Flight. Questar, 1998.

LESSON ④ When Freedom Came

Building Background

When misfortune occurs, most people find out just how important their families are to them. Family members comfort each other, keep each other's spirits up, give each other shelter, and help in rebuilding shattered lives. Just imagine how terrible it would be if you were suddenly disconnected from your family. That is the situation that confronts the main character in the story you are about to read. A newly freed slave, Jake, begins a desperate search for the people who mean the most to him—his family.

Think about what your own family means to you. What do you depend on them for? What would you miss most if you were suddenly cut off from them? On the lines below, list five reasons why your family is important to you. Consider all the needs they fill and what they add to your life.

1. _____
2. _____
3. _____
4. _____
5. _____

freedom

hoisted

plantation

stroll

toting

vicinity

Vocabulary Builder

1. The words in the margin are all from the story "When Freedom Came." As you read the story, use context clues to discover their meanings. But before you begin reading, concentrate on the first word on the list—*freedom*. It is a word that names something of great importance to most people. Freedom can mean different things to different people, however. To show what it means to you, create a concept map with the word *freedom* at its center. Around that central word, list ideas and feelings that you associate with freedom. Also list times when you feel most free and times when you don't feel free at all.

2. As you read the story, you might be reminded of other examples of what freedom is or is not. Add those examples to your concept map.

3. Then save your work. You will refer to it again in the Vocabulary Check.

Strategy Builder

Mapping the Elements of a Short Story

- "When Freedom Came" is a short story. A **short story** is a piece of fiction that usually can be read in one sitting. Because it is much shorter than a novel, a short story often has fewer characters and takes place over a briefer period of time.
- Short stories can be told from the first-person or the third-person point of view. The story you are about to read is written in the **third-person point of view**. That means that the **narrator**, who tells the story, is not a character in the story. He or she stands outside the action and comments on it, using words such as *he, she, his, her,* or *their.* The narrator in "When Freedom Came" can not only see what is happening but knows what Jake is thinking.
- The author of this story wants his readers to "hear" the voices of his characters. For that reason, the characters in this story—all freed slaves—speak in dialect. **Dialect** is a unique style of speech used by groups of people in particular places and times. The dialect in this particular story reflects the speech of Southern ex-slaves at the end of the American Civil War.
- One of the elements of every short story is its **setting**—the time and place in which the story occurs. Another element is the **plot**, or sequence of events. In most stories, the plot revolves around a problem and what the main characters do to solve it. Sometimes a problem's solution is satisfactory to the main characters—and sometimes it's not. Either way, it leads to the **conclusion**, or ending, of the story.
- A good way to keep track of what happens in a short story is to record its elements on a **story map**. Study the story map below. It lists and defines the elements that you should look for as you read.

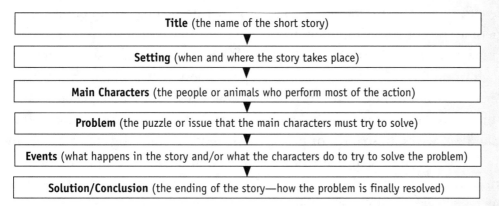

Title (the name of the short story)

▼

Setting (when and where the story takes place)

▼

Main Characters (the people or animals who perform most of the action)

▼

Problem (the puzzle or issue that the main characters must try to solve)

▼

Events (what happens in the story and/or what the characters do to try to solve the problem)

▼

Solution/Conclusion (the ending of the story—how the problem is finally resolved)

When Freedom Came

by Julius Lester

As you begin reading this short story, apply some of the strategies that you just learned. Keep track of the characters, the setting, and other elements. You may want to underline them as you read.

The Civil War is over and Jake is set free. He and his family had been owned by a Southern slaveholder. Several years before the war ended, Jake's wife and children were sold to someone else and taken away. Now Jake is free and sets out to find them.

Pulaski, Tennessee, was more than five hundred miles from Pine Bluff, Arkansas. Jake wished he was a bird and could have flown those miles in a couple of days. But he had to walk them, one step at a time, one foot in front of the other. And he couldn't walk every day, because he had to stop and work to get at least enough to eat. Sometimes he got paid in money, and for a few days he could travel and buy enough to eat.

There were a lot of ex-slaves traveling the roads. Some were also looking for children, wives, husbands, or parents who had been sold. It helped him to know that he wasn't the only one. Some he talked to hadn't seen their mothers since they were children. He knew how they felt. It helped a man to know where he was from if he knew where his mother was. His mother lay in the slave burying ground on the **plantation**.

He wondered sometimes how many people looking for loved ones would find them, including himself. In a way it was a foolish thing to do. But there was no way not to do it. Every day someone asked him if he knew such-and-such a person or if he had heard anything about them. After three months on the road he found that he had a vast store of information and several times was able to direct someone a little closer to the person he was looking for. And just as he was asked, he asked. But it wasn't until he had passed through Nashville, Tennessee, did he find someone who thought she knew Mandy. It was an old woman, who reminded him of Aunt Kate, walking down the road with a bundle on her head. Like many others, she didn't know where she was going but, "Where ain't as important as the going, son," she said, laughing. "You know when you let a chicken out of a coop, it don't have the slightest idea where it's going. Might run out in the woods and get eaten by a fox first thing. But all the chickens know is to get away from the coop."

He asked her about Mandy and gave a description of her.

The old lady nodded. "She got some children?"

Jake nodded.

"And she dark skin, you say? Like you is?"

"That's right," he said, getting excited.

"Well, if it's the same Mandy, she live on Mr. Jim Jenkenson's place on the other side of Pulaski. When you gets in the **vicinity**, son, you just ask somebody to direct you to Mr. Jim Jenkenson's place. Everybody 'round there know where it is. If it's the same Mandy, she be out there."

"How many days walking is that?"

"Three days if you **stroll**. Two and a half if you walk fast. And a day if you can hitch a ride on somebody's mule cart."

Jake tried not to let himself get too excited. It might be another Mandy. It was a common name. But the old woman said it was outside of Pulaski and that was where Mandy had been sold, too. Still, he kept his feelings

inside of him, as if they were a present tied up in a red ribbon which he could open only on Christmas.

It took him two days of fast walking with little sleep to get to Pulaski, and the first person he asked directed him to continue down the road for another two miles. He asked that person if he knew Mandy, and the person nodded and said Mandy had six children. Jake was disappointed. Mandy only had four. He almost didn't go any farther, but since he was so close, he decided to go on. Maybe the person had made a mistake about the number of children she had.

 Stop here for the Strategy Break.

Strategy Break

If you were to stop and begin a story map for "When Freedom Came," it might look like this:

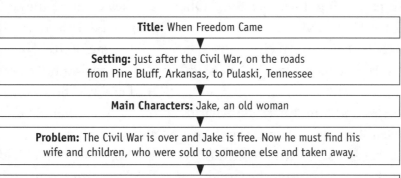

Title: When Freedom Came

Setting: just after the Civil War, on the roads from Pine Bluff, Arkansas, to Pulaski, Tennessee

Main Characters: Jake, an old woman

Problem: The Civil War is over and Jake is free. Now he must find his wife and children, who were sold to someone else and taken away.

Events:
1. Jake sets out walking from Arkansas to find his family.
2. After he passes through Nashville, he meets an old woman. She tells him where to find a woman named Mandy.
3. When someone in Pulaski tells Jake that Mandy has six children, he almost doesn't go any farther. But since he's so close, he decides to go on.

To be continued . . .

As you continue reading, keep paying attention to the events in this short story. You will use some of them to complete the story map in the Strategy Follow-up.

Go on reading to see what happens.

She was walking down the road carrying a bucket of water on her head when he saw her. He knew it was she, the one arm raised over her head, resting lightly against the bucket, the other arm swinging loosely at her side. He had always loved the easy way Mandy had of walking, even with a bucket of water on her head. She never looked like she was working. He started to call out her name, but stopped. It was just possible that it was somebody else. Sometimes every woman he saw looked like Mandy, so he started running to catch up with her.

The woman heard the hurried steps behind her and stopped to look back. Jake saw the soft black face he had loved all of his life and shouted, "It's you! It's you! Mandy!" He ran up to her, tears running down his face. "Oh, thank God. Mandy!"

"Jake? Is that you, Jake?"

"It ain't Abraham Lincoln," he said, laughing.

She gazed at him, uncertain what to do. Then, letting her hand drop from the bucket she screamed, "Jake!" as the bucket tumbled from her head and water splashed both of them. She flung her arms around him, laughing. "Jake, Jake, Jake. It is you, ain't it?"

And with the feel of her arms pressing against his back, Jake felt himself come to life for the first time since he'd last seen her. He buried his face in her neck. "I told you that if anything ever happened, I'd find you. I told you, didn't I?"

"You look just the same," Mandy said, looking at him. "Just the same." She stepped out of his arms and picked up the bucket, laughing. "Look what you made me do. Now I got to go all the way back to the spring and get some more."

"Well, come on. How's Charles and Mary Ann and Caesar and Carl?" he asked, referring to the children.

"Oh, they fine. You probably won't recognize none of 'em. They so big now."

He laughed. "And to think that I almost didn't come out here."

"What you mean?"

"Well, I asked after you in town and a man said he knew of a Mandy who had six children and since we only got four, I just figured it was another Mandy. I almost didn't come, till it occurred to me that he might have made a mistake."

They came to the spring and Mandy bent to fill the bucket.

"Let me do it," Jake said. "You ain't gon' be **toting** no more water now. And anyway, how come Charles or one of the other children didn't come and get it?"

"They out in the field."

"Well, from now on you ain't gon' be doing no more of that heavy lifting and work like that." Jake filled the bucket. "I never could carry it on my head like you."

"Jake? Set that bucket down." She laughed, looking at him trying to set it on his head.

"I'll carry it," Jake said proudly.

"Set it down," she said, suddenly sad.

He put it on the ground and looked at her. "Anything the matter?"

She nodded. "I ain't your wife no more, Jake," she said sadly, looking at her feet. "That man in town what told you I got six children now was telling the truth. I should've told you back on the road when you brought it up. But I didn't know how to tell you."

"You ain't married to somebody else?"

She nodded and broke into tears. "How was I to know for sure you'd find me, Jake? I could've waited for you until the day I died and you never showed up 'cause you was dead or had done married somebody else."

"Aw, Mandy," he cried, taking her in his arms. "But I told you I'd find you, didn't I? I told you that!"

"I know, Jake, and I wanted to believe you. God knows I did. But a woman gets lonesome, Jake. And Henry was a nice man. The children liked him, too. So we jumped the broom and I prayed that this time the Lord wouldn't let me or him be sold away from each other. And after we was freed, the first thing we done was to go and get married like white folks do, and get a piece of paper so couldn't nobody come and separate us. If I'd known, Jake, I wouldn't have done it. But a woman gets lonesome."

"So do a man," he sobbed. "So do a man."

They held each other tightly for a while. "I just wish I'd known, Jake," she whispered softly, stepping back and wiping her eyes.

"Mandy? You ain't got to stay, do you?" Jake said, getting excited. "Now that I'm here, you can leave and come with me."

Mandy shook her head. "I can't do that, Jake. I swore before God and the preacher to be with Henry until one of us died. And, plus, we got married by the paper, the way the white folks do. And when you get the paper, you married sho' 'nuf. It ain't like jumping the broom. Like we done in slavery time. We ain't slaves no more, Jake. We got to live by the paper now."

"But, Mandy, I love you! I ain't thought about nothing else for seven years but you!"

She started crying again. "I loves you, too, Jake. God knows I do. But Henry's a good man, and I don't love him like I do you, but I guess I love him. I loved him enough to get married by the paper."

Jake shook his head repeatedly, muttering, "No, no, no, no. It ain't right. First they come and take you away, sell you like a bale of cotton. They don't ask me how my heart feels about it. Just sell you away. Then you meets somebody you don't love like you love me, but they give you a piece of paper saying you got to be with him, though you love me. It ain't right, Mandy. It just ain't right."

"But that's the way it is, Jake. Wasn't right for us to be slaves all them years neither, but that was the way it was." She picked up the bucket of water and **hoisted** it to her head. "I—I got to be getting back, Jake. You want to come see the children? I know Henry wouldn't mind. I told him all about you and he say you sound like a very good man, the kind of man he'd like to know. I know you'd like him too Jake. Ain't none of this his fault."

"I know that, Mandy. But I reckon not. I don't think I could stand seeing another man happy with you."

She nodded. "I understands."

She started up the path from the spring to the road. Jake didn't move. He raised his head and watched the easy swaying of her body. When she got to the road she turned and looked at him. He could see the tears coming down her face.

"I wish I'd known, Jake."

"God knows, I wished you had too, Mandy," he said, biting his lip and sobbing as he watched her walk down the road and out of sight. ●

Strategy Follow-up

Now complete the story map for "When Freedom Came." First, on a large sheet of paper, copy the beginning of the story map from the Strategy Break. Then continue the story map, using the information below to help you. Don't forget to add any characters or settings that are introduced in the second part of the story.

> **Event 4:** Jake sees

⬇

> **Event 5:** Mandy hears

⬇

> **Event 6:** After Mandy and Jake walk back to the spring,

⬇

> **Event 7:** Jake cries and says

⬇

> **Event 8:** Mandy tells Jake that's the way it is. Then she asks

⬇

> **Event 9:**

⬇

> **Solution/Conclusion:**

✓Personal Checklist

Read each question and put a check (✓) in the correct box.

1. How well were you able to use what you wrote in Building Background to help you understand why Jake sets out to find his family?
   - ☐ 3 (extremely well)
   - ☐ 2 (fairly well)
   - ☐ 1 (not well)

2. In the Vocabulary Builder, how well were you able to create a concept map for the word *freedom*?
   - ☐ 3 (extremely well)
   - ☐ 2 (fairly well)
   - ☐ 1 (not well)

3. How well were you able to complete the story map in the Strategy Follow-up?
   - ☐ 3 (extremely well)
   - ☐ 2 (fairly well)
   - ☐ 1 (not well)

4. How well do you understand Mandy's feelings in this story?
   - ☐ 3 (extremely well)
   - ☐ 2 (fairly well)
   - ☐ 1 (not well)

5. How well do you understand why Mandy married Henry?
   - ☐ 3 (extremely well)
   - ☐ 2 (fairly well)
   - ☐ 1 (not well)

Vocabulary Check

Look back at the work you did in the Vocabulary Builder. Then answer each question by circling the correct letter.

1. What is a synonym for *freedom*?
   - a. plantation
   - b. slavery
   - c. liberty

2. When someone hoists something, what does he or she do with it?
   - a. spills it
   - b. lifts it up
   - c. carries it a long way

3. Which of these words describes something you could tote?
   - a. a bookbag
   - b. a song
   - c. an idea

4. In which situation would a person be most likely to stroll?
   - a. when trying to catch a train on time
   - b. when walking through a park
   - c. when walking on a very cold day

5. When someone is in the vicinity of a building, where is that person?
   - a. near the building
   - b. far away from the building
   - c. inside the building

Add the numbers that you just checked to get your Personal Checklist score. Fill in your score here. Then turn to page 215 and transfer your score onto Graph 1.

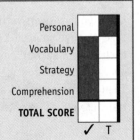

Check your answers with your teacher. Give yourself 1 point for each correct answer, and fill in your Vocabulary score here. Then turn to page 215 and transfer your score onto Graph 1.

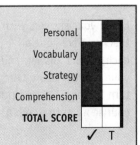

Strategy Check

Review the story map that you completed in the Strategy Follow-up. Also review the rest of the story. Then answer these questions:

1. Which main character or characters from the second part of "When Freedom Came" did you add to your story map?

   a. Henry

   b. Mandy

   c. Henry and Mandy's children

2. Which setting from the second part of "When Freedom Came" did you add to your story map?

   a. a spring in Pulaski, Tennessee

   b. a road outside Nashville, Tennessee

   c. Jim Jenkenson's place

3. What does Jake see in Event 4?

   a. Mandy walking down the road with her four children

   b. Mandy walking down the road with her six children

   c. Mandy walking down the road with a bucket of water on her head

4. Which sentence could you have written for Event 9?

   a. Mandy tells Jake that she's married "by the paper" to someone else.

   b. Mandy asks Jake if he wants to see the children.

   c. Jake tells Mandy that he couldn't stand seeing another man happy with her.

5. Which sentence tells the conclusion of this story?

   a. Jake sobs as he watches Mandy walk away.

   b. Jake is reunited with Mandy and his children.

   c. Jake and his family return home to Arkansas.

Comprehension Check

Review the story if necessary. Then answer these questions:

1. How had Jake and his wife been separated?

   a. They had gotten divorced.

   b. Mandy was sold to someone else.

   c. Mandy decided to move away from Jake.

2. How many children do Jake and Mandy have?

   a. three

   b. four

   c. six

3. What is Mandy doing when Jake first sees her?

   a. carrying a bucket of water on her head

   b. hanging laundry on a line

   c. working in the fields with a hoe

4. Why can't Mandy leave with Jake?

   a. She belongs to a new slave owner.

   b. She doesn't want to upset the children.

   c. She is married to another man now.

5. Which of these is *not* a reason why Mandy married another man?

   a. She was lonely.

   b. She never really loved Jake.

   c. Her children liked Henry.

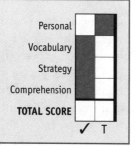

Check your answers with your teacher. Give yourself 1 point for each correct answer, and fill in your Strategy score here. Then turn to page 215 and transfer your score onto Graph 1.

Personal
Vocabulary
Strategy
Comprehension
TOTAL SCORE
✓ T

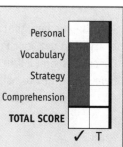

Check your answers with your teacher. Give yourself 1 point for each correct answer, and fill in your Comprehension score here. Then turn to page 215 and transfer your score onto Graph 1.

Personal
Vocabulary
Strategy
Comprehension
TOTAL SCORE
✓ T

Extending

Choose one or more of these activities:

CONTINUE THE STORY

When the story ends, Jake is sitting at the spring. What do you think he might do next? Might he find another woman to be his wife? Might he pine away from loneliness, dreaming only of Mandy? Might he travel West and become a cowboy or a goldseeker? Continue Jake's story and tell what he does as he tries to remake his life. You might want to use the resources listed on this page to find real stories on which to base Jake's story.

ILLUSTRATE THE STORY

Using details from the story to help you, draw a picture of the scene that stands out most in your mind. Try to convey the emotion of the moment.

READ OTHER WORKS BY JULIUS LESTER

Using the resources listed on this page, find and read other short stories or books by Julius Lester. Then choose your favorite story or book and report on it to the class. If you report on a short story, create a story map for it and use it to give your report.

Resources

Books

Lester, Julius. *Black Cowboy, Wild Horses: A True Story.* Dial Books, 1998.

————. *Black Folktales.* Grove Press, 1991.

————. *Long Journey Home: Stories from Black History.* Puffin, 1998.

Haskins, James, and Kathleen Benson. *Bound for America: The Forced Migration of Africans to the New World.* HarperCollins, 1999.

Web Sites

http://www.childrenslit.com/f_lester.html
This site provides a brief biography of Julius Lester and reviews of several of his books.

http://xroads.virginia.edu/~HYPER/wpa/wpahome.html
This Web site is a collection of oral narratives by former slaves who were interviewed during the 1930s.

Audio Recording

Berlin, Ira, Marc Favreau, and Steven F. Miller, eds. *Remembering Slavery: African Americans Talk About Their Personal Experiences of Slavery and Emancipation.* Norton, 1998.

Across the Frozen Sea

Building Background

There are only a few areas of our world that are still unexplored. For centuries, people have been busy making discoveries in the mountains, under the oceans, in the deepest jungles, and in the coldest polar regions of the earth. Their curiosity has led them to take incredible chances and to put themselves in unbelievable danger. Because of the efforts of those who have gone before us, there are fewer geographical mysteries left to be unraveled today.

Only about a century ago, however, the situation was different. For example, people knew little about the area around the geographic North Pole, the place where all the lines of longitude come together. Since no one had ever journeyed to the spot, no one could say for sure what it looked or felt like. People around the world raced to claim the honor of being the first to ever stand at that spot.

How much do you know about the North Pole and the first people who journeyed there? In "Across the Frozen Sea," you will learn about some of the experiences of that first expedition as you read excerpts from the journal of Matthew Henson, the first black man to reach the North Pole.

impassable

impatience

impossible

recrossed

unfurled

Vocabulary Builder

1. The words in the margin are from the article you are about to read. Each of the words contains a **prefix**—a word part added to the beginning of a root word to make a new word. Complete the following sentences with the vocabulary words. Notice how the prefix changes the meaning of each root word.

   a. You should be more patient. Your _____ is annoying.

   b. We folded the flag at night and _____ it in the morning.

   c. No one can accomplish this task. It is _____.

   d. In the summer this mountain road is open to traffic, but in the winter it is _____.

   e. Peary walked across the campsite twice. He crossed and _____ it.

2. As you read the article, look for other words that contain prefixes. Notice how the prefix added to each root word makes it a completely different word.

3. Save your work. You will refer to it again in the Vocabulary Check.

Strategy Builder

Following Sequence While You Read

- An **informational article** is nonfictional writing that gives facts and information about a particular topic. The topic is what the article is about. The **topic** is usually given—or referred to—in the article's **title**. For example, "Across the Frozen Sea" refers to a journey made across the frozen Arctic Ocean to the North Pole.

- As mentioned earlier, "Across the Frozen Sea" includes several entries from Matthew Henson's journal. In most **journals**, writers record the events that happen each day. People who take long trips often keep journals to help them remember their day-to-day experiences. The writer of this article has chosen to include entries from Henson's journal in order to give readers a first-hand, factual account of what happened on certain days.

- Since events in this article are described in the order in which they occurred, the organizational pattern of both the journal and the article is **sequence**, or chronological order. **Signal words** such as *soon, now, from 6 A.M. to 9 P.M.,* and *on April 6,* help make that order clearer.

- In order to track the article's sequence of events more clearly, you can use a **time line**. If you need help remembering how to use a time line, review the ones you worked on in Lesson 3.

Across the Frozen Sea

by Jessie V. Robinette

As you begin reading this article, apply some of the strategies that you just learned. Notice the point at which the article begins to focus on Matthew Henson's journal. In both parts of the article, look for signal words and dates that help you understand the order of events.

On July 6, 1908, dockside crowds cheered and tugboat whistles blew as a stubby 184-foot schooner-rigged steamship sailed out of New York harbor. She was named the *Roosevelt* for President Theodore Roosevelt, and the president himself saw her off. Aboard were Commander Robert E. Peary and a hand-picked crew to accompany him on his latest attempt to reach the North Pole.

The *Roosevelt* had been built in 1905 according to Peary's own specifications at a cost of one hundred thousand dollars. Peary called this forerunner of the modern icebreaker "a 1500-ton battering ram."

Northward along the shore of Greenland, stops were made at several Eskimo villages to take on board forty-nine Eskimo—twenty-two men to handle the sledges, seventeen women to sew winter garments for the party, and ten children.

"Now began 21 days of the hardest kind of work imaginable for a ship, actually fighting for every foot of the way against the **impassable** ice," wrote Matthew Henson. "The constant jolting, bumping, jarring, made work and comfort all but **impossible**." The ship smashed its way through the ice, its front rising up on the ice and then crashing through it to open the way.

On September 5, 1908, the *Roosevelt* reached Cape Sheridan on Ellesmere Island, where the crew would winter over. From there, once the dark winter ended but before the first Arctic thaw, Peary would set out for the Pole.

Preparation, timing, and speed all were important. They could not begin the trek until sunlight returned to the Arctic but had to finish before great sections of the polar ice melted in the Arctic summer. Peary's expedition consisted of five advance sledge teams, besides his own, which would take turns going ahead to break the trail and establish supply camps. As they finished their marches, each team would return to the supply ship. Only one of the team leaders would accompany Peary all the way to the Pole.

The journey began in February 1909:

FEBRUARY 18—The last of the advance parties, under Henson, left the ship for Cape Columbia, the last point of land before the ice pack of the arctic Ocean. Henson wrote, "The Arctic night still holds sway."

FEBRUARY 28—Peary called the expedition teams to his igloo for a final briefing. He defined the problems and explained what measures the teams could take to meet them. He expressed confidence in the venture but said, "From now on we will be indifferent to comfort. We must always be moving on."

MARCH 1—Henson wrote, "By 6 A.M. we were ready, standing at the upstanders of our sledges awaiting the command, 'Forward! March!'" With a crack of the whip and a "Huk! Huk!"

to the dogs, they were off—23 men, 19 sledges, and 133 barking dogs—across the Arctic Ocean.

An easy start soon turned rough, and the men used pickaxes to clear a path through ice ridges. Sledges broke and had to be repaired. Dead tired, they made only twelve miles.

 Stop here for the Strategy Break.

Strategy Break

If you were to create a time line for the main events in this article so far, it might look like this:

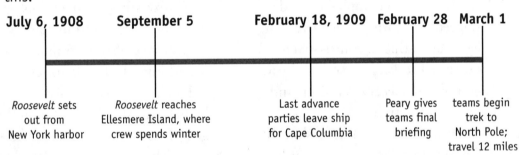

July 6, 1908	September 5	February 18, 1909	February 28	March 1
Roosevelt sets out from New York harbor	*Roosevelt* reaches Ellesmere Island, where crew spends winter	Last advance parties leave ship for Cape Columbia	Peary gives teams final briefing	teams begin trek to North Pole; travel 12 miles

As you continue reading, keep paying attention to the dates and events mentioned in this article. When you finish reading, you will use those dates and events to complete a time line of your own.

Go on reading.

MARCH 4—"Commander routed out all hands by 7 A.M. Best traveling on heavy old ice floes."

MARCH 5—"First view of the sun today. Made us all cheerful."

Cheer soon turned to worry, as progress was halted by the "Big Lead"—an open stretch of water a quarter mile wide. Instead of making the twenty to twenty-five miles they had hoped, they waited for days for the lead to freeze over. "We eat, sleep, and watch this lead," Henson wrote. "Are we to be repulsed again?"

The Eskimo complained and wanted to return. Some were sent back, and athletic contests were organized to keep the others busy. Commander Peary paced up and down in frustration.

MARCH 11—"The lead is shut, but Commander Peary would not let us take chances, until he was sure he could keep all the party together. Off we go. No halt. The ice is liable to open at any moment to let us sink in the cold, black water."

MARCH 22—"Daylight for full 24 hours. Marched from 6 A.M. to 9 P.M. —a full 15 hours."

On they went. Temperatures as low as forty degrees below zero froze their hoods to their beards.

APRIL 1—They were now at 88 degrees north latitude. Three teams had been sent back to the ship. Ship Captain Robert A. Bartlett's, Henson's, and Peary's teams were left. Peary would make the difficult decision to send back

the fourth. Which would it be? Henson wrote, "Today Capt. Bartlett is to be sent back to make the trail for our return. He has been a brave man, borne the brunt of all our hardships."

"Now we were 6—Peary, 4 Eskimos and myself," Henson wrote. "Peary and I looked at each other. We knew without speaking that the time had come to demonstrate that we were the men who should unlock the door which held the mystery of the Arctic."

APRIL 6—"The memory of the last 5 marches is a memory of toil, fatigue and exhaustion. Urged on by our relentless Commander we marched until it was impossible to go on. We were forced to camp in spite of the **impatience** of the Commander, who found himself unable to rest."

Finally, having reached a point that he believed should be close to his goal, Peary ordered the men to stop and make camp. Eyes red and burning, he took sightings of the sun and calculated that they had reached 89 degrees 57 minutes 11 seconds, about three miles from the Pole. Too tired to do anything more than eat, he crawled into an igloo to sleep. He gave orders to his crew not to let him sleep more than four hours.

When he awoke, Peary set out with a sledge and his instruments to find, as closely as possible, 90 degrees north. As he crossed and **recrossed** an area of several square miles, he knew that he must have passed directly "over or very near the point where north and south and east and west blend into one."

APRIL 7—"When Peary returned, he roused us all," Henson wrote, "and gave the word, 'We will plant the Stars and Stripes at the North pole.' And it was done. On the peak of a huge floeberg the glorious banner was **unfurled** in the breeze."

The sight meant different things to those present. Otah, speaking for the Eskimo, said, "There is nothing here. Just ice." Henson felt honored to be the first man of his race to reach the North Pole. And Peary wrote, "The Pole at last! The prize of 3 centuries, my dream and goal of 23 years. Mine at last! I cannot bring myself to realize it. It all seems so simple and commonplace."

The party spent only thirty hours at the Pole. Peary left a strip of flag in a glass jar and at 4 P.M. gave the order to depart, saying, "From now on it is a case of big travel, little sleep, and hustle every minute." They made it back to the *Roosevelt* in seventeen days. ●

Strategy Follow-up

Now complete the following time line for the second part of this article. Use a separate sheet of paper if you need more room to write. Some of the information has been filled in for you.

March 4, 1909   March 5   March 11   March 22   April 1   April 6   April 7   April 8   April 25

✓Personal Checklist

Read each question and put a check (✓) in the correct box.

1. How well were you able to use the information in Building Background to help you understand the importance of Peary's expedition?
    - ☐ 3 (extremely well)
    - ☐ 2 (fairly well)
    - ☐ 1 (not well)

2. How well were you able to complete the sentences in the Vocabulary Builder?
    - ☐ 3 (extremely well)
    - ☐ 2 (fairly well)
    - ☐ 1 (not well)

3. How well were you able to find other words with prefixes as you read this article?
    - ☐ 3 (extremely well)
    - ☐ 2 (fairly well)
    - ☐ 1 (not well)

4. How well were you able to complete the time line in the Strategy Follow-up?
    - ☐ 3 (extremely well)
    - ☐ 2 (fairly well)
    - ☐ 1 (not well)

5. How well could you explain why reaching the North Pole meant different things to each person present?
    - ☐ 3 (extremely well)
    - ☐ 2 (fairly well)
    - ☐ 1 (not well)

Vocabulary Check

Look back at the work you did in the Vocabulary Builder. Then answer each question by circling the correct letter.

1. In the words *impossible* and *impassable*, what does the prefix *im-* mean?
    - a. again
    - b. not
    - c. after

2. What does the prefix *un-* mean in the word *unfurled*?
    - a. in the style of
    - b. before
    - c. the opposite of

3. If snow blocked the only way through a mountain range, how would you describe those mountains?
    - a. impassable
    - b. unfurled
    - c. recrossed

4. Which word best describes someone who doesn't want to wait until his or her birthday to open presents?
    - a. impatient
    - b. recrossed
    - c. impassable

5. If you were told to unfurl a flag, what would you do?
    - a. fold it up
    - b. spread it out
    - c. run it down the flag pole

Add the numbers that you just checked to get your Personal Checklist score. Fill in your score here. Then turn to page 215 and transfer your score onto Graph 1.

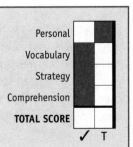

Check your answers with your teacher. Give yourself 1 point for each correct answer, and fill in your Vocabulary score here. Then turn to page 215 and transfer your score onto Graph 1.

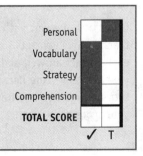

Strategy Check

Review the time line that you completed in the Strategy Follow-up. Then answer these questions:

1. Which of these events happened on March 5?
   a. Progress was halted when Bartlett's team was sent back.
   b. Progress was halted by 24 hours of sun.
   c. Progress was halted by a "Big Lead."

2. How many days did the expedition have to wait for the lead to shut?
   a. 6 days
   b. 17 days
   c. 30 days

3. On what day did the number of team members fall to only six?
   a. March 11
   b. March 22
   c. April 1

4. What happened on April 8?
   a. The team reached the North Pole.
   b. The team left the North Pole.
   c. The team made it back to the *Roosevelt*.

5. Which of the following sentences does *not* contain an example of signal words?
   a. Henson felt honored to be the first man of his race to reach the North Pole.
   b. They made it back to the *Roosevelt* in seventeen days.
   c. Peary left a strip of flag in a glass jar and at 4 P.M. gave the order to depart.

Comprehension Check

Review the article if necessary. Then answer these questions:

1. Why did Peary choose to make his journey in February?
   a. February was the month when the supplies were delivered.
   b. Peary's birthday was in February.
   c. February comes after the dark of winter but before the spring thaw.

2. What made the *Roosevelt* especially useful for the race to the North Pole?
   a. It could break through ice.
   b. It left from New York harbor.
   c. It was built in 1905.

3. What was the job of the advance teams?
   a. to find the North Pole first
   b. to break the trail and establish supply camps
   c. to report on ice and snow conditions

4. According to Henson's journal, who is the leader of the expedition?
   a. Robert Peary
   b. Theodore Roosevelt
   c. Matthew Henson

5. When the team reaches 88 degrees north latitude, where do they know they are?
   a. near Cape Sheridan
   b. near the North Pole
   c. near the *Roosevelt*

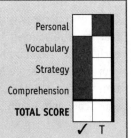

Check your answers with your teacher. Give yourself 1 point for each correct answer, and fill in your Strategy score here. Then turn to page 215 and transfer your score onto Graph 1.

Personal
Vocabulary
Strategy
Comprehension
TOTAL SCORE
✓ T

Check your answers with your teacher. Give yourself 1 point for each correct answer, and fill in your Comprehension score here. Then turn to page 215 and transfer your score onto Graph 1.

Personal
Vocabulary
Strategy
Comprehension
TOTAL SCORE
✓ T

Extending

Choose one or both of these activities:

RESEARCH MATTHEW HENSON AND ROBERT PEARY

These two brave explorers both reached the North Pole. However, they had very different backgrounds that led them to that point. Using the resources listed on this page as well as ones you find yourself, research the lives of both of these men. Then arrange what you find on a chart that lists such information as date of birth, families they were born into, early education, military background, or other categories that you think are important. Display your completed chart for others to see.

CREATE A "HELP WANTED" AD

Peary needed to find many hardy members for his polar expedition. The job he needed done was not a typical nine-to-five job, however. Decide what qualities a participant in this expedition would have needed, and write them in a list. Then use your list to write a want ad intended to attract the right people for the trip. Team members would need to help with the preparations and become part of the advance teams and the final expedition teams. Try to make the ad realistic but, at the same time, attractive to potential job applicants.

Resources

Books

Henson, Matthew A. *A Black Explorer at the North Pole.* Brompton Books, 1989.

Holland, Clive, ed., *Farthest North: The Quest for the North Pole.* Carroll & Graf, 1994.

Schlesinger, Arthur M., and Fred L. Israel. *Robert E. Peary and the Rush to the North Pole.* Cultural Geographic Exploration/Chronicals from *National Geographic.* Chelsea, 1999.

Web Sites

http://www.matthewhenson.com/chapter1.htm
Read the first chapter of the book *Dark Companion: The Story of Matthew Henson* on this Web site.

http://www.matthewhenson.com/matt2.htm
Discover more about Matthew Henson on this Web site.

http://www.robertepeary.com/index2.htm
This Web site focuses on the North Pole expeditions of Robert Peary.

Learning New Words

VOCABULARY

From Lesson 5
- impassable
- impossible
- impatience

Prefixes

As you know, a prefix is a word part that is added to the beginning of a root word. (*Pre-* means "before.") When you add a prefix, you often change the root word's meaning and function. For example, the prefix *re-* means "again." So adding *re-* to the root word *write* changes the meaning of the word to "write over or again."

im-

The prefix *im-* means "not" or "the opposite of." In Lesson 5 you read that the traveling conditions in the frozen arctic made comfort *impossible,* or not possible, and that sometimes the ice was *impassable,* or not able to be passed over or through.

Match each word with its definition.

1. immature   not able to be measured

2. immeasurable   not moveable

3. imprecise   not exact

4. impractical   not fully grown or developed

5. immobile   not useful or sensible

From Lesson 2
- disconnected

dis-

The prefix *dis-* means the same thing as *im-:* "not" or "the opposite of." It also can mean "lack of _____." In "Solo Flight," Keisha explains that it's easy to feel disconnected from reality in a sailplane because of the lack of light and noise. In this context, *disconnected* means "a lack of connection with reality."

Match each word with its definition.

1. disregard   lack of respect or attention

2. disarray   lack of confidence or courage

3. disagree   have the opposite opinion

4. discouragement   lack of order

Suffixes

A suffix is a word part that is added to the end of a root word. When you add a suffix, you often change the root word's meaning and function. For example, the suffix *-ful* means "full of," so the root word *respect* changes from a noun or verb to an adjective meaning "full of respect."

-ation

The suffix *-ation* usually turns words into nouns that mean "the act or process of _____" or "the condition or result of being _____." In "Solo Flight" Keisha describes riding in a sailplane as "a sensation most kids can only dream about." *Sensation* means "the act or process of sensing, or feeling."

Write the definition for each word below.

1. act or process of realizing   _____

2. result of being civilized   _____

3. act or process of admiring   _____

4. state of being cancelled   _____

Prefixes and Suffixes

Some root words have both a prefix *and* a suffix added to them. For example, in the word *impassable*, *im-* means "not" and *-able* means "able to be _____ed." So *impassable* means "not able to be passed over or through."

Match each word with its definition.

1. unwilling   in a way that's not convenient

2. inconveniently   a putting out of place or joint

3. dislocation   not willing

4. incompletely   in a way that's not complete

VOCABULARY

From Lesson 1
• sensation

From Lesson 4
• plantation

From Lesson 1
• decelerated

From Lesson 2
• disconnected

From Lesson 5
• impassable
• recrossed
• unfurled

Follow Your Dreams

Building Background

In 1909 Robert Peary and Matthew Henson were the first people to stand at the North Pole, the place where all the longitude lines come together at the top of the world. Their dangerous and amazing feat was celebrated around the world.

What other events have made international news? Some events have made the world rejoice, while others have plunged people into sorrow on many continents. Think about the biggest news events that have occurred during your lifetime. Then focus on one event, and write three questions that you would ask of one of the people involved. Be sure your questions require more than just a "yes" or "no" answer.

Q: _____

_____

Q: _____

_____

Q: _____

_____

controversy

frostbite

sledge

survive

trek

Vocabulary Builder

1. The words in the margin are from "Follow Your Dreams." Use your understanding of the words to decide if they are used correctly or incorrectly in the following sentences. Then write a **C** or an **I** on each line.

_____ a. The people involved in a **controversy** usually agree with one another.

_____ b. When you suffer from **frostbite**, your heart and lungs are damaged.

_____ c. A **sledge** is a type of large sled.

_____ d. After an expedition returns, funerals are held for those who **survive** it.

_____ e. Successfully completing a long **trek** takes a great deal of energy.

2. As you read the selection, look for the sentences containing the boldfaced vocabulary words. Use context to decide whether your answers above are correct. If necessary, change your answers.

3. Then save your work. You will refer to it again in the Vocabulary Check.

Strategy Builder

How to Read an Interview

- The selection you are about to read is an interview. An **interview** is like a conversation: one person asks **questions**, and the other person—usually a famous person or an expert in some field—gives **answers**. The person who asks the questions is called the **interviewer**. In "Follow Your Dreams," the interviewer asks Will Steger questions about his experiences as he traveled to the North Pole by dogsled.

- The purpose of an interview is to **inform** readers. For example, the interviewer in "Follow Your Dreams" wants to inform readers about Steger and his adventures.

- To get the most out of an interview, an interviewer asks questions that will provide information—not just "yes" or "no" answers. To get the most interesting information, interviewers often ask questions that begin with *Who, What, Where, When, Why,* and *How.* The interviewer's questions in this selection are set in boldface type. As you read this selection, you also will answer *Who, What, Where, When, Why,* and *How* questions. They will be about what you have learned.

- When interviewers record their subjects' answers, they are careful to use the subjects' exact words. If interviewers feel, however, that readers need a bit more information or clarification, they will insert their own words in brackets. For example, in "Follow Your Dreams," Steger mentions the IGY. Since many readers may not know what the IGY is, the interviewer inserted this explanation: [International Geophysical Year].

Follow Your Dreams

by Louise Tolle Huffman

When Will Steger was nine years old, he traded his hockey skates for a stack of *National Geographic* magazines. From that day, he was hooked on the outdoors. At the age of fifteen, he and his brother took a "Huckleberry Finn" boat trip from Minnesota, where he grew up, down the Mississippi River to New Orleans. Later his interests turned to cold and snow, and he began raising and training sled dogs. He has traveled thousands of miles on the Arctic ice by **sledge**. Steger is one of a few men who have been to both the North and South poles.

In 1986, Will Steger organized an expedition team with his co-leader, Paul Schurke. The team was made up of seven men and one woman. Their goal was to reach the North Pole by dog sled in a re-creation of Robert Peary's expedition. It would be the first dog sled **trek** since Peary's to reach the Pole without outside help. To ensure success, the team spent more than a year planning and training. During the trek, two men had to be flown to safety when one broke his ribs and the other suffered **frostbite**. On May 1, 1986, six of the original eight members triumphantly stood at the top of the world. Steger talks about the expedition:

When you were young, was there any one person or event that made you want to become an explorer?
When I was in fourth grade, Huck Finn made me want to travel down the Mississippi. That was my first trip. The IGY [International Geophysical Year] back in 1958, when I was fourteen, brought about a fascination for Antarctica. It was the first time they began exploring Antarctica internationally.

What were your qualifications for making the North Pole expedition?
I had twenty years of experience traveling in the north, of which fifteen were dog sled years. Also, I have the ability to raise money and run a business. I had run my own school for ten years prior to that. [Will organized a winter school where he taught his students how to run a dog sled team and **survive** outdoors without camping in tents. His "classroom" was the Minnesota and Canadian wilderness.] Exploring is a great big organizational and managerial feat. People don't realize you need those skills to be an explorer.

There were many dangers and hardships on your trek—the extreme cold, frostbite, and falling into open leads. Two of your team members were injured and had to be flown out. Your favorite dog, Zap, suffered a badly split front paw, and another dog, Critter, died. Why did you do it?
We did it because we wanted to go to the North Pole. It was pretty simple. For myself, I also was interested in the Peary **controversy**. I felt the best way to understand it was to travel in a

similar means. Too many people who had never experienced the polar sea or driven a dog sled were making sweeping statements. I felt I could do something more decisive by going on the trip. That was part of the reason, but I'd say the real motivation was the adventure of doing it.

 Stop here for the Strategy Break.

Strategy Break

Use what you've learned so far to answer these questions:

Q: Who is Will Steger? _____

Q: What did Steger do in 1986? _____

_____

_____

Q: When and why did Steger become fascinated with Antarctica?_____

_____

_____

 Go on reading.

On the expedition, you crossed an open lead by ferrying over on an ice block, just as Peary did on his expedition. Were other parts of your journey similar to Peary's?
Most of it. Once you're on the ice, it all has a common denominator—men, dogs, and struggle. The ice has not changed. We had some advantages in our clothing, but it was still men and dogs, and in this case we had one woman on the team.

Peary claimed to have traveled twenty-five to forty miles per day at the end of his journey. You felt your team was less rested than his, yet you traveled thirty-five miles on two days as you neared the Pole. Do you think Peary made it?
I think he came real close. I've always said I thought he got within twenty, maybe ten, miles. Now the Navigation Foundation has uncovered other evidence through shadows in old photographs that indicate he made it or at least was very close.

Another team member, Ann Bancroft, was the first woman to reach the North Pole. Do you have any special advice for girls today?
Don't limit your thinking. It's not just a man's world. Anybody can do this. Your thinking will be your biggest barrier. If you think you can't do something because you are a girl, you won't be able to do it. My advice to girls is the same as to boys—follow your dreams.

You used dogs to travel by sledge. Can you tell us about Sam?

Sam was a wild dog we found during a training expedition for the North Pole. We were along the north coast of Alaska. A little speck appeared on the trail way back on the pack ice. The speck got bigger and bigger until we could tell it was a dog. We thought it might be a wolf. He followed us, but he was shy and wouldn't allow us to get close. After three days, he walked up, and I harnessed him. I put him in the lead dog position, and he led to the North Pole and later to the South Pole.

What would you like to say to young people?

If you want to be an explorer or whatever, just go out and do it. It takes time to become a doctor or an explorer. You've got to put a lot of effort into it, but it's the effort that makes dreams come true.

Young people definitely need to be aware of the planet and take responsibility for it, maybe even more than adults. They may need to set aside some personal goals for the good of the earth. They should educate themselves to become aware of how we are all connected to this world.

Since going to the North Pole, you have completed another history-making trek—thirty-seven hundred miles across Antarctica. You also have written a book on the environment titled *Saving the Earth*. What do you plan to do now?

Unofficially, I will probably be going on an expedition to the Northwest Passage by dog sled and kayak, and I also might cross the Arctic Ocean. Some of the same effort I have put into organizing and launching expeditions will now be put into education. I want to help bring about an awareness of the environment. ●

Strategy Follow-up

Review the interview if necessary. Then answer these questions:

Q: In what two ways did Steger's trip to the North Pole make history? _____
_____

_____

Q: Since that trip, what other history-making trek did Steger make?

Q: What does Steger say it takes to make dreams come true? _____
_____

Q: Besides taking more trips in the future, what does Steger plan to do? _____
_____
_____

✓Personal Checklist

Read each question and put a check (✓) in the correct box.

1. How well do you understand why Will Steger became an explorer?
    - ☐ 3 (extremely well)
    - ☐ 2 (fairly well)
    - ☐ 1 (not well)

2. How well did the questions that you wrote in Building Background help prepare you for reading and understanding this interview?
    - ☐ 3 (extremely well)
    - ☐ 2 (fairly well)
    - ☐ 1 (not well)

3. How well were you able to complete the activity in the Vocabulary Builder?
    - ☐ 3 (extremely well)
    - ☐ 2 (fairly well)
    - ☐ 1 (not well)

4. How well were you able to answer the questions in the Strategy Break and Follow-up?
    - ☐ 3 (extremely well)
    - ☐ 2 (fairly well)
    - ☐ 1 (not well)

5. How well do you understand Steger's feelings about the environment?
    - ☐ 3 (extremely well)
    - ☐ 2 (fairly well)
    - ☐ 1 (not well)

Vocabulary Check

Look back at the work you did in the Vocabulary Builder. Then answer each question by circling the correct letter.

1. What is another word for *trek*?
    - a. race
    - b. track
    - c. journey

2. Steger traveled thousands of miles on the Arctic ice by sledge. In the context of this selection, what is a *sledge*?
    - a. a hammer
    - b. a sled
    - c. an argument

3. Which word means the opposite of *survive*?
    - a. exist
    - b. struggle
    - c. die

4. Where do you feel the effects of frostbite most?
    - a. on your skin
    - b. in your heart
    - c. in your stomach

5. When people are having a disagreement, what could you say they are involved in?
    - a. an expedition
    - b. a controversy
    - c. a sledge

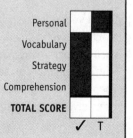

Add the numbers that you just checked to get your Personal Checklist score. Fill in your score here. Then turn to page 215 and transfer your score onto Graph 1.

Personal
Vocabulary
Strategy
Comprehension
TOTAL SCORE
✓ T

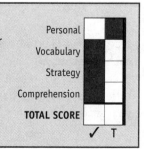

Check your answers with your teacher. Give yourself 1 point for each correct answer, and fill in your Vocabulary score here. Then turn to page 215 and transfer your score onto Graph 1.

Personal
Vocabulary
Strategy
Comprehension
TOTAL SCORE
✓ T

Strategy Check

Review the answers that you wrote in the Strategy Break and Follow-up. Then answer these questions:

1. What was one of the ways in which Steger's North Pole trip made history?

    a. It was the first time anyone ever reached the North Pole by dog sled.

    b. It was the fastest time anyone ever made to the North Pole by dog sled.

    c. Team member Ann Bancroft was the first woman to ever reach the North Pole.

2. Which word would you use to begin a question about the places that Steger has visited?

    a. How

    b. Where

    c. When

3. Which word would you use to begin a question about the reason Steger traveled by dogsled to the North Pole?

    a. Who

    b. When

    c. Why

4. What two things does Steger say it takes to make dreams come true?

    a. time and effort

    b. time and money

    c. money and friends

5. How old was Steger when he became fascinated with Antarctica?

    a. nine years old

    b. fourteen years old

    c. fifteen years old

Comprehension Check

Review the interview if necessary. Then answer these questions:

1. Where did Will Steger grow up?

    a. Canada

    b. Minnesota

    c. Alaska

2. How long did Steger spend preparing for his dog sled trip to the North Pole?

    a. more than a year

    b. fifteen years

    c. a few months

3. According to Steger, what skills don't people realize are necessary to be an explorer?

    a. the ability to organize and manage

    b. the ability to plan and dream

    c. the ability to get along with people

4. Why do you think Steger wants to involve young people in caring for the earth?

    a. He feels that the fate of the world is in their hands.

    b. He likes young people more than he likes adults.

    c. He knows that adults don't care about the environment.

5. Why do you think this selection is called "Follow Your Dreams"?

    a. Steger has been following his dreams all his life.

    b. That is his advice to boys and girls alike.

    c. Both of the above answers are correct.

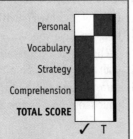

Check your answers with your teacher. Give yourself 1 point for each correct answer, and fill in your Strategy score here. Then turn to page 215 and transfer your score onto Graph 1.

Personal
Vocabulary
Strategy
Comprehension
TOTAL SCORE

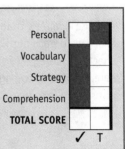

Check your answers with your teacher. Give yourself 1 point for each correct answer, and fill in your Comprehension score here. Then turn to page 215 and transfer your score onto Graph 1.

Personal
Vocabulary
Strategy
Comprehension
TOTAL SCORE

Extending

Choose one or more of these activities:

DO AN ACTUAL INTERVIEW

Interview a willing friend or family member about his or her life, job, or hobby. Be sure to prepare *Who, What, Where, When, Why,* and *How* questions before you begin the interview. Try to make your questions interesting for the interviewee as well as for yourself. If possible, tape record or videotape the interview. Then play it back and try to write the answers word for word. Write a final draft of the interview on a computer if you can. Use a different font for the questions to make them stand apart from the answers.

RESEARCH THE RACE TO THE SOUTH POLE

After Peary reached the North Pole, explorers' attention shifted to the South Pole. Read about the exciting race to the South Pole by Roald Amundsen from Norway and Robert Scott from Great Britain. Find out who won the race and the fate of the loser. Present a short report to the class on your findings.

READ ONE OF STEGER'S BOOKS

Locate one of Steger's books, and read all or part of it. (See the resources listed on this page.) Either orally or in writing, share what you've learned with the rest of the class. If other students read Steger's books too, you might hold a panel discussion to share opinions and information.

RESEARCH THE PEARY CONTROVERSY

At one point in the interview, Steger mentions "the Peary controversy." Find out about the issue at the heart of this controversy, and explain it to your classmates. Also tell whether or not Steger's trip to the North Pole helped clear up or shed any new light on the issue.

Resources

Books

Steger, Will, and Jon Bowermaster. *Crossing Antarctica.* Dell, 1993.

————. *Over the Top of the World: Explorer Will Steger's Trek Across the Arctic.* Bt Bound, 2001.

————. *Saving the Earth: A Citizen's Guide to Environmental Action.* Knopf, 1990.

Steger, Will, with Paul Schurke. *North to the Pole.* Times Books, 1990.

Web Sites

http://www.eyewitnesstohistory.com/scott.htm
This Web site offers an account of Robert Scott's 1912 expedition to the South Pole.

http://www.northpole1909.com/davies.html
A 1990 *National Geographic* article on the Peary controversy is found on this Web site.

http://www.pbs.org/wgbh/amex/ice/peopleevents/pandeAMEX87.html
Read a short biography of Roald Amundsen on this PBS Web site.

Sons and Daughters

Building Background

People from all over the world have come to America in search of a better life. They have brought with them all the customs and values of their native countries. Sometimes, the customs are soon forgotten. At other times, however, the customs become even more important, and they hold a group of immigrants together tightly. In the story you are about to read, one immigrant tries to hold on to the ideas that he had when he came to the New World—no matter what it costs him.

Consider the different immigrant groups that have come to America. If possible, survey your class and see if at least four different countries are represented. Find out what customs each group still honors, and if there is a particular time of year when the group practices the customs. Then fill in the chart below.

Country of Origin	Custom	When Practiced
1.	1.	1.
2.	2.	2.
3.	3.	3.
4.	4.	4.

discarded

mystified

peasants

spacious

summoned

Vocabulary Builder

1. The words in the margin are all found in "Sons and Daughters." Choose a **synonym** (a word with almost the same meaning) and an **antonym** (a word with the opposite meaning) for the boldfaced word in each row. Circle the synonym for each word, and underline the antonym.

a. **discarded**	drove a car	kept	threw away
b. **mystified**	informed	suspicious	puzzled
c. **peasants**	poor farmers	masters	birds
d. **spacious**	cramped	roomy	beautiful
e. **summoned**	called	blamed	sent away

2. As you read the story, find the sentences that contain the boldfaced vocabulary words. Use context to decide whether the choices you made above are correct. Change your answers if necessary.

3. Save your work. You will refer to it again in the Vocabulary Check.

Strategy Builder

Identifying Causes and Effects While You Read

- In many stories, events are connected by sequence, or time order: one event happens, and then another, and then another. In other stories, however, events are connected by **cause and effect**. One event will cause another event to happen, which will cause another event, and so on. The causes and effects in a story are often related to each other. Like the falling dominoes on this page, a single event can cause a chain reaction of more effects and causes.

- To find cause-and-effect relationships while you read, keep asking yourself, "What happened?" and "Why did it happen?" Doing this will help you understand what has happened so far. It also will help you predict what might happen next.

- As you read the following fable, look for the chain of causes and effects.

The Fox and the Crow

One day a fox was sitting near a tree in a sunny field. He saw a crow land on a branch of the tree. In her beak, the crow held a delicious piece of cheese. The fox thought to himself, *I am hungry. How can I get that cheese for myself?* The clever fox called to the crow, "I have heard that you sing more sweetly than any other bird. Would you please let me hear the music of your voice for even a few notes?"

The crow was so flattered that someone wanted her to sing that she immediately opened her beak, and out fell the cheese. The fox grabbed the cheese and ran away shouting over his shoulder, "Never trust a flatterer!"

- If you wanted to track the causes and effects in this fable, you could put them on a **cause-and-effect chain**. It might look like this:

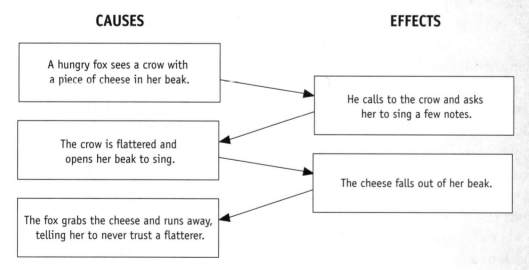

CAUSES

EFFECTS

A hungry fox sees a crow with a piece of cheese in her beak.

He calls to the crow and asks her to sing a few notes.

The crow is flattered and opens her beak to sing.

The cheese falls out of her beak.

The fox grabs the cheese and runs away, telling her to never trust a flatterer.

Sons and Daughters

by Paul Yee

As you read the first part of this story, apply the strategies that you just learned. To find the causes and effects, keep asking yourself, "What happened?" and "Why did it happen?"

If you had been in Chinatown in the early days, and if Merchant Moy had passed you on the thick wooden sidewalk, you would never have guessed that he was the richest Chinese in town. His face always wore a frown, even though his store and family name was carved into the largest wood scroll ever seen, painted with gleaming gold and hanging from the tallest building in Chinatown. Merchant Moy never spoke or joked, even when customers crowded around his counters from morning till midnight, peering into every rack and bin, into every stack and barrel.

No, Merchant Moy was not a happy man.

He was forty years old, and he had spent all his youth building his business. Still, he had one dream. More than anything in the world, he wanted a family. In particular, he wanted sons to carry on his family name. In China, the surname Moy was little known and linked only to poor **peasants**. Now Merchant Moy wanted everyone to know how rich his name and business had become.

Above his storefront, he had built **spacious** apartments large enough for many children and many more grandchildren. His wife was in China, and for a long time she was afraid to cross the ocean. So when she finally changed her mind and stepped off the steamship, there was no man happier than Merchant Moy.

Soon after her arrival, Madam Moy's belly swelled out broad and big, and Merchant Moy waited with bated breath. When the day came, he sat beside the bedroom door, and then he heard the loud wailings of a baby. The midwife hurried forth.

"Congratulations, sir!" she cried. "Twins have been born!"

"Twins?" Merchant Moy's heart skipped. "The gods are smiling to give me two babies at once!"

"Yes, sir," continued the midwife. "You have two healthy girls!"

"Girls?" Merchant Moy's heart sank. "How is my wife?" he asked.

The midwife shook her head sadly. "It was a difficult birth," she replied. "She lives, but she will never bear more babies."

Merchant Moy cursed. Without sons, the Moy family name would disappear. Without sons, he had no one to carry on his business. His entire life's work would be worthless.

Merchant Moy stood silent, thinking. Finally he spoke.

"Tell Chinatown that twin boys have been born," he ordered. "Tell Chinatown we will hold the biggest banquet ever seen. Tell Chinatown the gods have smiled on the Moy family today!" He told the midwife to register the birth of twin sons, and paid her well for her trouble. Then he went to his wife, who lay weak and weary in bed.

"My beloved," he said. "Let me take the children to China. My aged parents wish to see them, before it is too late. You rest here, and let the servants care for you."

Then Merchant Moy went down to the station. At one wicket he bought the steamship tickets. At another wicket he got the forms he would need when he returned from China. He filled out one form for himself, and then he filled out two for his children, putting in boy names for the babies. Then they all sailed for China.

Upon arriving, Merchant Moy **summoned** his servant to him. "Go out to the countryside," he ordered. "Find me a pair of baby boys and buy them for me. No price is too high."

The servant followed the dirt roads out to the fields and villages and went into the gray brick farmhouses to inquire among the peasants. Many had baby girls to sell, but even the hungriest fathers would try to keep a baby boy. Like Merchant Moy, they believed that only boys could keep the family name alive. And to them, after food

and shelter, there was nothing as important as the family name.

But eventually the servant found a family long without food and shelter—a family who could not resist Merchant Moy's money.

When the servant returned to his master, a broad smile crossed Merchant Moy's face. Without a second thought, he gave away his own two daughters and packed his bags.

Merchant Moy sailed for home with his new sons. At the station, inspectors checked his papers closely, but they found that the babies were indeed twin boys as the documents showed.

When Madame Moy discovered what her husband had done, she wept and wept and would not eat. She sat like a statue. She felt as if someone had cut her open and cast a piece of her into the cold dark ocean.

Then she heard the boy babies crying, crying for milk, crying to be fed. Her face softened, and she went to them.

Madame Moy raised the two boys as if they were her own. She brushed their cheeks to hers, nursed them and purred to them. She showered them with love and attention.

 Stop here for the Strategy Break.

Strategy Break

If you were to create a cause-and-effect chain for this story so far, it might look like this:

CAUSES   **EFFECTS**

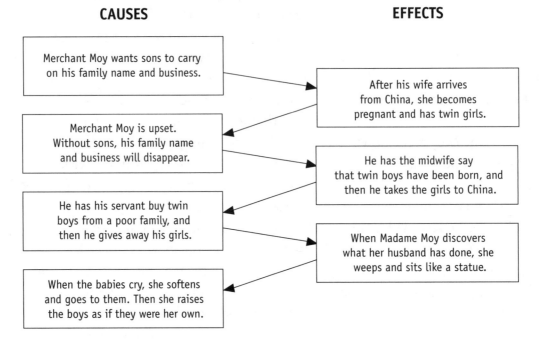

CAUSES	EFFECTS
Merchant Moy wants sons to carry on his family name and business.	After his wife arrives from China, she becomes pregnant and has twin girls.
Merchant Moy is upset. Without sons, his family name and business will disappear.	He has the midwife say that twin boys have been born, and then he takes the girls to China.
He has his servant buy twin boys from a poor family, and then he gives away his girls.	When Madame Moy discovers what her husband has done, she weeps and sits like a statue.
When the babies cry, she softens and goes to them. Then she raises the boys as if they were her own.	

As you continue reading, keep looking for causes and effects. At the end of this story you will create a cause-and-effect chain of your own.

 Go on reading to see what happens.

As the years went by, the two boys grew up bright and healthy. They worked hard at school and studied Chinese. On weekends they worked with the warehouse men and in their father's office, where they balanced the ledger books. Merchant Moy and his wife smiled softly, for they were very proud of their sons.

When the boys turned eighteen, Merchant Moy sent them to China to look for wives, for there were few unmarried women in Chinatown.

When the boys returned, a pair of twin sisters came with them. Madame Moy liked the girls immediately, for they were high-spirited, quick to laugh, and quick to learn. When the young people were married, all of Chinatown came to the gala banquet, with money and red-wrapped gifts to wish the Moy family well.

The sons and their wives moved into the family quarters above the store. A year passed, and Merchant Moy sat back to wait for grand-children. Another year passed, but still there were no babies. Merchant Moy began to fret and frown again.

He made sure the girls ate plenty of hot soup with life-giving seeds and herbs. Still, no new generation showed its head.

Merchant Moy sent his sons and their wives to the herbalist, the doctor who used wild herbs, preserved roots and dried animal parts to heal people according to ancient prescriptions. The wise old man listened carefully to their pulses and peered into their eyes, but he pronounced them all in perfect health.

Then Merchant Moy sent them to the western doctor at the city hospital. The efficient young man used his thermometer to take their temperatures while he poked and prodded high and low. He pronounced them all in perfect health.

Merchant Moy worried more and more. "Soon I will die," he thought. "I must have grandchildren!"

Finally he went to pray at the temple. He thrust two thick candles and three sticks of incense into the big brass urn. He offered wine to the gods above, and then he knelt before the altar and asked for answers.

The temple-keeper spoke. "The gods above, they say, no man can wed his sister."

Merchant Moy's face paled. Could it be? Could his sons have married the daughters he had **discarded** two decades earlier?

"But they are not true brothers and sisters," he prayed. "They come from different parents!"

"The gods say, they have the same name!" said the temple-keeper.

Merchant Moy bowed his head. "What can I do? My daughters were born with my name, but lost it when I gave them away. As for my boys, I gave them the Moy name. If I take it away now, the family name will be lost forever!"

But the gods would say no more.

As Merchant Moy left the temple, he knew that he alone had placed this curse on his children. In the following weeks his hair turned a snowy white. His head sagged from dread and his shoulders stooped. When he looked at his sons and daughters, he wanted to weep, but he could not.

Not long after, Merchant Moy died. When his will was read, everyone was puzzled. He had instructed that all his business and buildings and bank accounts be evenly divided between his two sons. But one strange condition was attached. His sons must give notice and change their family name.

The sons were **mystified**, but they obeyed the instructions. And so the Moy name was lost to the store, lost to the memory of the business that Merchant Moy had built. Only Madame Moy suspected why her husband had done this. She wept silently and drew her children close to her, but she told them nothing, for she wanted them to remember their father with love.

Soon the daughters gave birth—one boy, one girl. Madame Moy was overjoyed. She smiled and prayed for her husband's spirit to rest peacefully now. The name was lost, but the family would live on. ●

Strategy Follow-up

Work with one or two partners to create a cause-and-effect chain for the second part of "Sons and Daughters." To help identify the causes and effects, keep asking each other, "What happened?" and "Why did it happen?"

✓Personal Checklist

Read each question and put a check (✓) in the correct box.

1. How well do you understand what happened in this story?
   - ☐ 3 (extremely well)
   - ☐ 2 (fairly well)
   - ☐ 1 (not well)

2. How well do you understand why it was more important for Merchant Moy to have sons than daughters?
   - ☐ 3 (extremely well)
   - ☐ 2 (fairly well)
   - ☐ 1 (not well)

3. How well were you able to complete the chart in Building Background?
   - ☐ 3 (extremely well)
   - ☐ 2 (fairly well)
   - ☐ 1 (not well)

4. In the Vocabulary Builder, how well were you able to identify a synonym and an antonym for each vocabulary word?
   - ☐ 3 (extremely well)
   - ☐ 2 (fairly well)
   - ☐ 1 (not well)

5. In the Strategy Follow-up, how well were you able to help create a cause-and-effect chain for the second part of this story?
   - ☐ 3 (extremely well)
   - ☐ 2 (fairly well)
   - ☐ 1 (not well)

Vocabulary Check

Look back at the work you did in the Vocabulary Builder. Then answer each question by circling the correct letter.

1. Which word best describes how people feel when they watch a magician at work?
   - a. spacious
   - b. discarded
   - c. mystified

2. Where do peasants usually work?
   - a. on an assembly line
   - b. on a farm
   - c. on a riverboat

3. If you summoned your servants, what would you have done?
   - a. called them
   - b. discarded them
   - c. mystified them

4. Which word best describes a place that is spacious?
   - a. cramped
   - b. roomy
   - c. packed

5. How do you think Merchant Moy's daughters would feel if they discovered that he had discarded them?
   - a. angry and sad
   - b. proud and happy
   - c. lucky

Add the numbers that you just checked to get your Personal Checklist score. Fill in your score here. Then turn to page 215 and transfer your score onto Graph 1.

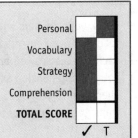

Check your answers with your teacher. Give yourself 1 point for each correct answer, and fill in your Vocabulary score here. Then turn to page 215 and transfer your score onto Graph 1.

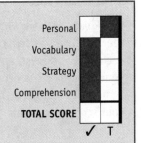

Strategy Check

Review the cause-and-effect chain that you helped create in the Strategy Follow-up. Also review the rest of the story if necessary. Then answer the following questions:

1. When the brothers go to China to look for wives, what is the effect?
   a. They return with a pair of twin sisters.
   b. They can't find anyone to marry.
   c. Madame Moy dislikes the girls immediately.

2. What causes Merchant Moy to send his sons and their wives to the herbalist?
   a. They need shots after returning from China.
   b. He wants to find out why they aren't having babies.
   c. They all get sick on the soup he makes them eat.

3. What causes Merchant Moy's hair to turn white and his shoulders to droop?
   a. He knows he has placed a curse on his children.
   b. He is getting extremely old and frail.
   c. He is worried about not having grandchildren.

4. What causes the daughters to finally give birth?
   a. The herbalist gives them the right herbs.
   b. The western doctor gives them the right medicine.
   c. The boys change their family name.

5. What is the final effect of Merchant Moy's actions in this story?
   a. The family fortune is lost after all.
   b. The family business is lost after all.
   c. The family name is lost after all.

Comprehension Check

Review the story if necessary. Then answer these questions:

1. What is most important to Merchant Moy?
   a. his name
   b. his wife
   c. his children

2. Why is Merchant Moy unhappy when his wife gives birth to twin daughters?
   a. He thinks that twins will bring him bad luck.
   b. Daughters won't work as hard as sons.
   c. Daughters can't pass on the family name.

3. How does Merchant Moy get sons?
   a. He trades them for his daughters.
   b. He has a servant buy them from a poor family.
   c. He persuades the parents to give away their sons.

4. Why do the gods prevent the sons' wives from having babies?
   a. The gods want to make the Moy family suffer.
   b. They are angry with Merchant Moy for not giving more money to charity.
   c. They are unhappy that the husbands and wives have the same family name.

5. At the end of the story, how does Madame Moy feel toward her husband?
   a. She loves him and wants him to rest peacefully.
   b. She is still angry with him for giving away her daughters.
   c. She is ashamed of him.

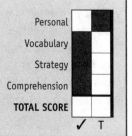

Check your answers with your teacher. Give yourself 1 point for each correct answer, and fill in your Strategy score here. Then turn to page 215 and transfer your score onto Graph 1.

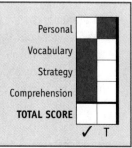

Check your answers with your teacher. Give yourself 1 point for each correct answer, and fill in your Comprehension score here. Then turn to page 215 and transfer your score onto Graph 1.

Extending

Choose one or more of these activities:

RESEARCH CHINESE AMERICANS

Life was not easy for any immigrant group that came to America, but it was particularly difficult for the Chinese. Search for information about the Chinese-American experience during the 19th and 20th centuries. (Use the resources listed on this page if you need a place to start.) How were the Chinese treated by other Americans? What kinds of jobs were they allowed to do? Where did they live? Give a short report of your findings to the class.

PREPARE A CHINESE BANQUET

"Sons and Daughters" mentions two gala banquets that Merchant Moy gives for his friends. Together with other classmates, re–create those parties by preparing your own Chinese banquet. Decide on authentic Chinese dishes to serve, decorate the room with Chinese artwork and signs with Chinese letters, and play Chinese music for entertainment.

READ OTHER BOOKS BY PAUL YEE

Locate one of Paul Yee's books, and read all or part of it. (See the resources listed on this page.) Either orally or in writing, share what you've read with the rest of the class. If other students have read any of Yee's books too, you might hold a panel discussion to share your opinions of them.

Resources

Books

Daley, William. *The Chinese Americans.* Chelsea House, 1995.

Moy, Tina. *Chinese Americans.* Cultures of America. Benchmark Books, 1995.

Wilson, John. *Chinese Americans.* American Voices. Rourke, 1991.

Yee, Paul. *The Boy in the Attic.* Groundwood Books, 1998.

———. *Ghost Trail.* Groundwood Books, 1996.

———. *Tales from Gold Mountain: Stories of the Chinese in the New World.* Groundwood Books, 1999.

Web Sites

http://home.ca.inter.net/~paulryee/
Paul Yee's Web site includes biographical information and short descriptions of his books.

http://www.angel-island.com/history.html
This Web site provides information on Angel Island—the immigration station in the San Francisco Bay where Chinese immigrants were detained in the early 1900s before they were allowed onto the U.S. mainland.

http://www.chinavoc.com/cuisine/recipe.asp
Look up recipes for Chinese dishes on this Web site.

LESSON **8** A Piece of Red Calico

Building Background

Different things make different people laugh. When you were young you probably thought that riddles were hilarious, and you laughed when cartoon characters fell into deep holes or were crushed by falling anvils. You may still think those things are funny now, but you probably enjoy other types of humor as well.

What makes you laugh? Is it physical humor, such as people slipping on banana peels? Is it word play, such as puns and words with double meanings? Do you find a particular television show funny, or a certain person's actions? How has your sense of humor changed as you have matured? Complete the concept map below to describe your own sense of humor.

When I was little, I laughed at . . .

My Sense of Humor

Now I laugh at . . .

The story you are about to read is a humorous story, but its humor is slightly different from that of other stories. The humor is found in the situation in which the narrator finds himself—and the frustrations that come along with it. See if you can relate to the narrator's feelings as you read.

Vocabulary Builder

calico

commission

floor-walker

goods

pen-wiper

plaits

upholsterer

1. The words in the margin are all found in "A Piece of Red Calico." Since this story was written many years ago, some of the vocabulary words are ones that we don't hear very often. Do your best to answer the following questions about the vocabulary words. Underline your answers.

   a. If you wanted help finding shoes in a large department store, would you talk to the **floor-walker** or the board of directors?

   b. Does an **upholsterer** deal with food or furniture?

   c. Would an example of dry **goods** be cloth or pickles?

   d. If you received a **commission**, would you be getting a letter or a job to do?

   e. Would a **pen-wiper** be used by someone who cleans pigpens or someone who uses a fountain pen filled with ink?

    f.   If you wanted to sew a fancy bridal gown, would you make it out of **calico** or silk?

    g.   If a girl wore her hair in **plaits**, would she be wearing a headband or braids?

2. As you read the story, find the sentences that contain the boldfaced vocabulary words. Use context to decide if the choices you made above are correct. Change your answers if necessary.

3. Save your work. You will refer to it again in the Vocabulary Check.

Strategy Builder

Following Sequence in a Short Story

- "A Piece of Red Calico" is a humorous short story. A humorous story often relies on a complicated or repetitive **plot** to make readers laugh. The author's purpose for writing this story was to **entertain** his readers. One of the ways he entertains his readers is to use exaggeration. When writers **exaggerate**, they overemphasize or overstate something. For example, someone who exaggerates may claim that he had to wait in line five hours when, in reality, the wait was only five minutes. In that particular situation, waiting for five minutes may not be funny or unusual, but waiting for five hours is.

- Another way the author entertains his readers is to use a humorous tone. The **tone** of a story is the attitude it conveys. As the narrator in this story gets more and more frustrated, his tone gets more sarcastic, thus adding to the humor.

- The events in this story are described in chronological order, or **sequence**, with each event building upon the one that came before it. Paying attention to the sequence of events will help you (1) follow what is happening, (2) predict what might happen next, and (3) see the humor in it.

- To make the sequence of events as clear as possible, authors often use **signal words**. Some examples of signal words are *first, next, then,* and *after a long time.*

- To help you keep track of the sequence of events in a story, you can use a **sequence chain**. For example, think about the popular story "Hansel and Gretel." Here is how you might put the story's main events on a sequence chain. Note the underlined signal words.

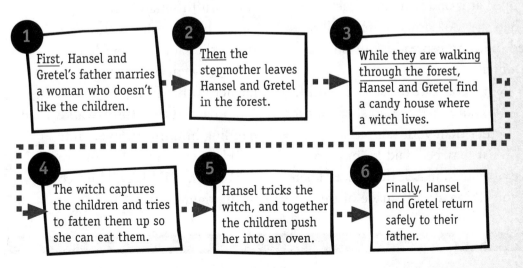

1. First, Hansel and Gretel's father marries a woman who doesn't like the children.

2. Then the stepmother leaves Hansel and Gretel in the forest.

3. While they are walking through the forest, Hansel and Gretel find a candy house where a witch lives.

4. The witch captures the children and tries to fatten them up so she can eat them.

5. Hansel tricks the witch, and together the children push her into an oven.

6. Finally, Hansel and Gretel return safely to their father.

A Piece of Red Calico

by Frank R. Stockton

As you read the first part of this story, apply the strategies that you just learned. Notice the underlined signal words. They will give you a more exact picture of the sequence of events.

I was going into town the other morning, when my wife handed me a little piece of red **calico**, and asked me if I would have time, during the day, to buy her two yards and a half of calico like that. I assured her that it would be no trouble at all; and putting the piece of calico in my pocket, I took the train for the city.

At lunch-time I stopped in a large dry-goods store to attend to my wife's **commission**. I saw a well-dressed man walking the floor between the counters, where long lines of girls were waiting on much longer lines of customers, and asked him where I could see some red calico.

"This way, sir," and he led me up the store. "Miss Stone," said he to a young lady, "show this gentleman some red calico."

"What shade do you want?" asked Miss Stone.

I showed her the little piece of calico that my wife had given me. She looked at it and handed it back to me. Then she took down a great roll of red calico and spread it out on the counter.

"Why, that isn't the shade!" said I.

"No, not exactly," said she; "but it is prettier than your sample."

"That may be," said I; "but, you see, I want to match this piece. There is something already made of this kind of calico, which needs to be made larger, or mended, or something. I want some calico of the same shade."

The girl made no answer, but took down another roll.

"That's the shade," said she.

"Yes," I replied, "but it's striped."

"Stripes are more worn than any thing else in calicoes," said she.

"Yes; but this isn't to be worn. It's for furniture, I think. At any rate, I want perfectly plain stuff, to match something already in use."

"Well, I don't think you can find it perfectly plain, unless you get Turkey red."

"What is Turkey red?" I asked.

"Turkey red is perfectly plain in calicoes," she answered.

"Well, let me see some."

"We haven't any Turkey red calico left," she said, "but we have some very nice plain calicoes in other colors."

"I don't want any other color. I want stuff to match this."

"It's hard to match cheap calico like that," she said, and so I left her.

I next went into a store a few doors farther up Broadway. When I entered I approached the "**floor-walker**," and handing him my sample, said:

"Have you any calico like this?"

"Yes, sir," said he. "Third counter to the right."

I went to the third counter to the right, and showed my sample to the salesman in attendance there. He looked at it on both sides. <u>Then</u> he said:

"We haven't any of this."

"That gentleman said you had," said I.

"We had it, but we're out of it <u>now</u>. You'll get that **goods** at an **upholsterer's**."

 Stop here for the Strategy Break.

Strategy Break

If you were to create a sequence chain for this story so far, it might look like this:

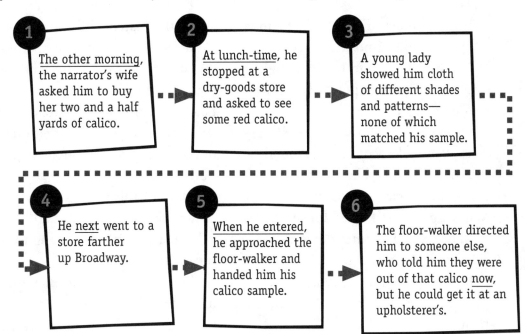

1 <u>The other morning</u>, the narrator's wife asked him to buy her two and a half yards of calico.

2 <u>At lunch-time</u>, he stopped at a dry-goods store and asked to see some red calico.

3 A young lady showed him cloth of different shades and patterns—none of which matched his sample.

4 He <u>next</u> went to a store farther up Broadway.

5 <u>When he entered</u>, he approached the floor-walker and handed him his calico sample.

6 The floor-walker directed him to someone else, who told him they were out of that calico <u>now</u>, but he could get it at an upholsterer's.

As you continue reading, keep paying attention to the sequence of events. At the end of the story, you will complete a sequence chain of your own.

 Go on reading to see what happens.

I went across the street to an upholsterer's.

"Have you any stuff like this?" I asked.

"No," said the salesman. "We haven't. Is it for furniture?"

"Yes," I replied.

"Then Turkey red is what you want?"

"Is Turkey red just like this?" I asked.

"No," said he; "but it's much better."

"That makes no difference to me," I replied. "I want something just like this."

"But they don't use that for furniture," he said.

"I should think people could use anything they wanted for furniture," I remarked, somewhat sharply.

"They can, but they don't," he said quite calmly. "They don't use red like that. They use Turkey red."

I said no more, but left. The next place I visited was a very large dry-goods store. Of the first salesman I saw I inquired if they kept red calico like my sample.

"You'll find that on the second story," said he.

I went upstairs. There I asked a man:

"Where will I find red calico?"

"In the far room to the left. Right over there." And he pointed to a distant corner.

I walked through the crowds of purchasers and salespeople, and around the counters and tables filled with goods, to the far room to the left. When I got there I asked for red calico.

"The second counter down this side," said the man.

I went there and produced my sample. "Calicoes downstairs," said the man.

"They told me they were up here," I said.

"Not these plain goods. You'll find 'em downstairs at the back of the store, over on that side."

I went downstairs to the back of the store.

"Where will I find red calico like this?" I asked.

"Next counter but one," said the man addressed, walking with me in the direction pointed out.

"Dunn, show red calicoes."

Mr. Dunn took my sample and looked at it.

"We haven't this shade in that quality of goods," he said.

"Well, have you it in any quality of goods?" I asked.

"Yes; we've got it finer." And he took down a piece of calico, and unrolled a yard or two of it on the counter.

"That's not this shade," I said.

"No," said he. "The goods is finer and the color's better."

"I want it to match this," I said.

"I thought you weren't particular about the match," said the salesman. "You said you didn't care for the quality of the goods, and you know you can't match goods without you take into consideration quality and color both. If you want that quality of goods in red, you ought to get Turkey red."

I did not think it necessary to answer this remark, but said:

"Then you've got nothing to match this?"

"No, sir. But perhaps they may have it in the upholstery department, in the sixth story."

So I got in the elevator and went up to the top of the house.

"Have you any red stuff like this?" I said to a young man.

"Red stuff? Upholstery department,—other end of this floor."

I went to the other end of the floor.

"I want some red calico," I said to a man.

"Furniture goods?" he asked.

"Yes," said I.

"Fourth counter to the left."

I went to the fourth counter to the left and showed my sample to a salesman. He looked at it, and said:

"You'll get this down on the first floor—calico department."

I turned on my heel, descended in the elevator, and went out on Broadway. I was thoroughly sick of red calico. But I determined to make one more trial. My wife had bought her red calico not long before, and there must be some to be had somewhere. I ought to have asked her where she bought it, but I thought a simple little thing like that could be bought anywhere.

I went into another large dry-goods store. As I entered the door a sudden tremor seized me. I could not bear to take out that piece of red calico. If I had had any other kind of a rag about me—a **pen-wiper** or any thing of the sort—I think I would have asked them if they could match that.

But I stepped up to a young woman and presented my sample, with the usual question.

"Back room, counter on the left," she said.

I went there.

"Have you any red calico like this?" I asked of the lady behind the counter.

"No, sir," she said, "but we have it in Turkey red."

Turkey red again! I surrendered.

"All right," I said, "give me Turkey red."

"How much sir?" she asked.

"I don't know—say five yards."

The lady looked at me rather strangely, but measured off five yards of Turkey red calico. Then she rapped on the counter and called out "cash!" A little girl, with yellow hair in two long **plaits**, came slowly up. The lady wrote the number of yards, the name of the goods, her own number, the price, the amount of the bank-note I handed her, and some other matters, probably the color of my eyes, and the direction and velocity of the wind, on a slip of paper. She then copied all this in a little book which she kept by her. Then she handed the slip of paper, the money, and the Turkey red to the yellow-haired girl. This young girl copied the slip in a little book she carried, and then she went away with the calico, the paper slip, and the money.

After a very long time,—during which the little girl probably took the goods, the money, and the slip to some central desk, where the note was received, its amount and number entered in a book, change given to the girl, a copy of the slip made and entered, girl's entry examined and approved, goods wrapped up, girl registered, plaits counted and entered on a slip of paper and copied by the girl in her book, girl taken to a hydrant and washed, number of towel entered on a paper slip and copied by the girl in her book, value of my note and amount of change branded somewhere on the child, and said process noted on a slip of paper and copied in her book,—the girl came to me, bringing my change and the package of Turkey red calico.

I had time for but very little work at the office that afternoon, and when I reached home, I handed the package of calico to my wife. She unrolled it and exclaimed:

"Why, this don't match the piece I gave you!"

"Match it!" I cried. "Oh, no! It don't match it. You didn't want that matched. You were mistaken. What you wanted was Turkey red—third counter to the left. I mean, Turkey red is what they use."

My wife looked at me in amazement, and then I detailed to her my troubles.

"Well," said she, "this Turkey red is a great deal prettier than what I had, and you've got so much of it that I needn't use the other at all. I wish I had thought of Turkey red before."

"I wish from my heart you had," said I. ●

Strategy Follow-up

Work by yourself or with a partner to complete the following sequence chain for the second part of this story. Use a separate sheet of paper if you need more room to write. Don't forget to use as many signal words as possible.

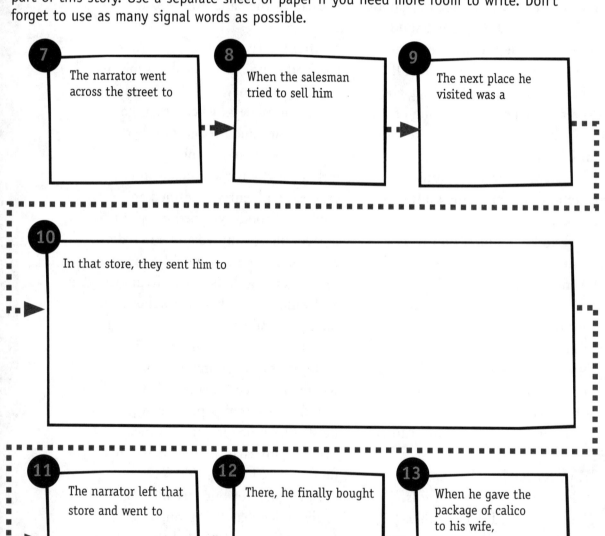

7 The narrator went across the street to

8 When the salesman tried to sell him

9 The next place he visited was a

10 In that store, they sent him to

11 The narrator left that store and went to

12 There, he finally bought

13 When he gave the package of calico to his wife,

✓Personal Checklist

Read each question and put a check (✓) in the correct box.

1. How well were you able to describe your changing sense of humor in Building Background?
   - ☐ 3 (extremely well)
   - ☐ 2 (fairly well)
   - ☐ 1 (not well)

2. How well do you understand the author's use of humor in this story?
   - ☐ 3 (extremely well)
   - ☐ 2 (fairly well)
   - ☐ 1 (not well)

3. How well do you understand why the author's use of exaggeration is so important in this story?
   - ☐ 3 (extremely well)
   - ☐ 2 (fairly well)
   - ☐ 1 (not well)

4. How well were you able to answer the questions in the Vocabulary Builder?
   - ☐ 3 (extremely well)
   - ☐ 2 (fairly well)
   - ☐ 1 (not well)

5. How well were you able to complete the sequence chain in the Strategy Follow-up?
   - ☐ 3 (extremely well)
   - ☐ 2 (fairly well)
   - ☐ 1 (not well)

Vocabulary Check

Look back at the work you did in the Vocabulary Builder. Then answer each question by circling the correct letter.

1. What does *calico* describe in this story?
   - a. a type of chair
   - b. a type of color
   - c. a type of cloth

2. What do floor-walkers do in this story?
   - a. tell people where to find things
   - b. work the cash registers
   - c. stock all the shelves with merchandise

3. Which meaning of the word *commission* fits this story?
   - a. put a ship into service
   - b. an assignment or task
   - c. an official document issued by the armed forces

4. One salesperson tells the narrator, "You'll get that goods at an upholsterer's." In the context of the salesperson's statement, what does *goods* describe?
   - a. cloth
   - b. a chair
   - c. a commission

5. If you wanted to hire someone to cover a chair with new material, whom would you call?
   - a. a pen-wiper
   - b. a floor-walker
   - c. an upholsterer

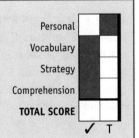

Add the numbers that you just checked to get your Personal Checklist score. Fill in your score here. Then turn to page 215 and transfer your score onto Graph 1.

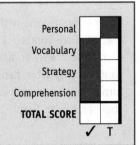

Check your answers with your teacher. Give yourself 1 point for each correct answer, and fill in your Vocabulary score here. Then turn to page 215 and transfer your score onto Graph 1.

Strategy Check

Review the sequence chain that you completed in the Strategy Follow-up. Also review the rest of the story. Then answer these questions:

1. What did the narrator do when the upholsterer tried to sell him Turkey red?

   a. He left and went to another dry-goods store.

   b. He bought the Turkey red from the upholsterer.

   c. He left and went back to the first store.

2. In the store after the upholsterer's, to how many places was the narrator sent?

   a. three places

   b. six places

   c. nine places

3. In that same store, after the narrator was told to go to the first floor, what did he do?

   a. He walked on his heels to the elevator.

   b. He took the elevator down to the first-floor calico department.

   c. He took the elevator down and walked out of the store.

4. What did the narrator end up buying at the last dry-goods store?

   a. 5 yards of Turkey red

   b. 2 ½ yards of Turkey red

   c. 2 ½ yards of calico to match the sample

5. What is ironic about the wife's last statement?

   a. If she had thought of Turkey red before, the narrator could have gotten it at the upholsterer's.

   b. If she had thought of Turkey red before, the narrator could have gotten it much earlier.

   c. If she had thought of Turkey red before, the narrator wouldn't have been looking for calico.

Comprehension Check

Review the story if necessary. Then answer the following questions:

1. For what did the narrator's wife say she needed more red calico?

   a. She needed it to mend a dress.

   b. She need it to mend a chair.

   c. She never said why she needed it.

2. How many yards of calico did she ask the narrator to buy?

   a. two yards

   b. two yards and a half

   c. five yards

3. What was beneficial about the amount of calico the narrator bought?

   a. He wouldn't lose as much money if his wife didn't like it.

   b. He bought so much that his wife didn't need to use the other calico.

   c. At that volume, he got a good discount on the calico.

4. What happened each time the narrator visited a new store?

   a. They tried to sell him everything except what he wanted.

   b. They were always out of the calico he wanted.

   c. They all tried to sell him Turkey red.

5. When the little girl took care of the narrator's purchase, he imagined the process. What made that scene humorous?

   a. He imagined they were doing everything in slow motion.

   b. He imagined they were doing all sorts of ridiculous things.

   c. He imagined they were doing everything backward.

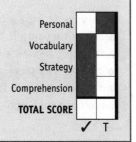

Check your answers with your teacher. Give yourself 1 point for each correct answer, and fill in your Strategy score here. Then turn to page 215 and transfer your score onto Graph 1.

Personal
Vocabulary
Strategy
Comprehension
TOTAL SCORE
✓ T

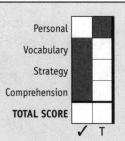

Check your answers with your teacher. Give yourself 1 point for each correct answer, and fill in your Comprehension score here. Then turn to page 215 and transfer your score onto Graph 1.

Personal
Vocabulary
Strategy
Comprehension
TOTAL SCORE
✓ T

Extending

Choose one or more of these activities:

ADAPT THIS STORY INTO A PLAY

Some of the scenes in "A Piece of Red Calico" would be especially humorous if performed on stage. Transform this short story into a play. Use the story's dialog to write lines for all the characters, and suggest how the actors should say them. For example, the narrator begins his adventure in a good mood, but he becomes more and more frustrated as he goes from store to store. After your play is written, ask some friends to help you perform it. Practice it several times before you finally put it on. If possible, have someone videotape your final performance.

RESEARCH THE FASHIONS OF THE 1880s

This story was written in the United States in the 1880s. Try to find out how some of its characters would have dressed. What styles did they wear, and what fabrics were most popular? You might begin your research with the encyclopedia. Try to find pictures of the typical outfits worn by people of that time. Create a poster display of your findings. Attach sketches and pieces of fabric if you can.

READ OTHER STORIES BY FRANK R. STOCKTON

Locate other short stories by Frank R. Stockton and read, view, or listen to several of them. (See the resources listed on this page for where to find them.) Either orally or in writing, share your stories with the rest of the class. If other students have read, watched, or heard any of Stockton's stories, you might hold a panel discussion to compare your favorites. Be sure to discuss what makes each story humorous.

Resources

Books

Stockton, Frank R. *Best Short Stories.* Scribner, 1957.

————. *The Lady or the Tiger? and Other Stories.* Tor, 1992.

————. *The Magic Egg, and Other Stories.* Indy Publishers, 2002.

Web Sites

http://selfknowledge.com/408au.htm
This Web site provides online versions of several works by Frank R. Stockton.

http://vintagegladrags.com/1880_1919_Vintage_Clothing.html
On this vintage clothing site, you can see photographs of clothing from the late 1800s and early 1900s.

http://www.tudorlinks.com/treasury/articles/#Victorian
This Web site offers information on clothing in the 1800s.

Audio Recordings

London, Jack, Rudyard Kipling, and Frank Stockton. *Tales of Adventure and Suspense.* Listening Library, 1987.

Stockton, Frank R. *The Lady or the Tiger?* Listening Library, 1995.

The Impossible Race

Building Background

Today, most families in the United States own a car. As a rule, we count on our cars to start in any weather, to brake quickly, and to be comfortable no matter what the traveling conditions are. We even expect our cars to be attractive, with eye-catching colors, shapes, and styles. However, when automobiles were new on the market, they didn't offer many of the features that we take for granted today.

How much do you know about the cars bought and sold around the year 1908? Fill in the Venn diagram below comparing cars sold in 1908 with cars sold today. In the left circle, list features that the cars of 1908 had that you no longer find in today's cars. In the right circle, list some of the features in today's cars that were not found in most cars in 1908. In the area where the circles overlap, list features that are common to cars from both eras. If you're not too familiar with cars of 1908, make logical guesses. After you've read this selection, you can see how accurate your guesses were.

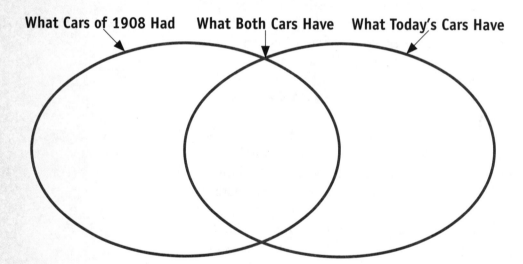

What Cars of 1908 Had   What Both Cars Have   What Today's Cars Have

Vocabulary Builder

1. The words in the margin are found in the following article. You can classify these words in two categories: **compounds**—words made up of two words that have been combined—or not compounds. Identify the compounds and write them on the first clipboard. Write the words that are not compounds on the second clipboard.

2. After each word, write a brief definition. If you need help with any of the words, find them in the selection and use context to figure them out. If context doesn't help, use a dictionary. If the dictionary has more than one definition, be sure to use the one that fits this selection.

3. Save your work. You will refer to it again in the Vocabulary Check.

Strategy Builder

Following Sequence in an Informational Article

- In Lesson 8 you learned to track the order of events in a short story. In this lesson, you will learn to chain to track the order of events in an informational article.

- You know that an **informational article** is nonfiction that gives facts and details about a particular topic. The topic of "The Impossible Race," as hinted at in the title, is an auto race from New York to Paris that took place in 1908.

- Since the author describes the events of the race in the order in which they happened, this article follows the main organizational pattern of **sequence**. In order to make that sequence as clear as possible, the author uses **signal words** such as *then, a few days before, meanwhile,* and *on February 12.*

- In order to track the article's sequence of events more clearly, you can use a **sequence chain**. If you need help remembering how to use a sequence chain, review the one that you completed in Lesson 8.

bankruptcy

breakdown

chauffeur

endurance

ingenuity

overland

penalized

railroad

showroom

snowdrifts

CLIPBOARD 1
Compounds

CLIPBOARD 2
Not Compounds

The Impossible Race

by Gary L. Blackwood

As you read the first part of this article, apply the strategies that you just reviewed. Notice the underlined signal words. They will give you a more exact picture of the sequence of events.

Even today, the idea would seem outrageous. In 1908, it was positively ridiculous. An automobile race all the way from New York to Paris? The route laid out by the sponsors—the *New York Times* and the French newspaper *Le Matin*—was enough to give even the most seasoned drivers second thoughts.

The race would take the cars across the northern United States in the dead of winter, over the Rockies and through Death Valley, across Alaska and the frozen Bering Strait, then through all of Asia and most of Europe. Much of the route was uninhabited—no gas stations, no hotels, often no real roads.

It would be more of an **endurance** contest than a race. Even the most luxurious cars had no heaters or air-conditioning, and only a folding canvas top kept out the weather. Automobiles weren't known for their reliability, either. After all, they had just been invented 20 years before. Autos were a rich man's toy, in a league with hot-air balloons. No one considered them a serious means of transportation like the horse.

The few car manufacturers who entered the race meant to prove otherwise—especially the Germans. They entered a huge, heavy car called the Protos, manned by three German army officers who meant to win the race at any cost. There were three French entries and one Italian.

Only a few days before the race, an American firm, the E. R. Thomas Company, decided to take part. The owners had no illusions of winning. They were close to **bankruptcy** and hoped that their car would make a respectable showing, enough to boost sales. They hadn't had time to build a special automobile as the foreign entrants had done; theirs was basically a stock Flyer, like the ones that sold on the **showroom** floor for $4,500—a *lot* of money in 1908.

The fact that people considered the New York to Paris route impossible didn't keep crowds from filling Times Square on February 12 for the start of the race. People continued to turn out in droves all along the route to cheer the drivers of the cars. The race was the biggest sporting event of its day—like the Super Bowl and the World Series rolled into one. The *New York Times* sent a special correspondent in the Thomas car and devoted a page or more in every day's paper to the autos' progress.

 Stop here for the Strategy Break.

Strategy Break

If you were to create a sequence chain for this article so far, it might look like this:

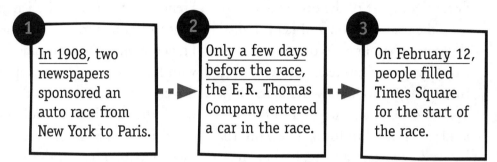

1 In 1908, two newspapers sponsored an auto race from New York to Paris.

2 Only a few days before the race, the E. R. Thomas Company entered a car in the race.

3 On February 12, people filled Times Square for the start of the race.

As you continue reading, keep paying attention to the sequence of events and the signal words. At the end of the article, you will complete a sequence chain of your own.

Go on reading.

The Thomas, which was lighter and faster than most of the other cars, took the lead early on and kept it all the way to San Francisco. It wasn't easy. The American team shoveled through eight-foot **snowdrifts** in New York and Ohio and slogged through ankle-deep mud in Iowa. The Thomas broke down again and again, but the Americans always managed to make the necessary repairs, sometimes through sheer **ingenuity**. Some of the other entrants were less lucky. One French car dropped out in New York State, another in Iowa.

Two of the German officers called it quits in Chicago, but the third, who still hadn't mastered the art of driving, hired a **chauffeur** and took the car on to Idaho. There the Protos had a major **breakdown**. By this time, the American car—which had crossed the continent in just 42 days, only 11 days short of the record—was on its way to Alaska by boat.

But when the Americans reached Valdez, they found that the spring thaw had turned the snow to mush. They couldn't even hope to drive **overland**, let alone cross the Bering Strait. There was nothing to do but turn back to Seattle.

The Italians, having survived an attack by wolves and narrowly escaping a plunge over a precipice, were waiting there. So was the German driver; determined not to be left behind, he had gotten permission to ship his disabled car by rail from Idaho. But the race committee had **penalized** him 15 days for it.

These three, plus the last remaining French team, crossed the Pacific by boat to Vladivostok. There the French manufacturer decided to withdraw his car. The disappointed driver, desperate to reach Paris, bought up all the gasoline in Vladivostok and offered it to the Americans in exchange for a seat in the Thomas. The Americans refused; they didn't want the extra weight. Luckily, the Frenchman had overlooked some American powerboats in the harbor. They furnished the Thomas with enough gas to go on.

Meanwhile, the Italian crew had run out of money and was forced to stay behind while the Protos and the Thomas headed for Paris. To avoid the muddy roads, the Germans and the Americans jolted along the ties of the Trans-Siberian Railroad, which had been built only a few years before.

In a **railroad** tunnel, the Thomas almost had a head-on collision with an oncoming train. The driver threw the car into reverse and backed up frantically. Just before the train overtook the Thomas, the driver found a spot wide enough to pull off the tracks.

The German team had lightened its load and was in the lead. The Americans lightened theirs even more; they shipped practically everything but the clothes on their backs ahead by rail. They nearly froze, but the strategy worked. They caught up with the Protos just as it was boarding a ferry to cross Lake Baikal. But the Americans were a few minutes too late. The ferry left without them, and they had to wait 12 hours for the next one.

Near Omsk, they caught up with the Protos again and, cheering wildly, passed it—only to fall behind again when they sank in a swamp. They broke a drive gear getting out and lost another five days.

The Protos reached Moscow almost two days ahead of the Thomas. To make sure they kept the lead, the Germans stripped their car down like a racing auto.

The Thomas, meanwhile, was being threatened by angry peasants waving sickles and throwing rocks. The American team had to swerve around broken bottles in the road. The reason? A year earlier, one of the contestants in an auto race from Peking to Paris had run down and killed a child in the same village.

The Americans poured on the speed, but it was no use. The Protos pulled up in front of the offices of *Le Matin* on July 26. It was the first car to reach Paris.

But it didn't win the race. Remember, the Germans had lost 15 days because they shipped the Protos by rail back in the United States. On top of that, the Thomas got a 15-day bonus for its side trip to Alaska. So, even though the Americans arrived in Paris four days behind the Protos, they took first place—over the loud protests of the Germans.

The American car—and, in fact, the automobile in general—had proven its worth. The proud manufacturer declared the Thomas was in such good shape that it "could start from Paris today and come back over the same route."

The exhausted crew wasn't so eager. "The trip," said the driver, "was a most remarkable one. . . . but none of the three of us would undertake it again for any consideration."

The men returned home as heroes, and the sales of the Thomas Flyer soared, saving the company from bankruptcy.

And what of the hapless Italians stranded in Vladivostok? They soon raised enough money to go on, but were plagued by illness and bad luck. Still, they managed to limp into Paris a month later, the third car to complete a race that nearly everyone had said was impossible. ●

Strategy Follow-up

First, go back and add to or revise the Venn diagram that you began in Building Background.

Then, complete the following sequence chain that tracks what happened to the Americans and their Thomas during the race. Use a separate sheet of paper if you need more room to write. Don't forget to use as many signal words as possible.

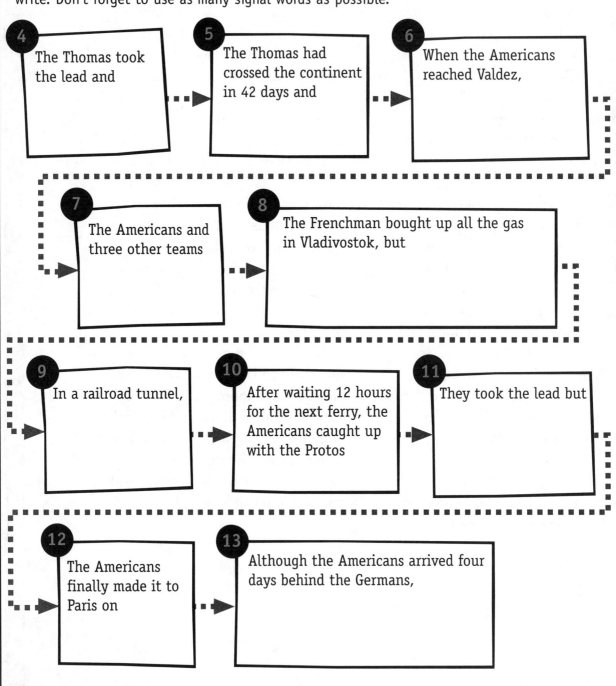

4 The Thomas took the lead and

5 The Thomas had crossed the continent in 42 days and

6 When the Americans reached Valdez,

7 The Americans and three other teams

8 The Frenchman bought up all the gas in Vladivostok, but

9 In a railroad tunnel,

10 After waiting 12 hours for the next ferry, the Americans caught up with the Protos

11 They took the lead but

12 The Americans finally made it to Paris on

13 Although the Americans arrived four days behind the Germans,

✓Personal Checklist

Read each question and put a check (✓) in the correct box.

1. How well do you understand the information presented in this article?
   - ☐ 3 (extremely well)
   - ☐ 2 (fairly well)
   - ☐ 1 (not well)

2. Now that you've read this article, how well were you able to add to or revise the Venn diagram you began in Building Background?
   - ☐ 3 (extremely well)
   - ☐ 2 (fairly well)
   - ☐ 1 (not well)

3. How well were you able to complete the activity in the Vocabulary Builder?
   - ☐ 3 (extremely well)
   - ☐ 2 (fairly well)
   - ☐ 1 (not well)

4. How well were you able to complete the sequence chain in the Strategy Follow-up?
   - ☐ 3 (extremely well)
   - ☐ 2 (fairly well)
   - ☐ 1 (not well)

5. Now that you've completed a sequence chain for the Americans and their Thomas, how well would you be able to complete a sequence chain for the Germans and their Protos?
   - ☐ 3 (extremely well)
   - ☐ 2 (fairly well)
   - ☐ 1 (not well)

Vocabulary Check

Look back at the work you did in the Vocabulary Builder. Then answer each question by circling the correct letter.

1. Which of these words did you list on the clipboard for compound words?
   - a. snowdrifts, breakdown, showroom
   - b. bankruptcy, overland, penalized
   - c. railroad, snowdrifts, endurance

2. Which compound word means "by or across land"?
   - a. railroad
   - b. showroom
   - c. overland

3. Which word describes what you use when you think of a clever way out of a difficulty?
   - a. penalized
   - b. ingenuity
   - c. endurance

4. Which word from the article describes a person who drives people around for a living?
   - a. manufacturer
   - b. correspondent
   - c. chauffeur

5. What is another word for *punished*?
   - a. overlooked
   - b. penalized
   - c. bankrupted

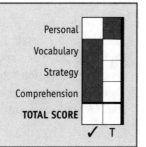

Add the numbers that you just checked to get your Personal Checklist score. Fill in your score here. Then turn to page 215 and transfer your score onto Graph 1.

Personal
Vocabulary
Strategy
Comprehension
TOTAL SCORE
✓ T

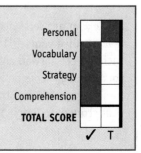

Check your answers with your teacher. Give yourself 1 point for each correct answer, and fill in your Vocabulary score here. Then turn to page 215 and transfer your score onto Graph 1.

Personal
Vocabulary
Strategy
Comprehension
TOTAL SCORE
✓ T

Strategy Check

Review the sequence chain that you completed for this article. Then answer these questions:

1. How long after the race began did the Americans keep the lead?
   a. until they reached Ohio
   b. until they reached Iowa
   c. until they reached San Francisco

2. What happened when the Americans reached Valdez, Alaska?
   a. They couldn't cross the Bering Strait, so they drove back to Seattle.
   b. The crossed the Bering Strait and continued on toward Paris.
   c. They fell behind when the Thomas sank in a swamp.

3. Which of these three events happened first?
   a. The Americans found gas in some powerboats and continued the race.
   b. The Americans and three other teams crossed the Pacific to Vladivostok.
   c. The Americans narrowly escaped colliding with a train in a tunnel.

4. Which of the following is *not* an example of signal words from the article?
   a. a month later
   b. in just 42 days
   c. but it was no use

5. Why did the Americans take first place in the race?
   a. because the Germans had received a 15-day penalty
   b. because the Americans had received a 15-day bonus
   c. because of both of the reasons above

Comprehension Check

Review the article if necessary. Then answer the following questions:

1. During which season was the race held?
   a. winter
   b. summer
   c. fall

2. Why did the E. R. Thomas Company enter a car in the race?
   a. They were doing so well that they wanted to spread sales to other countries.
   b. They wanted to start selling race cars, and the race would be good publicity.
   c. They hoped that a good showing would keep them from going bankrupt.

3. Where did the race begin and end?
   a. It began in New York and ended in Vladivostok.
   b. It began in Paris and ended in Valdez.
   c. It began in New York and ended in Paris.

4. Why did the German driver receive a 15-day penalty?
   a. He had tried to damage other cars in the race.
   b. He had shipped his car by rail for part of the race.
   c. He didn't follow the exact route of the race.

5. Why should the Italian team members have been proud of themselves?
   a. They won the race.
   b. They didn't give up in spite of their difficulties.
   c. They showed that their car was the best.

Check your answers with your teacher. Give yourself 1 point for each correct answer, and fill in your Strategy score here. Then turn to page 215 and transfer your score onto Graph 1.

Check your answers with your teacher. Give yourself 1 point for each correct answer, and fill in your Comprehension score here. Then turn to page 215 and transfer your score onto Graph 1.

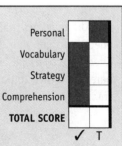

Extending

Choose one or both of these activities:

MAP OUT THE RACE ROUTE

On a globe or a world map, trace the route that the racers took. (Use the resources listed on this page to learn more about the race.) If possible, find and record the average winter temperature and snowfall in a few of the main cities that the race passed through. Use a scale of miles to figure approximately how many miles each car actually drove. Remember to include the Americans' side trip to Valdez and to subtract the miles between Idaho and Seattle for the Germans. Display your calculations on a bar or line graph.

ROLE-PLAY AN INTERVIEW WITH ONE OF THE RACE DRIVERS

What would you ask one of the drivers in this race if you met him today? What do you think his answers might be? Work with a partner to stage a mock interview with a driver from any of the teams. Together, plan the questions and write the answers. Try to make the personality of the driver obvious in his answers and his body language. Then present your interview to the rest of the class.

Resources

Books

Cole, Dermot. *Hard Driving: The 1908 Auto Race from New York to Paris.* Paragon House, 1991.

Jackson, Robert B. *Road Race Round the World: New York to Paris, 1908.* Hill & Wang, 1977.

Schuster, George, with Tom Mahoney. *The Longest Auto Race.* J. Day, 1966.

Web Site

http://www.thegreatautorace.com/
This Web site contains maps, photographs, and historical accounts of the 1908 auto race.

LESSON (10) The Long Carry

Building Background

One of the most colorful images from early 18th-century Canadian history is that of the voyageurs. *Voyageur* means "traveler" in French. Many of the men who made their living as voyageurs were of French descent. Their job was to transport goods to and from remote trading posts throughout Canada by way of canoe, using the vast system of rivers and lakes. Voyageurs had to be strong and resilient adventurers. The area they canoed through was wilderness. Voyageurs had to depend on their own strength, courage, and quick thinking to survive. They enjoyed reputations as cheerful, optimistic, and fun-loving men, famous for their wild senses of humor. Many of them dressed with flair and attention-getting style.

When railroads replaced canoes as the most economical method of transporting goods, the era of the voyageur soon ended. Even though the voyageurs are gone, the memory of their energetic and good-humored zest for life lives on.

doffed

elite

enormity

feat

hoisted

portage

Vocabulary Builder

1. The words in the margin are all from "The Long Carry." Match each word with its definition by writing the number of the correct definition on the line.

2. If you don't know the meaning of a word, find it in the story and use context to figure it out. If using context doesn't help, look up the word in a dictionary.

   a. _____ doffed   1) lifted

   b. _____ elite   2) hugeness

   c. _____ enormity   3) best or special

   d. _____ feat   4) took off

   e. _____ hoisted   5) accomplishment

   f. _____ portage   6) place where goods are carried overland from one body of water to another

3. Save your work. You will refer to it again in the Vocabulary Check.

Strategy Builder

Making Predictions While You Read

- While you read most stories, you probably try to **predict**, or guess, what will happen next. Almost like a detective, you piece together clues that the author gives, and you use them to make your predictions.

- The clues that the author gives are called context clues. **Context** is the information that comes before or after a word or a situation to help you figure it out. For example, read the following paragraphs. See if you can use the context clues to figure out what is happening and to predict what might happen next.

A tennis player, a snowman, a clown, and a vampire were sitting around a table. "Please pass that luscious slab of meat, would you please?" said the vampire.

"Why certainly. Please feast to your heart's content," said the snowman. "I'll take some of those blood-red beets, if you don't mind."

"I just love red. It's my favorite color," said the vampire while passing the beets.

"Oh, it's mine too," said the clown, "especially for noses and cheeks." Everyone at the table laughed.

"From now on, let's do this every October thirty-first!" said the tennis player. Suddenly there was a knock on the door . . .

- Can you predict who might be at the door? You can if you use context clues. By the end of these paragraphs, you probably figured out that the setting of this story is a Halloween dinner-party, and that the characters are all in costume. The strongest clue is the tennis player's line, particularly the words *every October thirty-first*. Without that clue, you might not be able to make an appropriate prediction about what might happen next. Now that you know that it's Halloween, however, you can use that information to predict that the person at the door will most likely be a trick-or-treater.

The Long Carry

by William Durbin

As you read this story, apply the strategies that you just learned. Look for context clues to help you predict what might happen next.

"Here it is—the Grand Portage." Marc turned from his friend, Henri Bonga, and studied the rocky trail. The nine-mile **portage** was the most famous and brutal carry in all the North West Territory.

This was the moment that Marc had been dreading since he left Montreal six weeks ago. In May 1800, he'd signed on as a voyageur with the North West Fur Company. His eight-canoe brigade had already paddled and portaged 50,000 pounds of trade goods across 1,200 miles of wilderness to reach the mid-summer rendezvous at Grand Portage. Rising each morning before 4 and laboring until dusk, the voyageurs were an **elite** corps who paddled 36-foot freight canoes up Canada's Ottawa River and across Lake Huron and Lake Superior. Though the trip had toughened Marc, he feared that tomorrow's carry would be more than he could handle.

"So what do you think?" Henri asked, gesturing up the hill. "Though we call it the Grand Portage, the Ojibwa know it as Kitchi Onigaming."

Marc glanced back at the gray waters of Lake Superior and then turned to measure the rise with his eye. "I can see why the voyageurs who've wintered in the North brag so much," Marc said, hoping his voice didn't betray his fear. Though Marc was only 13, he had managed every portage so far on their 1,200-mile paddle from Montreal. But the longest carry had been just over a mile. How could he portage his standard, two-pack load of 180 pounds up a "mountain" such as this? he thought. To make matters worse, he knew that each voyageur was required to make four trips, delivering two parcels of trade goods to Fort Charlotte—the departure point for brigades headed north—and returning to the Grand Portage depot with two bundles of furs each time.

"It's a tough one," Henri admitted. "The North West Company tried pack animals, but they decided it's cheaper to cripple men." He laughed and clapped Marc across his back. "And remember—you get a Spanish dollar for every extra parcel you carry."

Marc tried to laugh, but the best he could manage was a weak chuckle. The four trips up the hill and back would total more than 70 miles. Carrying anything "extra" was out of the question.

His friend Henri had nothing to worry about. Legendary for his strength, Henri was a mixed-blood voyageur who was part French, part Ojibwa, and part black. He never carried less than three packs—a 270-pound load—on any portage, yet he took even the steepest hills without effort. A quiet man, Henri prided himself on his bright red sash and his matching red cap. His cap was topped with a feather that made him look even taller than his 6 feet 6 inches.

"You've got lots of tough miles behind you, string bean," Henri said, as they paused before the company storehouse. Henri **doffed** his cap and ran his hand through his black hair. It was late afternoon, and the day was unusually warm for Superior's north shore. "Once you make the Grand Portage and paddle across the divide, you'll leave the pork eaters behind and become a Hivernant—a winterer."

Marc nodded. He didn't mind Henri teasing him about being skinny. He didn't mind his canoe mates kidding him about his blond hair and blue eyes either, because nearly all the voyageurs were dark-skinned and brown-eyed. But he was tired of being called a pork eater. That was the name given to men who paddled the Montreal to Grand Portage supply route and never ventured farther north. The name came from the fact that they mainly ate dried corn boiled with pork fat, while the men on the northern routes feasted on pemmican and wild game.

Marc and every French-Canadian boy dreamed of becoming *hommes du nord* or true men of the North, but his first step was to master the Grand Portage. Could he make it?

Marc and Henri paused before the squared-log storehouse. The double doors were both open, and there was a flurry of activity inside. Crude jokes and shouted oaths accompanied the work of the clerks who were sorting goods for the upcoming trading season.

"Of all the bumbling fools—" a self-important little clerk shouted, as he pulled a broken mirror from a pack. "Do you idiots kick your parcels across the portages?"

"We did you a favor by breaking that, sir," Henri said, staring the clerk straight in the eye.

"A favor?"

"That's right. We spared you the pain of looking at your ugly face." Henri threw back his head and laughed. Though the clerk looked ready to say more, after studying Henri's huge hands he thought better of it.

Marc knew that dozens of voyageur brigades passed through Grand Portage on their way to company trading posts scattered across the North West Territory. Some were traveling west to the Red River Valley, others to the Far North—the famed Athabasca. The assortment of kettles, blankets, beads, guns, iron works, mirrors, knives, cloth, and ribbons that the clerks packed depended on the destination of each brigade.

"We'd better get back to camp, Marc," Henri said. But Marc was looking over his shoulder at the portage again.

"What was that?" he apologized.

"Let's get back to camp," Henri repeated.

"O.K.," Marc agreed, but his mind was still on the nine-mile hike that awaited him tomorrow. Marc knew what tough carries could do. He'd never forget what happened to a man named Lucian Galtier back on the Grand Calumet Portage. Trying to lift more than his muscles could stand, he'd ripped open his stomach. Though the men pushed his intestines back in place and bandaged his middle with some gingham cloth, Galtier's death was slow and painful. Marc could still picture in his mind the lonely hillside where they tied a broken paddle blade into a cross to mark his grave.

When Marc and Henri returned to camp, all the voyageurs were talking about a carry that one of Roderick Mackenzie's men had completed that afternoon. According to the men, he'd portaged two parcels of trade goods to Fort Charlotte—a distance of nine miles—and returned with two bundles of furs in only five hours.

When the **feat** was mentioned again over supper, one of Henri's canoe mates, Martin Ballanger, declared in an intentionally loud voice, "I can't see why anyone would make a fuss over a little carry." Marc hated Ballanger. He was a greasy little man with close-set eyes who refused to mind his own business.

Mackenzie's men, who were camped next to Marc's crew, suddenly quieted. Finally a tall fellow stood up. "Would you like to match the effort, Ballanger?"

"Why waste my time?" Ballanger scoffed. "But I know someone who could double that weight."

When the man laughed, Ballanger bragged even more. "I'll bet he could even handle five packs."

"And who might that be? Your mother?"

Voyageurs from both camps roared. Bonga, guessing what was coming next, glared at Ballanger, but the weaselly man went on. "I was thinking of my friend here, Monsieur Bonga."

"Henri Bonga?"

Murmurs rose from the far side of the campfire, and a second man asked, "Did you have a wager in mind?"

"Put your money where your mouth is," Ballanger grinned. Though everyone had heard of Henri's legendary strength, the **enormity** of the task set the odds against him at three to one.

 Stop here for Strategy Break #1.

Strategy Break #1

1. What do you predict will happen next? _____

   _____

2. Why do you think so? _____

   _____

3. What clues from the story helped you make your prediction(s)? _____

   _____

   _____

➤ Go on reading to see what happens.

The contest began at dawn. Every man, woman and child in Grand Portage came out to watch. A chorus of encouragement rose from the crowd, as Ballanger helped Henri strap three bundles on his back and two across his chest.

Marc **hoisted** his own packs in place. The rest of Marc's brigade had already shouldered their own packs and headed up the trail.

Henri turned to Marc. "How are you feeling?" he asked. Marc couldn't believe Henri's kindness. He was taking on the carry of a lifetime, yet his main worry was his young friend.

"I'm as ready as I'll ever be," Marc lied, trying to show more confidence than he felt.

"Take it one pose at a time." Henri winked and started up the trail.

Marc was amazed at the big man's pace. He marched past the first poses, or resting places, without breaking stride. Two famous landmarks—the parting trees and the fountain—were soon left in the distance, and Marc had to jog to keep up. Only after Henri passed through an open meadow and reached the steepest part of the hill did he begin to breathe heavily. Marc noticed the backs of Henri's leggings were dark with sweat.

"You can make it," Marc called, looking down at the worn stones of the footpath. An hour later, the big man looked beaten. After balancing his load on a short resting pole at the next pose, Henri tried to sit down. But his packs tipped him over onto his side.

"Are you all right?" Marc asked. The big man was wheezing like a winded horse, but he still managed to nod and smile.

 Stop here for Strategy Break #2.

Strategy Break #2

1. What do you predict will happen next? _____

_____

2. Why do you think so? _____

_____

3. What clues from the story helped you make your prediction(s)?_____

_____

_____

 Go on reading to see what happens.

A few minutes later, Ballanger arrived. He had lagged behind, worried about losing his wager. "You can't quit now," he hollered. "The last flat is just over that hill."

"Why don't you shut—" Marc started to yell at Ballanger, but stopped when Henri once again rose to his feet.

"One pose at a time," he whispered to Marc.

The calmness of Henri's voice and the steadiness of his stride told Marc that the big man would make it. He knew there was no stopping Henri, for he was whistling softly now and walking with the ease of a gentleman strolling down a garden path.

Marc adjusted his packs and hurried past the astonished Ballanger. This was an event Marc didn't want to miss.

When Henri arrived at Fort Charlotte, cheers sounded throughout the stockade. Marc knew that he'd witnessed a carry that would forever remain a legend in the canoe country. Even before the freight was lifted from Henri's shoulders, Ballanger was collecting his bets.

"To the greatest voyageur ever," a man from Mackenzie's crew shouted. As the crowd pressed tightly around Henri and helped him with his packs, he looked worried. But as soon as he caught Marc's eye he smiled. "You made it, lad," he called out. Then he chuckled. "But don't you think it's time to set your parcels down?"

Marc suddenly felt the weight of his packs. He'd conquered the most famous portage in the North West without even thinking about it. Out of concern for Henri, he'd forgotten the pain of his own carry. Now for the first time he realized his calves were burning as if they'd been flogged, and his neck ached.

"Martin Ballanger," Henri spoke loud enough to get everyone's attention. Ballanger was counting his coins like a greedy child. He looked up as the crowd watched with interest.

"Turn around," the big man commanded.

To the amusement of both crews, Henri strapped a pack over Ballanger's shoulders. Ballanger frowned silently as Henri hooked a second pack around his front and placed a third across his shoulders. When Henri reached for the fourth parcel, Ballanger croaked, "No."

As Ballanger crumpled to his knees, Marc grinned. For once the fellow was getting what he deserved.

"Enough," Ballanger cried, wheeling his arms to balance himself, "enough!"

When Henri swung the last pack onto Ballanger's shoulders, the little man toppled face-first into the dust. The crowd roared. The only thing visible under the pile of packs was a single, coin-clutched hand.

"Now our work is done," Henri declared. Then grinning in Marc's direction, he added, "It's a fine day, indeed. What do you say we take a look at the Pigeon river?" ●

Strategy Follow-up

Now go back and look at the predictions that you wrote in this lesson. Do any of them match what actually happened in this story? Why or why not?_____

_____

_____

_____

_____

_____

_____

_____

_____

_____

_____

_____

_____

_____

_____

_____

_____

_____

_____

_____

_____

_____

_____

_____

_____

_____

_____

_____

✓Personal Checklist

Read each question and put a check (✓) in the correct box.

1. How well do you understand what happened in this story?
   ☐ 3 (extremely well)
   ☐ 2 (fairly well)
   ☐ 1 (not well)

2. After reading this story and the information in Building Background, how well could you explain who voyageurs were and what they did?
   ☐ 3 (extremely well)
   ☐ 2 (fairly well)
   ☐ 1 (not well)

3. In the Vocabulary Builder, how well were you able to match the words and their definitions?
   ☐ 3 (extremely well)
   ☐ 2 (fairly well)
   ☐ 1 (not well)

4. How well were you able to use context clues to make predictions while you read this story?
   ☐ 3 (extremely well)
   ☐ 2 (fairly well)
   ☐ 1 (not well)

5. How well would you be able to describe Henri Bonga?
   ☐ 3 (extremely well)
   ☐ 2 (fairly well)
   ☐ 1 (not well)

Vocabulary Check

Look back at the work you did in the Vocabulary Builder. Then answer each question by circling the correct letter.

1. When Marc realized the enormity of the task ahead of him, how did he feel?
   a. relieved
   b. confident
   c. fearful

2. Which word means the opposite of *hoist*?
   a. drop
   b. steal
   c. portage

3. If a person was accepted into an elite group, how would he or she probably feel?
   a. proud
   b. embarrassed
   c. silly

4. Which word means the same thing as *feat*?
   a. failure
   b. achievement
   c. laziness

5. What did Henri do when he doffed his cap?
   a. He put it on.
   b. He took it off.
   c. He put it on backward.

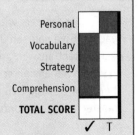

Add the numbers that you just checked to get your Personal Checklist score. Fill in your score here. Then turn to page 215 and transfer your score onto Graph 1.

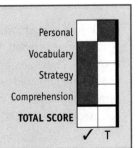

Check your answers with your teacher. Give yourself 1 point for each correct answer, and fill in your Vocabulary score here. Then turn to page 215 and transfer your score onto Graph 1.

Strategy Check

Review what you wrote at each Strategy Break. Then answer these questions:

1. At Strategy Break #1, which prediction would *not* have fit the story?

    a. Henri would not be in the contest.

    b. Henri would make Marc carry the packs.

    c. Henri would agree to take part in the contest.

2. At Strategy Break #1, if you had predicted that Henri would win the contest, which clue would have best supported your prediction?

    a. Ballanger bragged even more. "I'll bet he could even handle five packs."

    b. The enormity of the task set the odds against him three to one.

    c. Everyone knew Henri's legendary strength.

3. Which clue would have best supported your prediction that Henri would not make it?

    a. Marc remembered the man who ripped open his stomach trying to lift more than his muscles could stand.

    b. Henri never carried less than three packs . . . yet he took even the steepest hills without effort.

    c. Everyone knew Henri's legendary strength.

4. At Strategy Break #2, if you had predicted that Henri would win the contest, which clue would have best supported your prediction?

    a. An hour later, the big man looked beaten.

    b. He was wheezing like a winded horse.

    c. He still managed to nod and smile.

5. What did Henri say to Marc that might have helped you know Henri would win?

    a. "So what do you think?"

    b. "Take it one pose at a time."

    c. "It's a tough one."

Comprehension Check

Review the story if necessary. Then answer these questions:

1. Where does this story take place?

    a. at Grand Portage

    b. in Montreal

    c. along the Ottawa River

2. Why is Marc nervous when he reaches the nine-mile portage?

    a. He knows that Henri will make fun of him for his weakness.

    b. He doesn't want to deal with the clerk at the station there.

    c. He is afraid that he will fail at carrying his packs all the way.

3. Why does Marc hate Ballanger even before the bet?

    a. Ballanger always teases Marc and is mean to him.

    b. Ballanger doesn't mind his own business.

    c. Ballanger doesn't work as hard as Henri and Marc do.

4. Why doesn't Marc have any trouble making the nine-mile portage?

    a. He's so concerned about Henri that he doesn't pay attention to himself.

    b. Henri is carrying Marc's bags, so Marc doesn't have to struggle.

    c. Marc ate lots of pork before the trip, so he has extra energy.

5. Why does Henri place the five heavy packs on Ballanger?

    a. Henri wants to prove what a weak person Ballinger is.

    b. Henri wants Ballanger to carry the packs the rest of the way.

    c. Henri wants to hurt Ballanger.

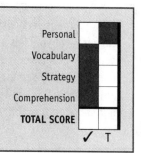

Check your answers with your teacher. Give yourself 1 point for each correct answer, and fill in your Strategy score here. Then turn to page 215 and transfer your score onto Graph 1.

	Personal
	Vocabulary
	Strategy
	Comprehension
TOTAL SCORE	

Check your answers with your teacher. Give yourself 1 point for each correct answer, and fill in your Comprehension score here. Then turn to page 215 and transfer your score onto Graph 1.

	Personal
	Vocabulary
	Strategy
	Comprehension
TOTAL SCORE	

Extending

Choose one or more of these activities:

CREATE A HELP-WANTED AD FOR A VOYAGEUR

Voyageurs were a special breed of worker. Not every person would want to take on the hard work and dangers that they faced every day. However, big companies like the North West Fur Company needed to find people who were willing to become voyageurs. Use what you know about the job to create a help-wanted ad for the position of voyageur in the early 1800s. Advertise the qualities that were needed for the job, and describe the type of person the company was seeking. Make sure your ad encourages applicants by pointing out the benefits of the job.

PLAN A TRIP THROUGH THE WATERWAYS OF CANADA

Using an encyclopedia, magazines, the Internet, or information that you get at a travel agency or Chamber of Commerce, plan a vacation to the area where the voyageurs worked. According to the story, Marc and Henri left Montreal and paddled their canoes up the Ottawa River and across Lake Huron and Lake Superior to a place called Grand Portage. What tourist attractions or natural wonders could a modern-day tourist see if he or she took the same route? Gather the information you find in a folder or scrapbook.

READ OTHER BOOKS BY WILLIAM DURBIN

Locate one of William Durbin's books, and read all or part of it. (See the resources listed on this page.) Either orally or in writing, share what you've read with the rest of the class. If other students have read any of Durbin's books, you might hold a panel discussion to share your opinions of them.

Resources

Books

Durbin, William. *The Broken Blade.* Yearling Books, 1998.

————. *Wintering.* Laure Leaf, 2000.

Into the Wilderness. National Geographic Society, 1978.

Web Sites

http://www.civilization.ca/vmnf/popul/coureurs/resident.htm
This article about voyageurs is on the Canadian Museum of Civilization Web site.

http://www.travelcanada.ca/travelcanada/app/en/us/home.do
Information about travel in Canada is available on this official Web site of the Canadian Tourism Commission.

http://www.williamdurbin.com/
This is William Durbin's Web site.

Learning New Words

VOCABULARY

From Lesson 9
• bankruptcy

Suffixes

A suffix is a word part that is added to the end of a root word. When you add a suffix, you often change the root word's meaning and function. For example, the suffix *-less* means "without," so the root word *pain* changes from a noun to an adjective meaning "without pain."

-cy

The suffix *-cy* turns words into nouns that mean "quality or condition of being _____" or "office, position, or rank of _____." In "The Impossible Race," you read that the E. R. Thomas company entered a car in the race because it was facing bankruptcy. The word *bankruptcy* means "condition of being bankrupt, or unable to pay debts."

Match each word below with its definition.

office or position of president   lunacy

condition of being legitimate   captaincy

condition of being a lunatic   legitimacy

rank of captain   presidency

From Lesson 9
• ingenuity

From Lesson 10
• enormity

-ity

The suffix *-ity* also turns words into nouns that mean "quality or condition of being _____."

Complete each sentence with one of the words below.

brevity   longevity   prosperity   sincerity

1. When people tell the truth, we admire their

_____.

2. When you wish people long life, you wish them

_____.

3. When you wish people success or good fortune, you wish them

_____.

4. When people say something briefly and concisely, they speak with

_____.

Compound Words

A compound word is made up of two words put together. When you read the interview with Will Steger in Lesson 6, you learned that frostbite was just one of the dangers that his team faced as they journeyed to the North Pole. *Frostbite* is made up of the words *frost* and *bite* and refers to damage done to the skin by severely cold, or biting, temperatures.

Fill in each blank with a compound word by combining a word from Row 1 with a word from Row 2.

Row 1:   rain   road   water   wrist

Row 2:   runner   watch   bow   way

1. speedy desert bird = _____

2. arch of colorful light = _____

3. river or canal that ships travel on = _____

4. clock worn on the arm = _____

Multiple-Meaning Words

You know that a single word can have more than one meaning. To figure out which meaning an author is using, you have to use context. Context is the information surrounding a word (or situation) that helps you understand it.

Use context to figure out the correct meaning of each underlined word. Circle the letter of the correct meaning.

1. Bill swung the <u>sledge</u> with both hands as he pounded the spike.

    a. large, heavy hammer

    b. heavy sled or sleigh

2. Our <u>calico</u> cat is white, black, and brown.

    a. patterned cotton cloth

    b. spotted in different colors

3. The pottery maker displayed his <u>goods</u> in the open-air market.

    a. personal belongings

    b. items for sale

VOCABULARY

From Lesson 6
• frostbite

From Lesson 9
• breakdown
• overland
• railroad
• showroom
• snowdrifts

From Lesson 6
• sledge

From Lesson 7
• summoned

Lesson 8
• calico
• commission
• goods

LESSON 11 The Craft of Writing

Building Background

Thank goodness we are all different from one another. One way we show our differences is in our choice of reading materials. While one person can't get enough of nonfictional biographies, another person's tastes might run to mysteries. And just as readers differ in what they like best, so do writers. One writer might write historical fiction nonstop, while another might enjoy writing poetry.

Complete the following statements about your reading and writing preferences. When you are finished, see how your choices compare with your classmates' choices. You will probably see a wide range of preferences.

1. In my spare time, I like to read _____

_____ .

2. The kind of material I like to write is _____

_____ .

3. My favorite author writes _____

_____ .

4. If I were to become a professional writer, I would write _____

_____ .

Vocabulary Builder

addiction

analysis

contradictory

dialog

perceptive

perfectionism

speculating

1. The words in the margin are found in the following essay. Use the words to complete the following sentences. Use a dictionary if you need help.

a. To do an _____ of something, you need to look at it part by part.

b. A monologue is a speech by one person, and a _____ is a conversation between two people.

c. I have a real _____ to chocolate and can't get enough of it.

d. Too much _____ can keep a person from being satisfied with anything.

e. I have been _____ about what I would do with the money if I ever won the lottery.

f. People who notice small details are very _____.

g. I'm puzzled by your _____ statements that first claim one thing and then another.

2. Save your work. You will refer to it again in the Vocabulary Check.

Strategy Builder

Summarizing an Essay

- An **essay** is a work of nonfiction in which the author focuses on a personal issue. The author might explain a point of view or might attempt to teach or persuade the reader. In fact, the word *essay* comes from a French word meaning "to try."

- Because essays are usually personal, they are most often written from the **first-person point of view.** The author uses words such as *I, me, my, and mine* to discuss his or her particular feelings and experiences.

- The organizational pattern of an essay will vary depending on the information the author is presenting, as well as his or her purpose for writing. In "The Craft of Writing," for example, the author uses the organizational pattern of **description** as she **informs** readers about why and how she became a writer—and how they, too, can become writers.

- Sometimes when you read a long essay, you're given a lot of information at once. To keep the information straight—and to remember it better—you might stop from time to time and **summarize** what you've read. When you summarize a section of text, you list or retell the most important ideas in your own words.

- Read the following paragraph from Jane's essay about her favorite childhood games. Then read how one student summarized the paragraph.

> I grew up in a neighborhood filled with children who loved to play games. After supper, we would gather in my big back yard. We might begin the evening's festivities with a loud game of the Mother May I? or the game I liked least, Red Rover, where I always ended up knocked on the ground. Before it got dark, we might launch into a long episode of Kick the Can. This game involved looking for a good place to hide while the player who was "It" counted to one hundred, and then noisily kicking a can before "It" could find you. The games continued until the street lights went on. Then everyone knew that it was time to head home.

Summary

As a child, Jane loved to play games with her neighbors. After supper, they would meet in her yard and begin with Mother May I? or Red Rover. Then they'd play Kick the Can. They'd continue playing games until the street lights went on. Then everyone knew it was time to go home.

The Craft of Writing

by Phyllis Reynolds Naylor

As you read the first part of this essay, think about how you might summarize it. Jot down your ideas on a separate sheet of paper. When you get to the Strategy Break, you can compare your summary with the sample provided.

The idea of being a writer never entered my mind when I was growing up. An occupation, I knew, was something that took years of preparation and hard work, and writing was simply too much fun. So I decided to become a teacher, actress, opera singer, tap dancer, or missionary.

My mother did not approve of my being an actress and told me I would probably faint under the bright lights. She did not like my becoming a tap dancer, either, so I was never allowed to take lessons. Missionaries, as everybody knew, were sometimes eaten alive, so that left teaching and opera singing. Writing was only my hobby.

My parents had always loved reading, so our family had books, but not a lot of them. I remember a set of encyclopedias, some red-bound Sherlock Holmes books, all of Mark Twain's works, and the voluminous Egermeier's *Bible Story Book*, which contained 233 stories about everything from the Garden of Eden to the Holy Ghost.

Mother read to us every night, almost until we were old enough to go out on dates. Occasionally my father did the reading, and these were wonderful times. He could imitate all kinds of voices, from Injun Joe's in *Tom Sawyer* to the runaway Jim's in *Huckleberry Finn*.

I began writing stories as soon as I could get the words down on paper, and by the age of ten, I was writing little books of my own. Each day I would rush home from school to see if the wastebasket held any paper with one side blank. I was not allowed to use new sheets for my writing and drawing, so books had to be made of scratch paper. I would staple the sheets together and sometimes paste a strip of colored paper over the staples to give the pages a bound appearance. Then I would grandly begin my story, writing the words at the top of each page and drawing an appropriate picture at the bottom. Sometimes I even cut old envelopes in half, pasted them on the inside covers as pockets, and slipped an index card in each one so I could check my books out to friends.

As I grew older, my desire to write became stronger. Eventually, after years of work and rejections, my stories were published in national magazines, and I began to write books as well.

 Stop here for the Strategy Break.

Strategy Break

Did you jot down your summary as you read? If you did, see if it looks anything like this:

When Naylor was growing up, writing was only her hobby. Her parents loved to read, and they read to the family every night. Naylor began writing little books by the age of ten. She would make them out of scratch paper and would staple and bind the pages to make them look like real books. Sometimes she put pockets inside her books so she could check them out to friends. Eventually, Naylor published her stories in magazines, and she began writing books too.

As you read the second part of this essay, think about how you would summarize it. When you get to the Strategy Follow-up, you will summarize a section of text.

 Go on reading.

Writing means remembering how you felt when you were small, being aware of how you feel right now, and **speculating** on how you will feel when you are old. It is a combination of real feelings and experiences all mixed up with imaginings, and one place to begin is yourself.

To write well, you must take a good look at yourself. What are your favorable qualities? Your faults? What do you like? Dislike? What makes you feel happy? Sad? Angry? What experiences may have helped to make you the way you are? Who else do you know well? What are they like? How do you feel about them? This **analysis** of yourself and your experiences will help you think of ideas for stories, poems, or articles, and will help you write about them convincingly.

"But how do the ideas keep coming?" people want to know. I asked an artist that same question once. Ideas, she told me, come with time and practice. Gradually she discovered that one idea led to another, and she became more **perceptive** about possibilities. A simple walk down the street gave her a dozen picture ideas—the pattern of light on a wall, the texture of somebody's stockings, or the tangle of branches against the sky. And so it is with writing. I now see story ideas in all sorts of things that earlier I would have dismissed as not worth writing about. It's not so much *what* one writes as *how* one writes.

Let's say you have an idea for a story. To make the most of your time, you will write on a regular schedule, setting aside an hour or more a day to be alone and concentrate. This is essential for any writer. To be sure you've written the best manuscript you can, you're prepared to revise it fifty times if necessary. If you've reached this point, you may not realize it, but you've already started as a writer.

Before you put any words down on paper, your theme and plot have to be clear in your mind. The theme is the main idea you want to convey, the meaning of your story—a moral perhaps, or a lesson you have learned that you think is important enough to write about. The plot is the way you are going to bring this theme to life—the action and conflict that will demonstrate it and make it real.

Beginning writers may choose one simple theme and one simple conflict. But as you grow as a writer, you will learn to make your stories richer by intertwining several themes and conflicts. One major problem may form the basis of your plot, but many minor problems may tangle with it.

Characters, too, must be somewhat **contradictory** if they are to seem true to life. Real people are mixtures of good and bad; they are both wise and foolish, generous and selfish. They may say they believe one way but act another. They may be loving and kind in one instance, but not in another. So when writing **dialog**, for example, you must always put yourself in the place of the speaker and think, "Now what would this person really, honestly say in a situation like this?"

Before they begin writing the actual story, some writers make a list of characters and describe them fully, then an outline of the plot with most of the details filled in. Other writers have only a general notion of what will

happen. They usually know how their story will start and how it will end and a few things that will happen along the way, but they prefer to write without a road map, letting the story develop as it will.

Characters tend to take over a story if you write about them convincingly. Sometimes when a writer tries to make characters do something that is not right for them, they will object. The writing will become very hard and laborious, the characters will turn into cardboard figures, and all the magic will go out of the pages. Then the writer must stop, go back, see where he or she went wrong, and put the characters in control again. But not completely. The writer's own hand must be kept on the pen enough to guide the characters to the final resolution he or she has in mind.

I have written books both ways, using an outline and doing without. Sometimes one method works better, sometimes another. Start with whichever method appeals more to you, and if you find yourself bogging down, switch to the other method, or to something in-between that you invent yourself.

I have found that the first and last paragraphs of each story require the most time and effort. And the first and last sentences are most important of all. I make it a point never to proceed with the rest of the first paragraph until the first sentence is perfect— until it says exactly what I want to say in exactly the right way. And I never continue the first page until the first paragraph is perfect. Sometimes I spend an entire morning on a first sentence or several days on a first paragraph. I go over it again and again, changing, rearranging, substituting words until I get just the effect I want, until I am convinced that no unnecessary words have been used, and that each word is exactly the right one.

Such **perfectionism** pays off. The first paragraph sets the tone and the style, and if I have succeeded in capturing precisely what I want, I have a model to follow for the rest of the story. But if my first paragraph is sloppy, if I wasn't quite sure whether to write it humorously or seriously, I tend to meander in the rest of the pages, and finally I realize that I don't have a style at all and must go back and start over.

Most good writers spend a lot of time rewriting their work before they come up with a finished copy. This is perhaps the most difficult thing for beginning writers to understand. All of us, of course, would like to write something down on paper and have it perfect the first time. But this rarely happens. There's always that urge to hurry, to trick oneself, to read rapidly over paragraphs that aren't quite right and pretend they are "good enough." A paragraph is never good enough until you know deep down in your heart that there is nothing, absolutely nothing, you can do to improve it—that you have replaced all the second-rate words with the best possible choices, that every sentence needs to be there, and that everything a character does or says somehow helps the story along.

When you have completed your manuscript, set it aside for a few days or weeks and then read it again. The passage of time will help you to approach the story with a fresh view, and glaring faults may be obvious. If there is something not quite resolved in your plot, something that doesn't quite make sense, correct it now. Don't think it is so small that no one will notice it. Someone will.

How can a young person prepare for a career as a writer? I think literature courses are far more helpful than writing classes. But nothing will be as helpful as living a full life with many types of experiences, good and bad. Everything that happens to you should be stored in your memory for use later on. In the past I read dozens of Russian and English novels, and I can see how my own writing has been influenced by them.

Reading will always help—good books as well as junk. How can you ever tell the difference if you spend all your time with one or the other? When you compare the two, you will see for yourself how rich and full the writing of great authors is, and how empty and repetitive the junk writing is.

In the long run, the best way to become a writer is to write, write, write. Read and observe and take classes and fill notebooks all you like, but eventually you will have to face up to the real work—writing in a disciplined way. Try different subjects and approaches, but concentrate first on what comes most naturally to you. If, at this time in your life, you have not had many experiences, write about what you do know, because then your stories will ring true, and other people will say when they read them, "Of course, that's just how *I've* felt sometimes. That's it exactly!"

Writing, for me, is an **addiction**. A story idea in my head is like a rock in my shoe—I just can't wait to get it out. And if you feel that way, too, you're on your way to becoming a true writer. ●

Strategy Follow-up

Work with a partner or two to complete this activity. On a separate sheet of paper, take turns writing a summary for the section of the essay that begins with the sentence *How can a young person prepare for a career as a writer?* and ends with *"That's it exactly!"* Use your own words as you summarize. Be sure to include only the most important ideas, and skip unnecessary details.

✓Personal Checklist

Read each question and put a check (✓) in the correct box.

1. How well do you understand the message of this essay?
   - ☐ 3 (extremely well)
   - ☐ 2 (fairly well)
   - ☐ 1 (not well)

2. After reading this essay, how well would you be able to summarize Naylor's advice to future writers?
   - ☐ 3 (extremely well)
   - ☐ 2 (fairly well)
   - ☐ 1 (not well)

3. In Building Background, how well were you able to identify your reading and writing preferences?
   - ☐ 3 (extremely well)
   - ☐ 2 (fairly well)
   - ☐ 1 (not well)

4. How well were you able to complete the sentences in the Vocabulary Builder?
   - ☐ 3 (extremely well)
   - ☐ 2 (fairly well)
   - ☐ 1 (not well)

5. In the Strategy Follow-up, how well were you able to help summarize a section of this essay?
   - ☐ 3 (extremely well)
   - ☐ 2 (fairly well)
   - ☐ 1 (not well)

Vocabulary Check

Look back at the work you did in the Vocabulary Builder. Then answer each question by circling the correct letter.

1. What is another word for *dialog*?
   - a. conversation
   - b. perfectionism
   - c. manuscript

2. What would a laboratory do to find out what a particular substance contained?
   - a. an experience
   - b. an addiction
   - c. an analysis

3. What is it called when you find something wrong with everything?
   - a. speculating
   - b. perfectionism
   - c. addiction

4. What kinds of statements does a person make who is always changing his or her mind?
   - a. dialog
   - b. perceptive
   - c. contradictory

5. What happens when you have an addiction?
   - a. You can't control your cravings.
   - b. You can't write clearly.
   - c. You can't read difficult material.

Add the numbers that you just checked to get your Personal Checklist score. Fill in your score here. Then turn to page 215 and transfer your score onto Graph 1.

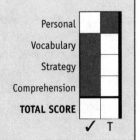

Check your answers with your teacher. Give yourself 1 point for each correct answer, and fill in your Vocabulary score here. Then turn to page 215 and transfer your score onto Graph 1.

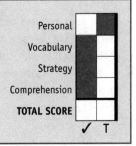

Strategy Check

Review the summary that you helped write in the Strategy Follow-up. Also review the rest of this essay. Then answer these questions:

1. Which sentence best summarizes how Naylor says a young person can prepare for a career as a writer?

   a. Take as many writing courses as you possibly can.

   b. Live a full life with many types of experiences.

   c. Read dozens of Russian and English novels.

2. What does Naylor say you should read to prepare yourself for being a writer?

   a. good books as well as junk

   b. dozens of Russian and English novels

   c. the works of many great authors

3. Which sentence best summarizes what Naylor says is the best way to become a writer?

   a. The best way to become a writer is to study, study, study.

   b. The best way to become a writer is to read, read, read.

   c. The best way to become a writer is to write, write, write.

4. What does Naylor say you need to do before you put any words down on paper?

   a. Have your theme and plot clear in your mind.

   b. Have all your characters clear in your mind.

   c. Be prepared to revise 50 times if necessary.

5. Which of the following best summarizes why Naylor wrote this essay?

   a. to explain why and how she became a writer

   b. to explain the craft of writing

   c. both of the above

Comprehension Check

Review the essay if necessary. Then answer these questions:

1. When Naylor was little, she thought of taking up many occupations. Which of the following was *not* one of them?

   a. teaching

   b. tap dancing

   c. writing

2. What does Naylor say you must do in order to write well?

   a. take a good look at yourself

   b. get a good computer or word processor

   c. take many classes on writing techniques

3. According to Naylor, what is a good way to get ideas for writing?

   a. Write about the same subject until you have explored it thoroughly.

   b. Read an encyclopedia to broaden your horizons.

   c. Notice what is all around you.

4. What does Naylor claim happens if a writer tries to make characters do what is not right for them?

   a. The story will be easier to write because the writer has taken control.

   b. The writer may have trouble writing, and the characters will lose their vitality.

   c. The story will become humorous.

5. Why does Naylor say that writing is an addiction for her?

   a. She wants to write all the time.

   b. Writing makes her feel sick.

   c. She has to write to make a living.

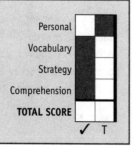

Check your answers with your teacher. Give yourself 1 point for each correct answer, and fill in your Strategy score here. Then turn to page 215 and transfer your score onto Graph 1.

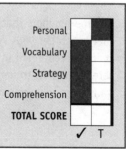

Check your answers with your teacher. Give yourself 1 point for each correct answer, and fill in your Comprehension score here. Then turn to page 215 and transfer your score onto Graph 1.

Extending

Choose one or more of these activities:

CHOOSE YOUR IDEAL OCCUPATION

Phyllis Reynolds Naylor says that she dreamed of many occupations while growing up. Think about what occupations might be best for you. First make a list of your strengths, such as creativity or patience or good math skills. Then make a list of your interests, such as caring for children, working with computers, or seeing the world. Analyze both lists, and then write at least three occupations that would make the best use of your strengths and interests.

WRITE ABOUT YOUR FIELD OF EXPERTISE

Naylor wrote about what she knows best—writing. Consider a subject that you know well, for example: gardening, skateboarding, working at a restaurant, or surfing the Internet. Write a short essay about the best way to prepare for and undertake that endeavor. Include information about the qualities that make you successful at that pastime, hobby, or job, as well as advice for anyone who would like to try it too.

ANALYZE NAYLOR'S WRITING

Read more by Phyllis Reynolds Naylor, and then analyze her writing. (See the resource section for several of her books.) Are her characters well-developed? Are her plots intriguing and easy to follow? Look for similarities and differences among her books, and discuss them with your classmates. What makes Naylor an award-winning author?

Resources

Books

Naylor, Phyllis Reynolds. *The Agony of Alice.* Aladdin, 1997.

———. *Alice on the Outside.* Simon Pulse, 2000.

———. *Saving Shiloh.* Aladdin, 1999.

———. *Send No Blessings.* Atheneum, 1990.

———. *Shiloh.* Aladdin, 2000.

Web Site

http://www.carolhurst.com/authors/pnaylor.html
Read more about Phyllis Reynolds Naylor on this Web site.

Video/DVD

Good Conversation! A Talk with Phyllis Reynolds Naylor. Tim Podell Productions, 1999.

calamity

curious

depression

desperate

determined

poverty

sneered

tightly

whirled

from Walking Through the Dark

Building Background

Sometimes an event has worldwide effects. Such an event was the stock market crash of 1929. Millions of Americans lost money when the stocks they had bought became almost worthless overnight. The country was forced to face up to the fact that businesses were in grave trouble. When businesses are in trouble, they close, and their employees find themselves out of work. Our nation's money troubles were mirrored in countries all around the world. In every country, people had to deal with poverty, unemployment, and homelessness.

Imagine that suddenly, as happened to so many families during the Great Depression, no one in your family had a job. What thoughts would go through your mind? How do you suppose your life would change? In the thought balloons below, write five thoughts or questions that would be on your mind if you found yourself in that situation.

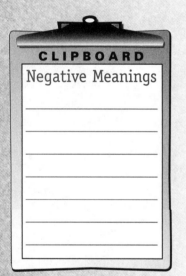

CLIPBOARD

Negative Meanings

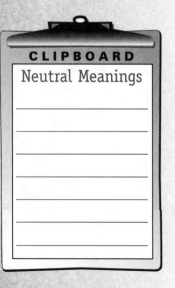

CLIPBOARD

Neutral Meanings

Vocabulary Builder

1. The words in the margin are from the story on page 122. Decide which of the words produce negative feelings in you and which words produce feelings that are neutral—neither negative nor positive. Then write each word on the appropriate clipboard.

2. As you read the selection, find the sentences that contain the boldfaced vocabulary words. After reading the words in context, would you still place them on the same clipboards? Change your answers if necessary.

3. Then save your work. You will refer to it again in the Vocabulary Check.

Strategy Builder

Drawing Conclusions about Characters

- As you know, the characters in a story are the people who perform the action. In some stories, the characters remain the same from the beginning to the end. These characters are called **static characters**. In other stories, however, the characters change. These characters are called **dynamic characters**.

- Dynamic characters usually change in response to events. You must keep track of those events and their effects on the characters. The author gives you clues about how and why the characters change throughout the story. From those clues, you can **draw conclusions** about the characters. A **conclusion** is a decision that you reach after thinking about information that the author gives you. You can draw conclusions about characters by looking at what they say, do, think, and feel.

- Read the following paragraphs. What conclusions can you draw about Laura based on what she says, does, thinks, and feels?

> Laura should have been enjoying her vacation, but she wasn't. She knew that everyone expected her to go on the canoe trip tomorrow, and she was dreading it. She had never been canoeing before and was afraid.
>
> When the time for the canoe trip came, Laura decided not to go. She would stay back at the cottage by herself. As everyone was preparing to leave, Laura walked down to the riverbank to wave goodbye. Soon everyone was laughing and having a good time—including Laura. *Maybe this wouldn't be so bad after all,* she thought. But at the last minute, she froze. She couldn't get into the canoe. Her best friend, Chris, held out her hand to help Laura in. Laura looked at the river, the canoe, and all her friends and then quickly climbed into the canoe.
>
> "Let's go," she said. "What's taking everyone so long?"

- If you wanted to track the changes in Laura's attitude, you could record them on a **character wheel** like the one below. The conclusions that one reader drew about Laura are in *italics.*

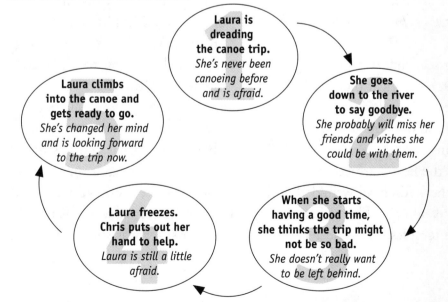

from Walking Through the Dark

by Phyllis Reynolds Naylor

As you read the first part of this selection, notice what Ruth says, does, thinks, and feels. What conclusions can you draw about her?

This selection is an excerpt from Naylor's novel, *Walking Through the Dark*, about a teenage girl growing up during the Great Depression. Notice how the author uses some of the techniques she described in "The Craft of Writing" in Lesson 11.

November 13, 1931
Dear Diary:

Today Father bought two boxes of apples from someone he knew on the corner of State and Madison. Mother says we'll have to use them for sauce, and I don't even like apples. Some birthday present!

For the first time I can remember, I'm not getting a new dress. Mother made over a dotted swiss of Aunt Marie's, but I don't think it looks right for winter. Oh, well. Maybe it's all because my birthday fell on Friday the thirteenth this time. . . .

"I don't see what was so wrong with it. *Cimarron* is a great picture. It won the Academy Award."

Ruth stood over the hot air register in the living room, her white dress billowing as the heat warmed her legs.

Her father's forehead wrinkled with impatience, and tiny blue veins stood out at the temples. Joe Wheeler was a small man, wiry and nervous, and now he sat on the edge of the sofa as though any moment he would spring forward.

"What's wrong is that you already saw it once! A waste of money!"

"But if I go every Saturday anyway, what difference does it make if I see the same movie twice?"

"I see her point, Joe," Mother commented from the dining room where she was addressing Christmas cards.

"She *has* no point!" Mr. Wheeler transferred his glare to his wife. "Millions of people without the price of bread, and this girl pays to see a movie twice. Like we're so rich we don't miss it. This is a **depression** Ruthie! You're fourteen now. Time you understood things like that." He stood up and thrust his hands in his pockets, shoulders hunched.

Ruth squatted down on the register to get her legs closer to the heat, hugging herself. "But if I go every Saturday anyway. . . ." she began.

"*Don't* go every Saturday!" her father exploded. "If you've seen a movie once, save your quarter for something else." He **whirled** suddenly toward the corner where Ruth's younger sister was sprawled on the rug listening to the radio. "Turn that thing down! Can't even hear *myself* above that noise."

Dawn stared back at him.

"Turn it down, Dawn," Mother urged, giving her a special look.

Joe Wheeler faced his wife. "It's up to you now, Grace. You've got to check how the girls handle their money. Don't spend a dime you don't have to." He bent over and picked up the pages of the *Chicago Tribune*, which had dropped from his lap, folding the edges meticulously together. "We don't know the meaning of want. Lewis Solomon didn't either, and now he's standing out there in his two-hundred dollar suits selling apples. A man never thinks he'll come to that. . . ."

He moved over to the window and stared at the street awhile. Then he went outside to check the car's radiator.

Ruth waited till the door closed behind him. She could hear the scratch of her mother's pen in the next room, and waited till it stopped.

"What's the matter with him, Mother? He's got the worst temper lately."

"He sure does!" Dawn agreed. She turned off the Philco and came over to share the heat with Ruth. "Yesterday he scolded me just because I lost three pennies."

"Your father has a lot to think about right now with business way down," Mother answered. "And he's right. We should be more careful with money."

Dawn caught sight of Ruth's bracelet. "Ruth! Where did you get this?" She knelt down and touched the gold leaves with her chubby fingers.

"Isn't it beautiful?" Ruth held out her arm. "Kitty gave it to me this afternoon as a birthday present."

Mrs. Wheeler got up and came over to look. "Why, Ruth! Her family can't afford presents like that! It looks terribly expensive."

"It is. It was her grandmother's."

"It's beautiful, dear, but I don't think you should have accepted it."

"Why *not*?" Ruth demanded. And suddenly, she'd had enough. There was something so joyless about her parents these days. Without waiting for an answer, she went upstairs to her room.

Had her parents always been so somber, she wondered, and she was just noticing it more as she got older? Or was there something about the year, the times, that made them so humorless?

Ruth finished dusting the living room and took the cloth upstairs. Mother liked to have the house clean before they took their Sunday drive so she could look forward to coming back. The nicest part about going anywhere, Mrs. Wheeler believed, was coming home again.

"Let's go for a ride," came Father's voice from the hallway below, but today it had a ring of duty about it, not of pleasure.

Ruth and Dawn got in the back seat and took turns holding the door shut. The car had been dented two months ago and still had not been fixed. It was easier holding the door than reminding Father to have it repaired.

The raccoon collar on Mother's coat blocked the view out the front, so Ruth watched through the side window. Usually the Sunday route was the same—straight east to the lake, then up through Jackson Park, Grant Park—past the Field Museum and Buckingham Fountain—still north till they reached Navy Pier. Then they would turn west, into the heart of the city, and finally head south on Halsted, which ran the length of Chicago. But today the Pontiac turned west immediately.

"Joe?" Mother said questioningly.

"We're going to see a Hooverville," Father replied. "It's time they knew what it's like."

Ruth was **curious**. She'd heard the word at school. No matter what happened, it was blamed on the President. Newspapers used for covers were called Hoover blankets. Shanty towns were Hoovervilles. Father said that if the Mississippi flooded, they'd blame that on Hoover, too. But this time he used the word himself.

"What's a Hooverville?" Dawn asked.

"A place where people live when they don't have homes," her father replied.

"Joe, they're so young . . ." Mother murmured.

"These are hard times, Grace, and the girls have got to know."

They all fell silent then.

 Stop here for the Strategy Break.

Strategy Break

What conclusions can you draw about Ruth so far? If you were to begin a character wheel for her, it might look like this:

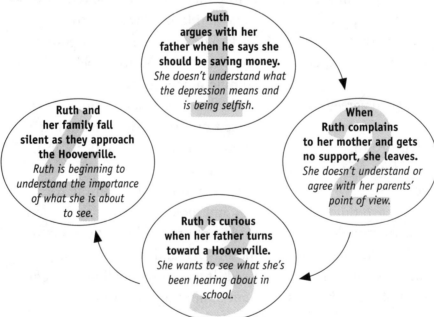

1. **Ruth argues with her father when he says she should be saving money.** *She doesn't understand what the depression means and is being selfish.*

2. **When Ruth complains to her mother and gets no support, she leaves.** *She doesn't understand or agree with her parents' point of view.*

3. **Ruth is curious when her father turns toward a Hooverville.** *She wants to see what she's been hearing about in school.*

4. **Ruth and her family fall silent as they approach the Hooverville.** *Ruth is beginning to understand the importance of what she is about to see.*

As you continue reading, keep drawing conclusions about Ruth. At the end of the selection, you will finish her character wheel. Does she continue to change?

Go on reading to see what happens.

It was not as though Ruth had never seen **poverty**. She had seen the bread lines on Maxwell Street, the soup kitchens, the men asleep under the Michigan Avenue bridge. But somehow it had all seemed transitory. Somewhere, she had felt, there was a home waiting—and after a week or two looking for work, the men would go back to wherever they came from and get jobs somewhere else.

The houses became grayer and shabbier as the car rattled on, then disappeared abruptly as warehouses and factories took their place. For half an hour Ruth watched as sidewalks gave way to crumbling curbstones, and newsstands to broken glass. And suddenly there it was, on a once-vacant lot—a Hooverville built around one side of an abandoned icehouse.

At first Ruth thought it was a city dumping ground. And then she saw people moving about and realized that to them it was home. It was as though the icehouse, beset by old age, had developed tumors that crept out from one wall and oozed people. Sheets of corrugated tin leaned against its walls forming metal tents for the families huddled underneath. A family "hooked on" to its neighbors with whatever it could find—a slab of plywood, a few two-by-fours covered with layers of cardboard, a surplus army tent, a box. . . .

Off to one side, a family lived in a deserted streetcar, the elite of Hooverville.

"Is this it?" Dawn whispered to Ruth.

She nodded.

Slowly the Pontiac circled the lot. Dawn sat with her face against the window, frankly staring, while Mother said nothing, lost, it seemed, in her raccoon collar. Ruth's eyes searched through the makeshift city, amazed at the **desperate** creativity of those who slept in concrete drainage ducts or discarded bathtubs, looking for the place where, if such a **calamity** happened to her, she would choose to make a nest. She realized that only the streetcar would do.

The Pontiac came back to the place where it began and started around the lot a second time.

"Oh, Joe!" Mother said quickly.

"Dad! They'll all stare at us!" Ruth protested, pressing back against the seat to escape their faces. But her father was **determined**.

"Take a good look," he said. "This is hard times. Don't ever forget it."

As the car moved around again, it was not the housing so much or the makeshift clothing that captivated Ruth, but the faces—dull, blank faces that seemed frozen with poverty.

They were passing a family of four living in an open piano crate. The mother nursed the baby, the father lay either sick or asleep. But standing outside, leaning against her home, was a girl slightly younger than Ruth, staring back at her without blinking. And then, as their eyes met, the girl **sneered**. Not openly—just a curling of the lips, a narrowing of the eyes, a haughtiness of the brows—and Ruth

closed her eyes **tightly** and did not
open them again till they were finally
heading home. ●

Strategy Follow-up

Work with a partner to complete this activity. On a large sheet of paper, copy the character
wheel below. Then fill in ovals 5–8 with information from the second part of the selection.

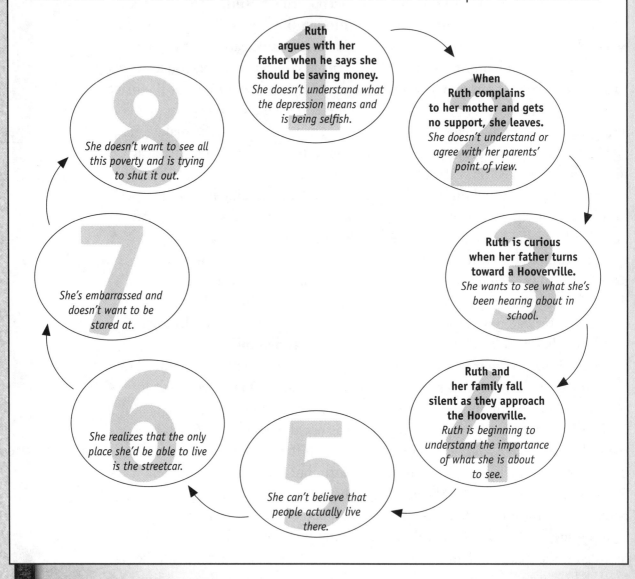

Ruth argues with her father when he says she should be saving money.
She doesn't understand what the depression means and is being selfish.

When Ruth complains to her mother and gets no support, she leaves.
She doesn't understand or agree with her parents' point of view.

Ruth is curious when her father turns toward a Hooverville.
She wants to see what she's been hearing about in school.

Ruth and her family fall silent as they approach the Hooverville.
Ruth is beginning to understand the importance of what she is about to see.

She can't believe that people actually live there.

She realizes that the only place she'd be able to live is the streetcar.

She's embarrassed and doesn't want to be stared at.

She doesn't want to see all this poverty and is trying to shut it out.

✓Personal Checklist

Read each question and put a check (✓) in the correct box.

1. How well did what you wrote in Building Background help you understand Ruth's feelings?
   - ☐ 3 (extremely well)
   - ☐ 2 (fairly well)
   - ☐ 1 (not well)

2. By the time you finished this selection, how well were you able to put the vocabulary words on the appropriate clipboards?
   - ☐ 3 (extremely well)
   - ☐ 2 (fairly well)
   - ☐ 1 (not well)

3. How well were you able to complete Ruth's character wheel in the Strategy Follow-up?
   - ☐ 3 (extremely well)
   - ☐ 2 (fairly well)
   - ☐ 1 (not well)

4. How well do you understand why Ruth's father is angry with her at the beginning of this selection?
   - ☐ 3 (extremely well)
   - ☐ 2 (fairly well)
   - ☐ 1 (not well)

5. How well do you understand why Ruth's father takes the family to a Hooverville?
   - ☐ 3 (extremely well)
   - ☐ 2 (fairly well)
   - ☐ 1 (not well)

Vocabulary Check

Look back at the work you did in the Vocabulary Builder. Then answer each question by circling the correct letter.

1. If you heard about a calamity that happened to a good friend, how would you feel?
   a. joyful
   b. sorry
   c. neutral

2. Which phrase best describes the word *whirled*?
   a. spun around quickly
   b. walked away
   c. thought deeply

3. Which meaning of the word *depression* matches the context of this selection?
   a. a place that is pressed down lower than the surrounding area
   b. a time when businesses are failing and unemployment is up
   c. a feeling of overwhelming sadness

4. What is a synonym for *determined*?
   a. curious
   b. lazy
   c. insistent

5. When someone sneers, what emotion is he or she showing?
   a. surprise
   b. happiness
   c. dislike

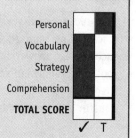

Add the numbers that you just checked to get your Personal Checklist score. Fill in your score here. Then turn to page 215 and transfer your score onto Graph 1.

Personal
Vocabulary
Strategy
Comprehension
TOTAL SCORE
✓ T

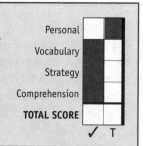

Check your answers with your teacher. Give yourself 1 point for each correct answer, and fill in your Vocabulary score here. Then turn to page 215 and transfer your score onto Graph 1.

Personal
Vocabulary
Strategy
Comprehension
TOTAL SCORE
✓ T

Strategy Check

Review the character wheel that you completed in the Strategy Follow-up, and the rest of the selection if necessary. Then answer these questions:

1. At first, what is Ruth's attitude about the depression?

   a. She understands why her parents don't want her to spend her money.

   b. She understands completely why her parents are taking it so seriously.

   c. She doesn't pay much attention to it because it doesn't affect her personally.

2. Why do you think Ruth's father takes the family to a Hooverville?

   a. He wants to try a new route during their weekly car trip.

   b. He wants them to see firsthand how the depression is affecting people.

   c. He got lost while they were out.

3. When Ruth first sees the Hooverville, why does she think it's a dumping ground?

   a. because she can't believe that people actually live there

   b. because she'd been there before to dump the family's trash

   c. because there were only piles of trash

4. Why do you think Ruth closes her eyes until they are on their way home?

   a. She is suddenly very sleepy.

   b. She wants her father to think that she didn't see the Hooverville.

   c. She doesn't want to see the poverty and is trying to shut it out.

5. What do you predict Ruth will do next Saturday?

   a. stay home and save her quarter

   b. go back and see *Cimarron* again

   c. take another trip to a Hooverville

Comprehension Check

Review the selection if necessary. Then answer these questions:

1. What is special to Ruth about November 13?

   a. It is her birthday.

   b. It is the day she goes to the movies.

   c. It is the day she goes to a Hooverville.

2. What does Mr. Wheeler want Ruth to understand?

   a. that she needs to start saving for college

   b. that she doesn't deserve to be happy when others are sad

   c. that the depression has been difficult for everyone

3. Where does the Wheeler family live?

   a. Chicago

   b. Hooverville

   c. Michigan

4. Why do the girls become quieter when they visit the Hooverville?

   a. They are afraid of being attacked.

   b. Their father told them to be quiet.

   c. They are stunned by what they see.

5. What emotions might Ruth be feeling when she meets the eyes of the sneering girl in Hooverville?

   a. confusion and guilt at her own good fortune

   b. anger and hatred toward the girl

   c. a feeling that she's better than the girl

Check your answers with your teacher. Give yourself 1 point for each correct answer, and fill in your Strategy score here. Then turn to page 215 and transfer your score onto Graph 1.

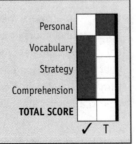

Check your answers with your teacher. Give yourself 1 point for each correct answer, and fill in your Comprehension score here. Then turn to page 215 and transfer your score onto Graph 1.

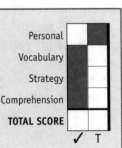

Extending

Choose one or more of these activities:

INTERVIEW SOMEONE WHO LIVED THROUGH THE GREAT DEPRESSION

The Great Depression had a tremendous impact on those who lived though it. Interview an older relative or family friend about life during the Depression. Ask questions such as these: How was your family affected by the hard times? What jobs did family members have, or how did they look for jobs? What cost-cutting measures did you use? What was your role in saving or earning money for the family? How did friends and neighbors help each other? Tape record your conversation if possible. With permission, play it for your classmates.

FIND OUT ABOUT HOMELESSNESS TODAY

During the Great Depression, homeless people gathered in Hoovervilles like the one that Ruth and her family visit. There are still homeless people today. Do some research on what your local community does to help the homeless. You may try calling various social service agencies or newspapers to find out this information. Prepare a short report for the rest of the class, and explain what you have learned.

LEARN MORE ABOUT THE GREAT DEPRESSION

Using the resources listed on this page or ones you find yourself, learn more about the Great Depression. As you do your research, try to find the answers to these questions:

- What caused the Great Depression?
- How long did it last?
- Who was affected by it?
- Was everyone affected equally?
- What did the Federal government do to try to end the depression?
- How did it finally end?
- Has the government taken any precautions to ensure that the United States won't have another Great Depression?

Resources

Books

Bendiner, Robert. *Just Around the Corner: A Highly Selective History of the Thirties.* Dutton, 1988.

Hard Times, the 30s. Our American Century. Time-Life Books, 1998.

Naylor, Phyllis Reynolds. *Walking Through the Dark.* Atheneum, 1976.

Nishi, Dennis. *Life During the Great Depression.* The Way People Live. Lucent, 1998.

Wormser, Richard. *Growing Up in the Great Depression.* Atheneum, 1995.

Web Sites

http://memory.loc.gov/ammem/fsowhome.html
On this Library of Congress Web site, you can view photographs taken during the period from the Great Depression to World War II.

http://users.snowcrest.net/jmike/20sdep.html
Scroll down to the "Great Depression" section on this site for links to resources about the period.

http://www.nationalhomeless.org/
Get information about homelessness today on this Web site of the National Coalition for the Homeless.

http://www.pbs.org/wgbh/amex/rails/index.html
This is a companion Web site to *Riding the Rails,* a PBS program about the 250,000 teenagers who lived on the road during the Great Depression.

Audio Recording

Brother, Can You Spare a Dime? American Song During the Great Depression. New World Records, 2001.

Video/DVD

Just Around the Corner. Republic Entertainment, 1991.

Building Background

Throughout "The Storm" Mom uses the expression, "The third time is the charm." What does that expression mean? Do you agree or disagree with it? On the lines below, first explain what you think the expression means. Then explain why you agree or disagree with it. If you agree, try to cite at least one example that supports your opinion.

_____

_____

_____

_____

_____

_____

chirrup

clutch

katydids

nasturtium

pretty

Vocabulary Builder

1. The words in the margin are found in "The Storm." Use the words to complete each of the following sentences.

2. If you need help with any of the words, find them in the story and use context to figure them out. Be careful—the word *pretty* is used differently from the way it's usually used today.

   a. A duck will quack, and a cricket will _____.

   b. When you throw something, you hurl it. But when you hold something tightly, you _____ it.

   c. A robin is a bird, and a _____ is a flower.

   d. You do a job with a tool, but you play with a _____.

   e. Maples are trees, and _____ are insects.

3. Save your work. You will refer to it again in the Vocabulary Check.

Strategy Builder

Observing Characters

- When you **observe** something, you study it in detail. You can learn about the characters in a story by observing what they say, do, think, and feel. You also can learn about characters by observing what other characters say *about* them. In "The Storm," for example, you will learn about Mom and Pa by observing what one of their children says about them. Shan—narrating the story from the **third-person point of view**—reveals what Mom and Pa say, do, think, and feel throughout the story.

- Now read the following paragraphs. Use the clues provided to help you learn about Lisa.

> Everyone was anxiously awaiting Lisa's return from college. The youngest children got out the board games that Lisa always played with them. They also prepared the playhouse in which Lisa liked to join them for tea parties.
>
> Lisa's teenage brother made a list of the movies that he wanted to rent while she was home. *It's always fun to watch with someone else who enjoys a good comedy*, he thought.
>
> Lisa's best friend prepared a surprise party for her, knowing that people always enjoyed socializing with Lisa. Most of Lisa's friends were eager to see her in person again, after communicating with her only by e-mail for months.

- You can learn a great deal about Lisa from this paragraph, even though she has not done or said anything in it. If you wanted to record your observations on a **concept map**, it might look like this:

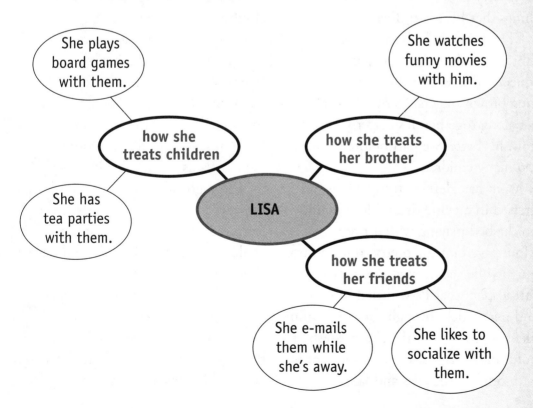

The Storm

by Jesse Stuart

As you read "The Storm," apply the strategies that you just learned. Observe the clues that Shan provides to help you learn about Mom and Pa.

"I can't stand it any longer, Mick," Mom says. "I'm leaving you. I'm going home to Pap. I'll have a rooftree above my head there. Pap will take me in. He'll give me and my children the best he has."

Mom lifts the washrag from the washpan of soapy water. She washes my neck and ears. Mom pushes the warm soft rag against my ears. Drops of warm water ooze down my neck to my shirt collar. Mom's lips are drawn tight. Her long fingers grip the washrag like a chicken's toes **clutch** a roost-limb on a winter night.

"We're different people," says Pa. "I'm sorry about it all, Sal. If I say things that hurt you, I can't help it."

"That's just it," Mom says as she dips the washrag into the pan and squeezes the soapy water between her long brown fingers. "Since we can't get along together, it's better we part now. It's better we part before we have too many children."

Mom has Herbert ready. He is dressed in a white dress. He is lying on the bed playing with a **pretty**. Mom gave him the pretty to keep him quiet while she dressed me. It is a threadspool that Pa whittled in two and put a stick through for me to spin like a top. I look at the pretty Herbert holds in his hands. Herbert looks at it with bright little eyes and laughs.

"Mom, he has the pretty Pa made for me," I say. "I don't want him to have it."

"Quit fussing with your baby brother," Mom says as she puts my hand into the washpan and begins to scrub it.

"Pa made it for me," I say, "and I want to take it with me. I want to keep it."

Pa looks at the top Herbert has clutched in his young mousepaw-colored fingers. Pa moves in his chair. He crosses one leg above the other. He pulls hard on his pipe. He blows tiny clouds of smoke into the room.

"You're not going to take all the children and leave me alone!" he says.

"They are mine," says Mom, "and I intend to have all three of them or fight everybody in this hollow. They are of my flesh and blood and I gave them birth—and I remember—and—I'm going to hold them." Mom looks hard at Pa as she speaks these words.

"I thought if you'd let Sis stay," says Pa, "she'd soon be old enough to cook for me. If it's anything I hate, it's cooking. I can't cook much. I'll have a time eating the food I cook."

"Serves you right, Mick," says Mom.

"It doesn't serve me right," says Pa. "I intend to stay right here and see that this farm goes on. And if I'm not fooled an awful lot, you'll be back, Sal."

"That's what you think," Mom storms. "I'm not coming back. I do not want ever to see this shack again."

"It's the best roof I can put over your head," Pa says.

"It's not the roof that's over my head," Mom says. "Mick, it's you. You can be laughing one minute and the next minute you can be raising the roof with your vile oaths. Your mind is more changeable than the weather. I never know how to take you, no more than I know how the wind will blow tomorrow."

"We just aren't the same people," Pa says. "That's why I love you, Sal. You're not like I am. You are solid as a mountain. I need you, Sal. I need you more than anyone I know in this world."

"I'm leaving," Mom says. "I'm tired of this. I've been ready to go twice before. I felt sorry for you and my little children that would be raised without a father. This is the third time I've planned to go. Third time is the charm. I'm going this time."

"I'm ready, Mom," says Sis as she climbs down the ladder from the loft. "I'm ready to go to Grandpa's with you."

Sis is dressed in a blue gingham dress. Her ripe-wheat-colored hair falls over her shoulders in two plaits. A blue ribbon is tied on each plait and beneath the ribbons her hair is not plaited. Her hair is bushy as two cottontails.

Pa cranes his autumn-brown neck. He looks at Sis and blows a cloud of smoke slowly from his mouth. Pa's face is brown as a pawpaw leaf in September. His face has caught the spring sunshine as he plowed our mules around the mountain slope.

"Listen," says Pa, "I hear something like April thunder!"

Pa holds his pipe in his hand. He sits silently. He does not speak. Mom squeezes the washrag in the water again. Now she listens.

"I don't hear anything," says Mom. "You just imagined you heard something."

"No, I didn't," Pa answers.

"It can't be thunder, Mick," says Mom. "The sky is blue as the water in the well."

Pa rises from his chair. He walks to the door. He cranes his brown neck like a hen that says "qrrr" when she thinks a hawk is near to swoop down upon her biddies.

"The rains come over the mountain that's to our right," Pa says. "That's the way the rains come, all right. I've seen them come too many times. But the sky is clear—all but a maretail in the sky. That's a good sign there'll be rain in three days."

"Rain three days away won't matter much to us," says Mom. "We just have seven miles to walk. We'll be at Pap's place in three hours."

"Listen—it's thunder I hear," Pa says loudly. "I didn't think my ears fooled me a while ago. I can always hear the foxhounds barking in the deep hollows before Kim and Gaylord can. Can't beat my ears for hearing."

"I don't hear it," says Mom as she takes the pan of water across the dog-trot toward the kitchen.

"You will hear it in a few minutes," says Pa. "It's like potato wagons rolling across the far skies."

"Third time is the charm for me," says Mom as she returns from the kitchen without the washpan. "Ever since I can remember, the third time has been the charm for me. I can remember once setting a hen on guinea eggs. A blacksnake that you kept in the corncrib crawled through a crack to my hen's nest. He crawled under the hen and swallowed the eggs. He was so full of eggs that when he tried to crawl out of the nest he fell to the ground. I saw him fall with his sides bulged in and out like wild frostbitten snowballs. I took a hoe and clipped his head. Then I set my hen on goose eggs and soon as they hatched my old hen pinched their necks with her bill like you'd do with a pair of scissors. I set her on her own kind of eggs—and she hatched every one of the eggs and raised all her biddies. Third time was the charm."

"See the martins hurrying to their boxes," says Pa. "Look out there, Sal! That's the sign of an approaching storm."

The martins fly in circles above our fresh-plowed garden. They cut the bright April air with black fan-shaped wings. They chatter as they fly—circle once and twice around the boxes and alight on the little porches before the twelve doors cut in each of the two big boxes. Martins chatter as they poke their heads in at the doors—draw them out one and chatter again—then silently slip their black-preening feathered bodies in at the small doors.

Mom looks at the long sagging martin boxes—each pole supported by a corner garden post. Mom watches the martins hurrying to the boxes. She listens to their endless chatter to each other and their quarreling from one box of martins in the other box.

"Listen, Sal—listen—"

"It's thunder, Mick! I hear it."

"Will we go, Mom?" Sis asks.

"Yes, we'll go before the storm."

"But it's coming fast, Sal, or the martins wouldn't be coming home to their nests of young ones like they are. Are you going to take our children out in a storm? Don't you know as much as the martin birds?"

I know what Mom is thinking about when she looks at the martin boxes. She remembers the day when Pa made the boxes at the barn. She held the boards while he sawed them with a handsaw. She remembers when he cut the long chestnut poles and peeled them and slid them over the cliffs above the house. They slid to the foot of the mountain like racer snakes before a new-ground fire. She held the boxes when Pa nailed them to the poles. Mom helped him lift the poles into the deep post holes and Mom helped him wrap the baled-hay wire around the poles and the corner garden posts to hold them steady when the winds blew. I'd just got rid of my dresses then and starting wearing rompers.

Mom turns from the front door. She does not speak to Pa. She walks to the dresser in the corner of the room. She opens a dresser drawer. She lifts clothes from the dresser drawer. She stacks them neatly on the bottom of a hickory-split-bottomed chair. She looks at the chair.

"I know what Mom is thinking," I think as she looks at the chair. "She remembers when she grumbled about the bad bottoms in the chairs and Pa says: 'Wait till spring, Sal—wait until the sap gets up in the hickories until I can skin their bark. I'll fix the chair bottoms.'"

And when the sap got up that early spring in the hickories, Pa took a day off from plowing and peeled hickory bark and scraped the green from the rough side of the bark and laced bot-toms across the chairs. I know Mom remembers this, for she helped Pa. I held the soft green, tough slats of bark for them and reached them a piece of bark as they needed it.

 Stop here for the Strategy Break.

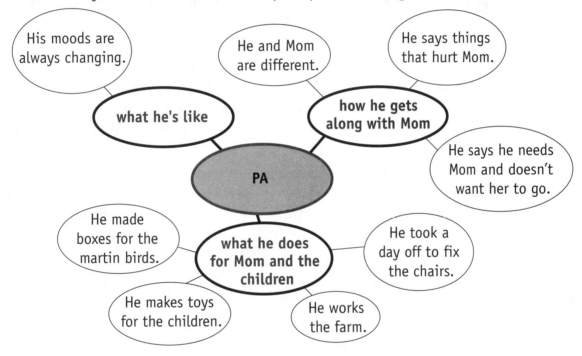

Strategy Break

Although Pa has not said or done much in the story so far, Shan has revealed quite a bit about him. If you wanted to make a concept map for Pa, it might look like this:

His moods are always changing.

He and Mom are different.

He says things that hurt Mom.

what he's like

how he gets along with Mom

PA

He says he needs Mom and doesn't want her to go.

He made boxes for the martin birds.

what he does for Mom and the children

He took a day off to fix the chairs.

He makes toys for the children.

He works the farm.

As you continue reading, keep making observations about what both Mom and Pa say, do, think, and feel. At the end of this story, you will create a concept map for Mom.

 Go on reading to see what happens.

Pa fills his pipe with bright burley crumbs that he fingers from his hip overall pocket with his rough gnarled hand. His index finger shakes as he tamps the tobacco crumbs into his pipe bowl. Pa takes a match from his hat band and strikes it on his overall leg and lights his pipe. I never saw Pa smoke this much before at one time. I never saw him blow such clouds of smoke from his mouth.

"The sun has gone from the sky, Sal," Pa says. His face beams as he speaks. "See, the air is stilly blue—and yonder is a black cloud racing over the sky faster than a hound dog runs a fox."

Mom does not listen. She lifts clothes from the dresser drawer. She closes the empty dresser drawers. Mom never opens the top dresser drawer. That is where Mom puts Pa's clothes.

"Bring me the basket, Shan," Mom says.

I take the big willow basket off the sewing-machine top where Mom keeps it for an egg basket. When I gather eggs, I put them in this basket.

"Where will Pa put the eggs, Mom?" I ask.

"Never mind that, Shan," she says. "We'll let him find a place to put the eggs."

Mom stacks our washed and ironed clothes neatly into this big willow basket. I see her looking at this basket. I remember when Mom told me how long it took Pa to make this basket. It was when Sis was the baby. Every Saturday Mom and Pa went to town and took this willow basket filled with eggs and traded the eggs at the stores for salt, sugar, coffee, dry goods, thread, and other things we needed.

"Listen to the rain, Sal," Pa says. "Hear it hitting the clapboards!"

Big waves of rain driven by puffs of wind sweep across our garden. We can barely hear the martins chattering in their boxes now. Their chattering sounds like they are hovering their young birds and talking to them about the storm.

Mom has our clothes in the big willow basket. She has Herbert's dresses on top of the basket. Herbert is asleep now. He does not hear the big raindrops thumping the dry-sounding clapboard roof. It sounds like you'd thump with your knuckles on the bottom of a washtub.

Mom walks to the door. She looks at the clothesline Pa made from baled-hay wire. He carefully put the pieces of wire together so that they wouldn't hook holes in the clothes Mom hung to dry. Mom watches the water run along the line and beads of water drop into the mouths of the fresh spring-growing grasses. The clothesline is tied to a plum-tree limb on one end and a white-oak limb on the other. There is a forked sour-wood bush that Pa cut and peeled for a clothesline prop between the plum tree and the white oak. It is to brace the clothesline when Mom has it loaded with the wet clothes.

The rain pours from the drainpipe in a big sluice into the water barrel Mom keeps at the corner of the house. "You won't wash my hair in rain water any more," says Sis. "Will hard water keep my hair from being curly, Mom?"

"I don't know," says Mom.

"You used to say hard water would hurt my hair," Sis says.

"I don't care whether Mom washes my hair in hard water or not," I say. "I'd as soon have it washed in well water as in water from the rain barrel."

Mom walks from the front room to the dog-trot. She looks at the rock cliffs over the mountainside. I know Mom remembers holding the lantern for Pa on dark winter nights when the ewes were lambing in these cliffs and they had to bring the baby lambs before the big log fire in the house and warm them.

Mom looks at the snow-white patches of bloodroot blooming around these cliffs. She sees the pink sweet Williams growing by the old logs and rotted stumps on the bluffs. Mom is thinking as she looks at these. I know what she is thinking. "Mick has picked bloodroot blossoms and sweet Williams for me many evenings with his big rough hands after he'd plowed the mules day long around the mountain slopes. Yes, Mick, bad as he is to cuss, loves a wild flower."

Mom walks from the dog-trot into the big kitchen.

"Aren't we going to Grandpa's, Mom?" I ask as I follow Mom.

"Bad as it is raining," Mom answers, "you know we're not going."

"If we go, Mom, who'll cook for Pa?"

Mom does not answer. She looks at the clapboard box Pa made for her and filled with black loam he gathered under the big beech trees in the hollow back of the house. Pa fixed this for a **nasturtium** seed-box for Mom. Pa put it in the kitchen window where it would catch the early morning sun.

"I have my little basket filled with my dollie's dresses," Sis says as she comes running across the dog-trot to Mom. "I'm ready too, Mom. I'm not going to leave my doll. There won't be anybody left to play with her. You know Pa won't play with her. Pa won't have time. Pa plays with the mules and pets them and calls them his dolls."

"Yes," Mom says, "your Pa—"

The sky is low. The rain falls in steady streams. The thin tender oak leaves, the yard grass, the bloodroot, sweet Williams, and the plum-tree leaves drink in the rain. They look clean-washed as Mom washed my face, hands, neck, and ears.

"God must have turned his water bucket over so we couldn't get to Grandpa's, Mom," I say.

It never rained like this before. It's raining so hard now we cannot see the rock cliffs. We cannot see the plum tree and the clothesline wire. We cannot see the martin-box poles at the corners of the garden.

"It's a cyclone, Sal," says Pa as he walks across the dog-trot into the kitchen. "I told you a while ago when I saw the martins making it for their boxes a storm was coming. Now you see just how much sense a bird has!"

"Yes, Mick, I see—"

"What if you had taken little Herbert out on the long road to your pap's place—a tree with leaves as thin as they are this time of spring wouldn't have made much of a shelter and there aren't any rock-cliff shelters close along that lonesome road."

Mom looks at the dim blur of wood-ash barrel that Pa put under the big white-oak tree where Mom washes our clothes. Pa carries the wood ashes from the kitchen stove and the fireplace and puts them in this barrel for Mom. She makes lye soap from these wood ashes.

"Don't talk about the road," says Mom.

"Where is my pretty, Pa?" I ask.

"Herbert is asleep with it in his hand," Pa answers.

"When we go to Grandpa's I'm going to take it with me. Pa made it and I intend to keep it."

Damp cool air from the rain sweeps across the dog-trot.

"The rain has chilled that air so," says Pa, "a person needs a coat."

Through the rain-washed window-pane, Mom sees the little bench Pa made. Mom and Pa would sit on this little bench at the end of the grape arbor and string beans, peel potatoes, and shuck roasting ears. They sit here on the long summer evenings when the **katydids** sing in the garden bean-rows and the crickets **chirrup** in the yard grasses. Pa smokes his pipe and Mom smokes her pipe and we play around them. We hear the whippoor-wills singing from mountain top to mountain top and we hear the mar-tins chattering to one another in their boxes. We see the lightning bugs lighting their way in the summer-evening dusk above the potato rows— and we hear the beetles singing sadly in the dewy evening grass.

"The sun, Mom," I say. "Look—we can go now."

Pa looks at the red ball of sun hang-ing brightly in the blue April sky above the mountain. It is like a red oak ball hanging from an oak limb by a tiny stem among the green oak leaves. A shadow falls over Pa's brown, weather-beaten face.

"The third time," says Mom, "that I've got ready to go. Something has happened every time. I'm not going."

"Aren't we going to Grandpa's, Mom?" Sis asks.

"No, we're not going."

"What will I do with my basket of doll clothes?"

"Put them back where you got them."

Pa puts his pipe back in his pocket. His face doesn't have a shadow over it now. Pa looks happy. There is a smile on his September pawpaw-leaf-colored face.

"Come, Sal," says Pa. "Let's see if our sweet potatoes have sprouted yet."

Mom and Pa walk from the kitchen to the dog-trot. They walk up the bank where Pa has his sweet-potato bed. Pa has his arm around Mom. They walk over the clean-washed yard grass as green and pretty as if God had just made it over new.

"I think the potatoes have sprout-ed," I hear Pa say.

Sis starts upstairs with her basket of doll clothes and her doll. I go into the front room to see if Herbert has my top in his hand. It is my top, for Pa made it for me. ●

Strategy Follow-up

On a separate sheet of paper, work with a partner to create a concept map of your observa-tions about Mom. Before you begin your concept map, skim the story. As you skim, jot down notes about Mom. When you have finished, arrange your notes into different categories, such as "how she feels about Pa," "why she wants to leave," and "why she decides to stay." Make each category a separate oval on your concept map, and then add examples or reasons around each oval. If you need help, use the concept map in the Strategy Break as a model.

✓Personal Checklist

Read each question and put a check (✓) in the correct box.

1. How well do you understand what happens in this story?
   - ☐ 3 (extremely well)
   - ☐ 2 (fairly well)
   - ☐ 1 (not well)

2. How well were you able to complete the activity in Building Background?
   - ☐ 3 (extremely well)
   - ☐ 2 (fairly well)
   - ☐ 1 (not well)

3. How well were you able to complete the sentences in the Vocabulary Builder?
   - ☐ 3 (extremely well)
   - ☐ 2 (fairly well)
   - ☐ 1 (not well)

4. In the Strategy Follow-up, how well were you able to create a concept map for Mom?
   - ☐ 3 (extremely well)
   - ☐ 2 (fairly well)
   - ☐ 1 (not well)

5. How well could you explain why Mom finally decides to stay?
   - ☐ 3 (extremely well)
   - ☐ 2 (fairly well)
   - ☐ 1 (not well)

Vocabulary Check

Look back at the work you did in the Vocabulary Builder. Then answer each question by circling the correct letter.

1. Which of the following words has the same meaning as *toy* in this story?
   - a. nasturtium
   - b. pretty
   - c. chirrup

2. Which meaning of the word *clutch* best fits the context of this story?
   - a. grasp tightly
   - b. pedal used to shift a car
   - c. dangerous situation

3. What is a nasturtium?
   - a. a type of flower
   - b. a type of insect
   - c. a type of bird

4. Which word sounds like the noise a cricket makes?
   - a. purr
   - b. quack
   - c. chirrup

5. What is a katydid?
   - a. a fancy toy
   - b. a noisy insect
   - c. a farm machine

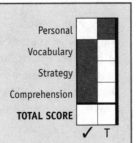

Add the numbers that you just checked to get your Personal Checklist score. Fill in your score here. Then turn to page 215 and transfer your score onto Graph 1.

Personal
Vocabulary
Strategy
Comprehension
TOTAL SCORE
✓ T

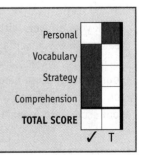

Check your answers with your teacher. Give yourself 1 point for each correct answer, and fill in your Vocabulary score here. Then turn to page 215 and transfer your score onto Graph 1.

Personal
Vocabulary
Strategy
Comprehension
TOTAL SCORE
✓ T

Strategy Check

Review the concept map that you created in the Strategy Follow-up. Also review the rest of the story. Then answer the following questions:

1. How does Pa describe Mom?

    a. She's as solid as a mountain.

    b. Her mind is more changeable than the weather.

    c. She's tired all the time.

2. How does Shan let us know how Mom feels about leaving?

    a. Shan describes how Mom packs the things she is taking to Pap's.

    b. Shan describes how much Mom dislikes Pa and the farm.

    c. Shan imagines what Mom is thinking when she looks around the farm.

3. For what reason does Mom decide to stay with Pa?

    a. She believes that the rain is the third sign telling her she shouldn't go.

    b. Herbert won't let go of the pretty that Pa made, so Mom decides to stay.

    c. She doesn't want to leave Sis, so she stays to keep the children together.

4. From all the clues that Shan gives, how do you think Mom really feels about Pa?

    a. She hates him.

    b. She loves him.

    c. She doesn't care about him.

5. Based on the clues that Shan gives, how do you think Mom feels after she says she won't be leaving?

    a. disappointed

    b. angry

    c. relieved

Comprehension Check

Review the story if necessary. Then answer these questions:

1. Why does Mom want to leave Pa at the beginning of the story?

    a. She doesn't like Pa's changeable behavior.

    b. She misses her father and wants to live with him again.

    c. Pa doesn't ever help her or show any kindness toward the children.

2. What does Pa hear that makes him think Mom should postpone her trip?

    a. He hears high winds.

    b. He hears the baby crying.

    c. He hears the thunder of an approaching storm.

3. How many children do Mom and Pa have?

    a. two

    b. three

    c. four

4. How many times has Mom threatened to leave before this?

    a. once

    b. twice

    c. three times

5. Why do you think Mom really changes her mind about leaving?

    a. She is afraid of thunderstorms.

    b. She recalls how helpful and loving Pa has been over the years.

    c. She doesn't want her father to raise her children.

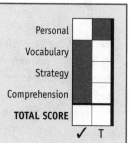

Check your answers with your teacher. Give yourself 1 point for each correct answer, and fill in your Strategy score here. Then turn to page 215 and transfer your score onto Graph 1.

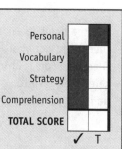

Check your answers with your teacher. Give yourself 1 point for each correct answer, and fill in your Comprehension score here. Then turn to page 215 and transfer your score onto Graph 1.

Extending

Choose one or both of these activities:

DESCRIBE A FATHER'S JOB

In "The Storm," Pa is responsible for many tasks, from making toys for the children to plowing the fields. Even though times have changed, fathers still have many responsibilities. Make a list of all the tasks that fathers are usually expected to complete. Think of their responsibilities when their children are young and as they grow up. Get together with others in a small group and compile a complete list. Then share your list with other groups. Did everyone come up with similar ideas? How do people differ in their opinions about this topic?

READ ALOUD OTHER STORIES BY JESSE STUART

Use the resources listed on this page to find other stories by Jesse Stuart. Choose the story that you like best, and read it aloud to the rest of the class. If there are several characters, you might ask some classmates to read the dialogue for those characters. When you have finished reading, discuss the elements of the story that made it particularly appealing to you.

Resources

Books

Stuart, Jesse. *Clearing in the Sky, and Other Stories.* University of Kentucky Press, 1984.

————. *Harvest of Youth.* Jesse Stuart Foundation, 1998.

————. Ed. Paul Douglass. *Cradle of the Copperheads.* McGraw-Hill, 1988.

————. Ed. Richardson, H. Edward. *Best-Loved Short Stories of Jesse Stuart.* Jesse Stuart Foundation, 2000.

Web Site

http://www.morehead-st.edu/projects/village/jshome.html
On this Web site, you can find a short biography of Jesse Stuart and links to a poem and a short story by Stuart.

LESSON 14 Elegy for Woodward

Building Background

No matter where you live, you risk experiencing a natural disaster. Hurricanes, blizzards, drought, flooding, mudslides, and tornadoes are threats at various times in various places. If you have lived through one of these calamities, you will never forget it.

Think back to a time when you watched or experienced a natural disaster of some kind. Describe the disaster and your reaction to it by completing the concept map below. Add more ovals as necessary.

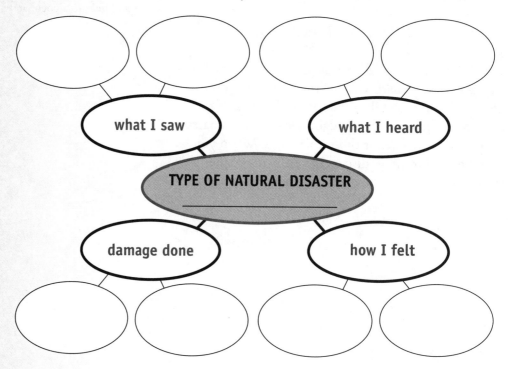

cowering

debris

eerie

grimly

incredible

rubble

tornado

torrents

twister

Vocabulary Builder

1. The words in the margin are all found in the following informational article. Use as many of the words as possible to write a story or a news article about a tornado. (Use a dictionary for any words you don't know.) Write your story or article on a separate sheet of paper.

2. As you read "Elegy for Woodward," find the sentences containing the bold-faced vocabulary words. Did you use the words in the same way that they are used in the selection?

3. Save your work. You will refer to it again in the Vocabulary Check.

Strategy Builder

Identifying Main Ideas and Supporting Details

- You know that an **informational article** presents facts and information about a particular topic or event. Before beginning an informational article, a writer does a great deal of research and organization. For example, for the article you are about to read, the writer searched through the records of a terrible tornado that hit Woodward, Oklahoma, in 1947. He then selected the facts and information that would tell his story best, and he arranged them in a way that would help readers understand what happened.

- Since the writer describes the events in this article in the order in which they happened, the main organizational pattern of this article is **sequence**. Within that sequence, the author uses **main ideas** and **supporting details** to describe the events in detail.

- Read the following paragraph about clouds. Try to identify the main idea and the details that support, or explain, it.

> Clouds can be good indicators of the weather to come. A tall cumulus cloud often signals that conditions are right for a thunderstorm. A cumulonimbus cloud may bring tornadoes. Low stratus clouds can bring rain or snow. Stratocumulus clouds signal that rainy weather is settling in for a while.

- If you wanted to arrange this paragraph's main idea and supporting details on a graphic organizer, you could use a **main idea table**. It would look like this:

Clouds can be good indicators of the weather to come.			
Detail #1	**Detail #2**	**Detail #3**	**Detail #4**
tall cumulus: thunderstorms	cumulonimbus: tornado	low stratus: rain or snow	stratocumulus: rainy weather settling in

- Some informational articles present facts in more than one way. In addition to providing facts in the text, this article includes a **map** showing the path of the storm. One map shows the midsection of the United States and highlights a square for you to concentrate on. The other map focuses on the specific area where the tornado touched down. As you read about the different places mentioned in this article, be sure to refer to the map to see where they are located.

Elegy for Woodward

By Richard Bedard

As you begin reading "Elegy for Woodward," apply the strategies that you just learned. Use the map to help you locate the places mentioned in the article. Note that an *elegy* is a tribute written for someone or something that has died.

The chilling blackness of the sky was broken only by the ceaseless strobing of white-hot lightning. By 8:30 p.m. on April 9, 1947, the flashing cloud-to-ground bolts southwest of Woodward, Oklahoma, were so intense it hurt your eyes to look at them.

The weather had been strange all day. In the morning and afternoon, a nagging, wind-whipped drizzle had chased townspeople indoors. Then, about dinnertime, the clouds had finally broken, revealing a dying sun that flared violent coppery red. Meanwhile, more than 100 miles away, a huge thunderstorm had formed and begun tearing across the Texas panhandle. A **tornado** snaked down from the storm northeast of Amarillo amid a barrage of golfball-sized hail. The **twister** was not very wide, and after raging briefly, slimmed to a curling thread, then vanished.

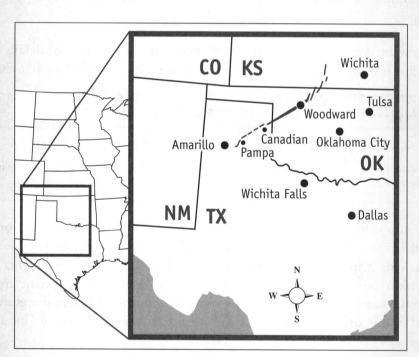

The path of the tornado covered at least 98 miles as it blasted through three states. The dashed portion in the Texas Panhandle reflects the uncertainty over its path. (This map is based on a map that appeared in the February 1988 *Monthly Weather Review,* p. 499.)

Before the storm reached the Texas-Oklahoma border, however, it put down a new tornado, and this one was a multi-vortex monster 1.5 miles wide and whirling at more than 200 m.p.h.

With an earsplitting roar the tornado bore down on two Texas towns. As it tore through Glazier and Higgins, laundromat washing machines rained from the sky, a lifted house crashed down to straddle a highway, and combines rolled across fields like tumbleweeds.

Large fires burned through the wreckage in the twister's wake. Stunned survivors, their clothes shredded by the wind, wailed and wandered aimlessly through streets reduced to **rubble**.

The tornado raced northeastward, blasting into Oklahoma. Woodward, a hardscrabble community of 5,500 souls, was the only large town on the vast, harsh plains in the desolate northwest corner of the state. There worshipers were praying at the dozen or so Wednesday evening church services, while moviegoers were enjoying two feature films. One happened to be titled *Rage in Heaven*.

When the power winked off at one of the movie theaters, the owner drove over to flip the electrical breaker back on. As he did, he was startled to see an inky river of cloud streaming along overhead, pressing down on the building tops. It was so thick and substantial, he thought he could reach up and cut it with a knife.

About this time, a telephone operator got a worried call from a fellow worker in a town 25 miles to the southeast.

"There's a black cloud over Woodward," she said. "It looks terrible."

In Woodward, the snapping south wind suddenly shifted to the east, then the southwest. Quick bursts of rain, then hail followed, giving way to an **eerie**, gathering calm.

The tornado hit Woodward at 8:43 p.m. The monster twister was now 1.8 miles wide, with winds near 300 m.p.h. It smashed into the northwest half of Woodward like a giant, whirling wrecking ball. As if made of rubber, house windows bowed in crazily before exploding into glass bullets. Airborne tin roofs became as lethal as giant buzzsaw blades. Steel I-beams floated like feathers. **Cowering** men, women, and children were plucked from houses that seemed to explode and flung into the night.

 Stop here for the Strategy Break.

Strategy Break

Read the previous paragraph again. It describes the tornado that struck Woodward, Oklahoma, in 1947. If you wanted show the main idea and supporting details in the paragraph, you could arrange them on a main idea table like this:

The tornado hit Woodward at 8:43 p.m.			
Detail #1	**Detail #2**	**Detail #3**	**Detail #4**
1.8 miles wide, with winds near 300 m.p.h.	smashed into northwest Woodward	house windows exploded; airborne material became lethal	people plucked from houses and flung into the night

As you continue reading, keep looking for main ideas and supporting details. At the end of the article, you will use some of them to create a main idea table of your own.

 Go on reading.

A Blazing River of Fire

In Gill's Cafe, fronting Main Street, a barometer needle took a sudden nose-dive, prompting a customer to go to the door to look down the street. He was shocked to see a blazing river of fire generated by flying scraps of tin, nails, and other metal objects striking the pavement at such horrific speeds they threw off great cascading plumes of sparks. He also heard a peculiar humming noise.

The ominous weather had been worrying Agnes Hutchison, a 28-year-old waitress at the Oasis steakhouse. She couldn't stop fretting, wondering why her husband hadn't come by with their two sons for his customary evening cup of coffee.

Suddenly the frame of the building began to creak and shudder. Dishes jitterbugged off kitchen shelves and crashed to the floor. The front door kept flapping open, and at the cash register, a flurry of receipts swirled around the owner's head.

Seeing the frightened expressions of the grown-ups around her, a little girl calmly asked her grandmother, "It's time to die, isn't it?"

Seconds later, the building broke up and suddenly there was nothing there but a lightning-streaked black night and a terrible wind. Agnes bearhugged a still-standing telephone pole as the whirlwind enveloped her.

"I had no control," she later recalled, ". . . it was blowing my flesh every which way. . . . I couldn't hold my mouth shut, I couldn't breathe, I couldn't see."

Agnes hung on **grimly**. Then the big wind passed. The flashes of lightning revealed wheat straws sticking arrow-straight out of the trunks of leafless trees. Broken pipes gushed water. Piles of shattered glass and brick, intertwined with power and telephone lines, choked the streets. Woodward looked alien and unreal, like something in a horrible nightmare.

A Death Smell

A rank, musty odor hung over the ruins. "It was an eerie smell, of old dirty plaster and things under houses that had been aged there a long time," Agnes recalled. "I almost want to call it a death smell. I'll never forget it."

She groped toward home using the lightning's illumination. One flash revealed only a jumble of boards where the house her husband had built with his own hands had stood. She found her husband Olan and their two sons, Jimmie Lee and Roland, in a ditch about a block away. Roland was crying for help and Jimmie Lee was unconscious. Olan was dead, the crown of his head crushed in.

The rain began to spill down in **torrents**, making the night even more miserable. Agnes flagged down a motorist picking his way through the **debris**-clogged streets and took her sons to a makeshift emergency station, one of many hastily set up and lit only by lantern and candlelight. There she discovered that Jimmie Lee, age five, was already dead. As she peeled off his muddy, soaking clothes and tenderly wrapped him in a blanket, she was overwhelmed by a paralyzing sense of disbelief. "Please God, let me wake from this nightmare," she begged silently.

She passed Jimmie Lee to a man on the back of a pickup already piled with bodies. He reached to take the blanket, gently telling Agnes it could no longer do her son any good, but she snapped angrily, "I'll pay for the damn blanket. The blanket stays." Then the truck pulled away, disappearing into the night.

The storm's terrible human toll was evident at Woodward's crowded red-brick hospital. Moans and cries echoed through the halls as the injured writhed on the floor. The hospital staff temporarily stuffed the dead under beds to make room for the living. The staff—some with World War II combat experience—had never seen anything like this.

Eye whites contrasted starkly with blackened, mud-smeared faces. Small children stared straight ahead with sad, glazed eyes. Shattered bones, cuts, and wounds caused by hard objects driven into soft flesh were too numerous to even begin to count.

A TWA pilot flying over the area heard an emergency radio plea for pounds of anti-infection, blood-clotting, and bacteria-fighting drugs. On landing in Kansas City he reported "There was so much smoke hanging over Woodward I couldn't see exactly what had happened there, but I could tell the damage was enormous."

The Cruel Light of Dawn

Just how enormous was revealed by the cruel light of dawn. In some of the 200 damaged blocks, only scattered boards remained to remind homeowners where their houses had stood just the day before. Bits of trash and unlikely objects such as fur coats and bathtubs decorated leafless tree tops. A car had landed upside down in a neighbor's living room, its wheels pointing to the sky. Giant, tangled balls of debris as huge as houses littered the countryside.

Survivors' stories were **incredible** and unsettling. A man in Glazier, Texas, for example, claimed to have been snatched from his basement and carried almost a quarter mile before the tornado gently lowered him head-first into a wild plum thicket.

The vast majority of survivors, however, had far grimmer tales to tell. One woman had been buried alive and now suffered dim vision as gravel worked itself out from behind her right eye. Her nose, jaw, and three ribs were broken and her right arm dislocated. The flesh on her arm felt like raw hamburger.

A young mother who had lost her baby daughter was full of wooden splinters. After extracting nearly all of them, her doctor joked that if he had known how many there were, he would have saved them for her to build a house.

A vigorous, dark-eyed boy who lost his father and his lower leg to the tornado would years later write of himself in a school essay: "He is known for his way of being so jolly and always looking forward instead of looking back on that time when he had two feet and legs of flesh instead of what is now and always will be."

In the days of recovery following the tornado, the fervor to rebuild was focused as much below ground as above: storm shelters, or "fraidy holes," became essential for peace of mind.

Meanwhile, there were so many funerals they often were sparsely attended. Agnes Hutchison watched the service for her husband and youngest son in a daze. "I couldn't cry," she said. "It was beyond crying. I was numb, a walking zombie."

Agnes's bad weather luck had not ended. Eight years later, remarried and living in Udall, Kansas, she saw in the distance what looked like a grain elevator spinning like a top. This tornado tore the roof off her house as she and her new family huddled in fear on the floor. Now Agnes always sleeps with a window open, even in the dead of winter, to detect any damp, dangerously shifting wind.

The funerals were supposed to provide closure, but no one ever claimed the bodies of three girls, the youngest less than a year old, the oldest about 12. Each was laid to rest in an anonymous grave.

By their very nature, tornadoes sow mystery and confusion, and there is no precise death toll for the six separate twisters spawned by the parent thunderstorm over a 221-mile trail of destruction during the outbreak of April 9, 1947. At least 107 people perished in Woodward alone, victims of the largest tornado, which was on the ground for some 98 miles.

Years later, that twister was classified an F5 tornado, the highest possible damage ranking. Of the many tornadoes that have scoured the Sooner State before and since, it is still the deadliest.

An old timer once told me that Woodward had seen cyclones before, but not tornadoes. Of course "cyclone" technically refers to a low-pressure system. Out on the prairie, however, the word often seems to connote a mischievous, almost friendly natural phenomenon.

This is shown by a story, set in Woodward, a daughter told about her pioneer mother. That hardy woman refused to budge from her open doorway as a "cyclone" bore down on her—even after it snatched up a neighbor's claim shanty. As the twister swirled almost to her fence, she hollered sternly, "Don't you drop that house down on my garden!"

The whirl dipped and lifted, then obediently flung the shanty down outside the fence. "Not a bean in Mama's garden was disturbed," reported the daughter.

For many prairie inhabitants, that tale described a cyclone: frisky and quirky, a skyborne, superstrong prankster. But the furious black wall of wind that blasted Woodward on April 9, 1947—savaging wood and brick and flesh and bone, and leaving acres of rubble resembling a bombed-out European city of World War II—that was definitely a tornado. ●

Strategy Follow-up

Now, with a partner, fill in the main idea table below for the first paragraph of the section labeled "The Cruel Light of Dawn." Remember to list only the important details.

The enormity of damage was revealed by the light of dawn.			
Detail #1	**Detail #2**	**Detail #3**	**Detail #4**

✓Personal Checklist

Read each question and put a check (✓) in the correct box.

1. How well do you understand the information presented in this article?
   - ☐ 3 (extremely well)
   - ☐ 2 (fairly well)
   - ☐ 1 (not well)

2. How well were you able to use what you wrote in Building Background to help you understand the author's description of the storm?
   - ☐ 3 (extremely well)
   - ☐ 2 (fairly well)
   - ☐ 1 (not well)

3. In the Vocabulary Builder, how many words were you able to use in your story or article about a tornado?
   - ☐ 3 (7–9 words)
   - ☐ 2 (3–6 words)
   - ☐ 1 (0–2 words)

4. How well were you able to create a main idea table in the Strategy Follow-up?
   - ☐ 3 (extremely well)
   - ☐ 2 (fairly well)
   - ☐ 1 (not well)

5. How well do you understand why the author called this article "Elegy for Woodward"?
   - ☐ 3 (extremely well)
   - ☐ 2 (fairly well)
   - ☐ 1 (not well)

Vocabulary Check

Look back at the work you did in the Vocabulary Builder. Then answer each question by circling the correct letter.

1. Which two vocabulary words are synonyms?
   - a. *twister* and *tornado*
   - b. *torrents* and *rubble*
   - c. *eerie* and *grimly*

2. Which of these scenes would you describe as eerie?
   - a. a busy office filled with the sound of workers and telephones
   - b. a sunny meadow filled with wildflowers
   - c. a deserted town with only the sound of the wind to break the stillness

3. When people start cowering, how are they feeling?
   - a. confident
   - b. afraid
   - c. angry

4. The opposite of *grimly* is
   - a. joyfully
   - b. charmingly
   - c. incredibly

5. What is another word for *debris*?
   - a. clothing
   - b. garbage
   - c. yarn

Add the numbers that you just checked to get your Personal Checklist score. Fill in your score here. Then turn to page 215 and transfer your score onto Graph 1.

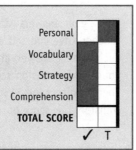

Check your answers with your teacher. Give yourself 1 point for each correct answer, and fill in your Vocabulary score here. Then turn to page 215 and transfer your score onto Graph 1.

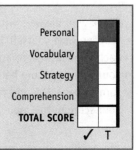

Strategy Check

Review the main idea table that you created in the Strategy Follow-up. Also review the rest of the article. Then answer these questions:

1. Which of these supporting details should you *not* have included on your main idea table?

    a. Bits of trash and decorated leafless trees.

    b. Giant balls of debris littered the countryside.

    c. Many people were injured by the wind.

2. Which supporting detail *should* you have included on your main idea table?

    a. Giant balls of debris littered the countryside.

    b. Building "fraidy holes" was essential for peace of mind.

    c. Survivors' stories were incredible.

3. How does the detail *A car had landed upside down in a neighbor's living room,* support the main idea of your table?

    a. The detail is one example of the damage the tornado created.

    b. The detail shows that some residents of Woodward owned cars.

    c. The detail shows that the houses of Woodward were flimsy.

4. If you created a main idea table for the second through fifth paragraphs under "The Cruel Light of Dawn," what would be your main idea?

    a. A mother who had lost her baby daughter was full of wooden splinters.

    b. Survivors' stories were incredible.

    c. "He is known for his way of being so jolly and always looking forward."

5. What would the legs of your table contain?

    a. a description of the tornado

    b. examples of survivors' stories

    c. a description of the death smell

Comprehension Check

Review the article if necessary. Then answer these questions:

1. At what time did the tornado hit Woodward?

    a. 8:30 A.M.

    b. 8:30 P.M.

    c. 8:43 P.M.

2. About how many miles did the tornado travel on the ground?

    a. 1.5

    b. 98

    c. 200

3. What happened to Olan Hutchinson?

    a. His head was crushed, and he died.

    b. He saw his wife and children killed.

    c. He survived for a while but died in the hospital.

4. What are "fraidy holes"?

    a. holes that frightened animals dug in the ground

    b. holes that the tornado dug

    c. storm shelters that people dug into the ground

5. What does the F5 rating given the Woodward tornado mean?

    a. The Woodward tornado had the lowest possible damage ranking.

    b. The Woodward tornado had a medium damage ranking.

    c. The Woodward tornado had the highest possible damage ranking.

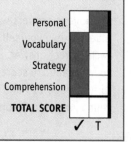

Check your answers with your teacher. Give yourself 1 point for each correct answer, and fill in your Strategy score here. Then turn to page 215 and transfer your score onto Graph 1.

Personal
Vocabulary
Strategy
Comprehension
TOTAL SCORE

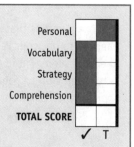

Check your answers with your teacher. Give yourself 1 point for each correct answer, and fill in your Comprehension score here. Then turn to page 215 and transfer your score onto Graph 1.

Personal
Vocabulary
Strategy
Comprehension
TOTAL SCORE

Extending

Choose one or both of these activities:

RESEARCH RECORD-BREAKING DISASTERS

Use a book of facts, an encyclopedia, or the Internet to research the five most destructive storms or natural disasters in history. Find out about the toll they took on human lives, as well as the damage they did to buildings, roads, and bridges. Compile your findings on a poster that you display in the classroom. Use a bar graph and pictures, if possible, to present the information.

LEARN MORE ABOUT TORNADOES

What causes tornadoes? Why do they tend to appear in certain areas of the country and not in others? What do the terms *tornado watch*, *tornado alert*, and *tornado warning* mean? What should you do in each situation? Use the resources listed on this page and ones you find yourself to learn more about tornadoes and what to do if one is headed your way.

Resources

Books

Allaby, Michael. *Tornadoes*. Dangerous Weather. Facts on File, 1997.

Bluestein, Howard B. *Tornado Alley: Monster Storms of the Great Plains*. Oxford University Press, 1999.

Burby, Liza N. *Tornadoes*. Extreme Weather. Rosen Publishing, 2003.

Web Sites

http://www.btinternet.com/~mike.ferris/naturaldisasters.htm
This Web page offers information on some major natural disasters in history.

http://www.crh.noaa.gov/lmk/tornado/whatis.htm
Learn about tornadoes on this Web site of the National Weather Service Forecast Office.

Videos/DVD

Cyclone! Nature at Its Most Terrifying. National Geographic Society, 2003.

Extreme Disaster: Nature's Deadly Force. Unapix, 1998.

The Homesick Chicken

Building Background

The short story you are about to read is a mystery. A **mystery** always contains some kind of puzzle that needs to be solved. Think about some mysteries that you have read or seen lately. What puzzle were the characters trying to solve? What clues helped them solve it? Get together with a partner and talk about your favorite mysteries. Then, on the concept map below, list several words or phrases that describe the characteristics of a mystery. Some examples are provided. Add more ovals as necessary.

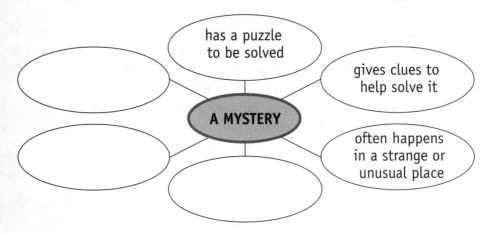

depressions

hybrid

imprinting

motivation

surreptitiously

tranquilize

Vocabulary Builder

1. The words in the margin are all found in "The Homesick Chicken." Think about what the words mean, and then use them to complete the following sentences.

    a. The key was stolen in secret, when no one was looking. In other words, the theft was done _____.

    b. We want this animal to quiet down so we can run some tests on it. Let's _____ it.

    c. This chicken is a blend of different types of chickens and was bred for strength. It is a _____ chicken.

    d. Through the process of _____, our cat now comes running when it hears the electric can opener.

    e. The heavy sofa that rested in one spot for years left four deep _____ in the carpet.

    f. The detective wanted to understand why the criminal committed the crime. She looked for the criminal's _____.

2. Save your work. You will refer to it again in the Vocabulary Check.

Strategy Builder

Identifying Problems and Solutions in Stories

- The characters in science fiction often have **problems** just like other fictional characters do. Throughout a particular story, the characters try to solve the problem. They may try different **solutions** until they find one that works, or they may solve the problem in stages, as in this story. Through the work and intelligence of the characters, necessary information is gathered bit by bit until the final solution—the **end result**—is reached.

- As you read the following paragraphs, notice Kate's problem and the information that she gathers to solve it.

Kate bought a bag of trail mix and put it in the top drawer of her desk. She was planning to eat it later on, while she worked on a term paper.

When Kate came back from the library a few hours later, she found the bag on top of her desk, half-empty and neatly resealed. Who had eaten half of her trail mix?

Kate asked her mother—who dislikes that kind of snack—who had been in the house that day. Her mother replied that she had been there alone, except for when Kate's brother from college stopped in for a few minutes. Kate asked if he had gone upstairs near her room, and her mother said that he had. Since no one else could have eaten the mix, Kate knew that it must have been her brother. *Jack owes me a new bag of trail mix,* she thought.

- If you wanted to show the problem and solutions in the paragraphs above, you could create a **problem-solution frame**. It would look like this:

What is the problem?
Someone ate half of Kate's trail mix.

Why is it a problem?
Kate doesn't know who ate it, and she was saving it for when she wrote her term paper.

Solutions	Results
1. Kate knows that her mother doesn't like trail mix.	**1.** She knows that her mother didn't eat it.
2. Kate asks who has been in the house.	**2.** She learns that her brother was there.
3. She asks if her brother went near her room.	**3.** **END RESULT:** Her mother says yes, so Kate concludes that Jack ate half of her trail mix.

The Homesick Chicken

by Edward D. Hoch

As you read the first part of this story, apply the strategies that you just learned. Look for the problem, or mystery, in this story and what the investigator does to solve it.

Why did the chicken cross the road?

To get on the other side, you'd probably answer, echoing an old riddle that was popular in the early years of the last century.

But my name is Barnabus Rex, and I have a different answer.

I'd been summoned to the Tangaway Research Farms by the director, an egg-headed old man named Professor Mintor. After parking my car in the guarded lot and passing through the fence—it was an EavesStop, expensive, but sure protection against all kinds of electronic bugging—I was shown into the presence of the director himself. His problem was simple. The solution was more difficult.

"One of the research chickens pecked its way right through the security fence, then crossed an eight-lane belt highway to the other side. We want to know why."

"Chickens are a bit out of my line," I replied.

"But your specialty is the solution of scientific riddles, Mr. Rex, and this certainly is one." He led me out of the main research building to a penned-in area where the test animals were kept. We passed a reinforced electric cage in which he pointed out the mutated turkeys being bred for life in the domes of the colonies of the moon.

Further along were some leggy-looking fowl destined for Mars. "They're particularly well adapted to the Martian terrain and environment," Professor Mintor explained. "We've had to do very little development work; we started from desert roadrunners."

"What about the chickens?"

"The chickens are something else again. The strain, called ZIP-1000, is being developed for breeding purposes on Zipoid, the second planet of Barnard's star. We gave them extra-strength beaks—something like a parrot's—to crack the extra-tough seed hulls used for feed. The seed hulls in turn were developed to withstand the native fauna like the space-lynx and the ostroid, so that—"

"Aren't we getting a little off course?" I asked.

"Ah—yes. The problem. What *is* a problem is the chicken that crossed the road. It used its extra-strength beak to peck its way right through this security fence. But the puzzling aspect is its **motivation**. It crossed that belt highway—a dangerous undertaking even for a human—and headed for the field as if it were going home. And yet the chicken was hatched right here within these walls. How could it be homesick for something it had never known?"

"How indeed?" I stared bleakly through the fence at the highway and the deserted field opposite. What was there to attract a chicken—even one of Professor Mintor's super-chickens—to that barren bit of land? "I should have a look at it," I decided. "Can you show me the spot where the chicken crossed the highway?"

He led me around a large pen to a spot in the fence where a steel plate temporarily blocked a jagged hole. I knelt to examine the shards of complex, multiconductor mesh, once more impressed by the security precautions. "I'd hate to meet your **hybrid** chickens on a dark night, Professor."

"They would never attack a human being or even another creature," Mintor quickly assured me. "The beak is used only for cracking seed hulls, and perhaps in self defense."

"Was it self-defense against the fence?"

He held up his hands. "I can't explain it."

I moved the steel plate and stooped to go through the hole. In that moment I had a chicken's-eye view of the belt highway and the barren field beyond, but they offered no clues. "Be careful crossing over," Mintor warned. "Don't get your foot caught!"

Crossing a belt highway on foot—a strictly illegal practice—could be dangerous to humans and animals alike. With eight lanes to traverse it meant hopping over eight separate electric power guides—any one of which could take off a foot if you misstepped. To imagine a chicken with the skill to accomplish it was almost more than I could swallow. But then I'd never before been exposed to Professor Mintor's super-chickens.

The empty lot on the other side of the belt highway held nothing of interest to human or chicken, so far as I could see. It was barren of grass or weeds, and seemed nothing more than a patch of dusty earth dotted with a few pebbles. In a few sunbaked **depressions** I found the tread of auto tires, hinting that the vacant lot was sometimes used for parking.

 Stop here for the Strategy Break.

Strategy Break

If you were to create a problem-solution frame for this story so far, it might look like this:

What is the problem?
One of the research chickens pecked its way through the security fence and crossed the road.

Why is it a problem?
Any abnormal behavior worries the scientists who work with the chickens on this secret project.

Solutions	Results
1. The scientists decide they need help.	**1.** They call Barnabus Rex.
2. Rex asks Professor Mintor about the chicken.	**2.** He begins gathering information that will help him.
3. Rex investigates the scene.	**3.** He finds the tread of auto tires.

As you continue reading, keep paying attention to what Barnabus Rex does to solve the problem. At the end of this story, you will complete the problem-solution frame.

 Go on reading to see what happens.

I crossed back over the belt highway and reentered the Tangaway compound through the hole in the fence. "Did you find anything?" Mintor asked.

"Not much. Exactly what was the chicken doing when it was recovered?"

"Nothing. Pecking at the ground as if it were back home."

"Could I see it? I gather it's no longer kept outside."

"After the escape we moved them all to the interior pens. There was some talk of notifying Washington since we're under government contract, but I suggested we call you in first. You know how the government is about possible security leaks."

"Is Tangaway the only research farm doing this sort of thing?"

"Oh, no! We have a very lively competitor named Beaverbrook Farms. That's part of the reason for all this security. We just managed to beat them out on the ZIP-1000 contract."

I followed him into a windowless room lit from above by solar panes. The clucking of the chickens grew louder as we passed into the laboratory proper. Here the birds were kept in a large enclosure, constantly monitored by overhead TV. "This one," Mintor said, leading me to a pen that held but a single chicken with its oddly curved beak. It looked no different from the others.

"Are they identified in any way? Laser tattoo, for instance?"

"Not at this stage of development. Naturally when we ship them out for space use they're tattooed."

"I see." I gazed down at the chicken, trying to read something in those hooded eyes. "It was yesterday that it crossed the highway?"

"Yes."

"Did it rain here yesterday?"

"No. We had a thunderstorm two days ago, but it passed over quickly."

"Who first noticed the chicken crossing the road?"

"Granley—one of our gate guards. He was checking security in the parking lot when he spotted it, about halfway across. By the time he called me and we got over there it was all the way to the other side."

"How did you get it back?"

"We had to **tranquilize** it, but that was no problem."

"I must speak to this guard, Granley."

"Follow me."

The guard was lounging near the gate. I'd noticed him when I arrived and parked my car. "This is Barnabus Rex, the scientific investigator," Mintor announced. "He has some questions for you."

"Sure," Granley replied, straightening up. "Ask away."

"Just one question, really," I said. "Why didn't you mention the car that was parked across the highway yesterday?"

"What car?"

"A parked car that probably pulled away as soon as you started after the chicken."

His eyes widened. "My God, you're right! I'd forgotten it till now! Some kids; it was painted all over stripes, like they're doing these days. But how did you know?"

"Sunbaked tire tracks in the depressions where water would collect. They told me a car had been there since your rain two days ago. Your employees use the lot here, and no visitors would park over there when they had to cross the belt highway to reach you."

"But what does it mean?" Professor Mintor demanded.

"That your mystery is solved," I said.

"All right. Why *did* the chicken cross the road?"

"Because somebody wanted to play back the contents of a tape recorder implanted in its body. For some time now you've been spied upon, Professor Mintor—I imagine by your competitor, Beaverbrook Farms."

"Spied upon! By that—*chicken*?"

"Exactly. It seemed obvious to me from the first that the fence-pecking chicken was not one of your brood. It was much too strong and much too homesick. But if it wasn't yours it must have been added to your flock **surreptitiously**, and that could only have been for the purposes of industrial espionage. Since you told me Beaverbrook was doing similar work, this has to be their chicken. I think an X-ray will show a micro-miniaturized recorder for listening in on your secret conversations."

"It was a simple task for them to drop the intruding chicken over your fence at night, perhaps lassoing one of your birds and removing it so the count would be right. Those fences are all right for detecting any sort of bugging equipment, but they aren't very good at stopping ordinary intrusion—otherwise that wandering chicken would have set off alarms when it started to cut a hole there. Beaverbrook has been recording your conversations, probably trying to stay one jump ahead on the next government contract. They couldn't use a transmitter in the chicken because of your electronic fence, so they had to recover the bird itself to read out the recording. At the right time, the chicken pecked its way through the fence and started across the highway, but when the guard spot-ted it the waiting driver panicked and took off. The chicken was left across the road without any way to escape."

"But how did the chicken know when to escape?" asked Mintor. "Could they have some kind of electronic honing device . . . ?"

"That was the easiest part," I said at last. "**Imprinting**."

"But . . ."

"Exactly. The highly distinctive stripes on the car. The Beaverbrook people evidently trained the chicken from—ah—hatching to associate that pattern with home and food."

A technician trotted up to the professor, waving a photographic negative. "The X-rays—there *was* something inside that chicken!"

"Well, Mr. Rex, you were right," the professor conceded.

"Of course, in a sense the chicken *did* cross the road to get to the other side," I admitted. "They always do."

"Have you solved many cases like this one?"

I merely smiled. "Every case is different, but they're always a challenge. I'll send you my bill in the morning—and if you ever need me again, just call." ●

Strategy Follow-up

On a separate sheet of paper, complete a problem-solution frame for the second half of the story. Compare your completed frame with a partner's.

✓Personal Checklist

Read each question and put a check (✓) in the correct box.

1. How well do you understand what happens in this story?
   - ☐ 3 (extremely well)
   - ☐ 2 (fairly well)
   - ☐ 1 (not well)

2. In Building Background, how well were you able to complete the concept map with the characteristics of a mystery?
   - ☐ 3 (extremely well)
   - ☐ 2 (fairly well)
   - ☐ 1 (not well)

3. In the Vocabulary Builder, how many sentences were you able to complete correctly?
   - ☐ 3 (5–6 sentences)
   - ☐ 2 (3–4 sentences)
   - ☐ 1 (0–2 sentences)

4. How well were you able to complete the problem-solution frame in the Strategy Follow-up?
   - ☐ 3 (extremely well)
   - ☐ 2 (fairly well)
   - ☐ 1 (not well)

5. How well do you understand what makes this story science fiction?
   - ☐ 3 (extremely well)
   - ☐ 2 (fairly well)
   - ☐ 1 (not well)

Vocabulary Check

Look back at the work you did in the Vocabulary Builder. Then answer each question by circling the correct letter.

1. What does it mean when something is done surreptitiously?
   - a. It is done repeatedly.
   - b. It is done in secret.
   - c. It is done out in the open.

2. What does the word *imprinting* mean in the context of this story?
   - a. the process of engraving a number on the inside of a machine
   - b. the process of marking or depressing something through pressure
   - c. a learning process that establishes a particular pattern of behavior

3. What does the word *depressions* mean in the context of this story?
   - a. low or hollow places in the ground
   - b. sad or gloomy feelings
   - c. serious reductions of business activity

4. When you want to know why a person did a certain thing, what are you trying to understand?
   - a. the person's depressions
   - b. the person's hybrid
   - c. the person's motivation

5. Which phrase best describes a hybrid animal?
   - a. an animal mixture
   - b. bigger than usual
   - c. smarter than normal

Add the numbers that you just checked to get your Personal Checklist score. Fill in your score here. Then turn to page 215 and transfer your score onto Graph 1.

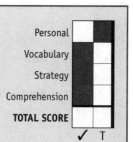

Check your answers with your teacher. Give yourself 1 point for each correct answer, and fill in your Vocabulary score here. Then turn to page 215 and transfer your score onto Graph 1.

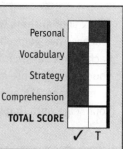

Strategy Check

Review the problem-solution frame that you completed in the Strategy Follow-up. Also review the rest of the story if necessary. Then answer these questions:

1. When Rex asks what the chicken was doing when it was recovered, what does he learn?
   a. that it was pecking as if it were back home
   b. that it was trying to chase after the striped car
   c. that it was trying to get back across the road

2. When Rex asks if the chickens are identified in any way, what does he learn?
   a. that they aren't marked for identification
   b. that their identification marks are hard to detect
   c. that they aren't tattooed until they're shipped

3. What information does Rex gain from Granley the security guard?
   a. The chicken was running toward a striped car that was parked across the street.
   b. Granley had not been paying attention.
   c. The chicken had been pecking at the ground as if it were back home.

4. Which piece of information did the striped car help Rex figure out?
   a. that the car belonged to some teenagers who wanted to hurt the chicken
   b. that the chicken had been imprinted to associate the stripes with home
   c. that the last rain fell on the car two days ago

5. How does Barnabus Rex solve the problem?
   a. He uses his amazing ability to sense activities that happened in the past.
   b. He finds someone who saw the competitor throw a chicken over the fence.
   c. He gathers all kinds of information and uses it to make a logical guess.

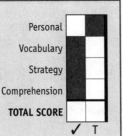

Check your answers with your teacher. Give yourself 1 point for each correct answer, and fill in your Strategy score here. Then turn to page 215 and transfer your score onto Graph 1.

Personal
Vocabulary
Strategy
Comprehension
TOTAL SCORE
✓ T

Comprehension Check

Review the story if necessary. Then answer the following questions:

1. Where are the hybrid chickens supposed to be taken after they leave the research farm?
   a. to a dome on Mars
   b. to a colony on the moon
   c. to Zipoid, the second planet of Barnard's star

2. Why are the scientists upset that the chicken broke through the fence?
   a. The chicken was not bred to use its beak that way.
   b. The chicken's beak was damaged in the breakout.
   c. The chicken has become violent ever since that day.

3. Who are the competitors of the Tangaway Research Farms?
   a. Mintor's Farms
   b. Beaverbrook Farms
   c. Zipoid Farms

4. Why is it significant that the last rain was two days ago?
   a. It means that the chicken might have crossed the road because it was thirsty.
   b. It means that the earth around the farm was dry.
   c. It means that the tire depressions were made after the rain.

5. Why did the competitors implant a tape recorder in the chicken?
   a. They wanted to send it aggressive messages to make it fight.
   b. They wanted to use it to spy on the Tangaway scientists.
   b. They wanted to use it to spy on the Tangaway chickens.

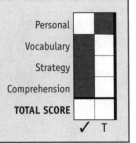

Check your answers with your teacher. Give yourself 1 point for each correct answer, and fill in your Comprehension score here. Then turn to page 215 and transfer your score onto Graph 1.

Personal
Vocabulary
Strategy
Comprehension
TOTAL SCORE
✓ T

Extending

Choose one or more of these activities:

CREATE A HYBRID ANIMAL

Imagine that you work with hybrid animals at the Tangaway Research Farms. What animal might you want to develop, and why? "Design" a science fiction animal that is equipped to survive in a certain environment or do certain tasks. Then draw, sculpt, or create the animal from pictures that you cut from magazines. Write a brief description of your animal and explain its special features and abilities.

CREATE A STORYBOARD

When directors plan a movie, they often post pictures of the most important scenes in the movie, in chronological order. Draw at least five pictures for a storyboard for this story. Each picture should depict a different setting and event than the one before. Together, the pictures should tell the entire story.

READ OTHER SCIENCE-FICTION STORIES

Use the resources on this page to locate other science fiction stories. After reading a few, make a chart that compares the stories' settings (both time and place) characters, and problems and solutions. What similarities, if any, do you find among the stories?

Resources

Books

Hoch, Edward D. *Diagnosis: Impossible; The Problems of Dr. Sam Hawthorne.* Crippen & Landru, 1996.

————. *The Night, My Friend: Stories of Crime and Suspense.* The Mystery Makers. Oxford University Press, 1992.

————. *The Ripper of Storyville, and Other Ben Snow Tales.* Crippen & Landru, 1997.

Williams, Sheila, and Charles Ardai, eds. *Why I Left Harry's All-Night Hamburgers, and Other Stories from Isaac Asimov's* Science Fiction *Magazine.* Delacorte, 1990.

Web Site

http://www.freesfonline.de/Home2.html
This Web site offers a selection of science fiction stories.

Learning New Words

VOCABULARY

From Lesson 14
- debris/rubble
- tornado/twister

From Lesson 11
- contradictory

Synonyms

A synonym is a word that means the same thing—or close to the same thing—as another word. For example, the author of "Elegy for Woodward" uses the synonyms *tornado* and *twister* to describe the storm that devastated Woodward. He also uses *debris* and *rubble* to describe what the storm left behind.

Draw a line from each word in Column 1 to its synonym in Column 2.

Column 1	Column 2
curious	elated
joyful	faithful
calm	rare
loyal	tranquil
unique	nosy

Suffixes

As you know, a suffix is a word part that is added to the end of a root word. When you add a suffix, you often change the root word's meaning and function.

-ory

The suffix *-ory* has several meanings. Two of them are "place for _____" or "having to do with _____tion." A word ending in *-ory* can also mean the same thing as a word ending in *-ing*. For example, *contradictory* = *contradicting*.

Complete each sentence with one of the words below.

depository   mandatory   conciliatory   preparatory

1. Alex went to a _____ school before he entered college.

2. The assembly is _____, so we all have to go.

3. I dropped my check into the _____ to add more money to my account.

4. To apologize, John shook my hand in a _____ gesture.

Multiple-Meaning Words

From Lesson 12
• depression

From Lesson 13
• clutch
• pretty

From Lesson 15
• depressions
• imprinting

You know that a single word can have more than one meaning. For example, in Lesson 12 the word *depression* refers to the Great Depression of the 1930s—a worldwide reduction of business activity that resulted in much poverty and homelessness. In Lesson 15, however, the word *depressions* refers to hollow grooves in the ground caused by automobile tires. To figure out which meaning of *depression* each author was using, you had to use context. Context is the information surrounding a word or situation that helps you understand it.

Now use context to figure out the correct meaning of each underlined word. Circle the letter of the correct meaning.

1. As she approached the stop sign, Bonnie engaged the clutch.

   a. pedal used to shift a car

   b. brood of chickens

2. Well, this is a pretty mess that you've gotten us into!

   a. pleasing to the eye or ear

   b. not at all pleasing

3. I'm imprinting all of these places so I can remember them when I get home from vacation.

   a. learning process occurring in very young animals

   b. fixing firmly in the mind

4. Both sides of the debate team argued their points very well.

   a. main ideas

   b. tiny dots

5. We dubbed my sister "Grace" after she stumbled up the stairs.

   a. added music or voices

   b. gave a nickname

Zoo's New Top Banana

Building Background

Animals can seem almost human sometimes. We look into the eyes of our pets and seem to detect emotions such as happiness, sadness, and worry. We talk to them, and sometimes they seem to respond as if they understand. But in our hearts we know that animals are different from us in countless ways.

The chart below lists several animals. Complete the chart by listing ways in which each animal is like and unlike humans.

Animal	Like Humans	Unlike Humans
gorilla		
dog		
cat		
bird		
fish		
ant		

celebrity

endangered

instinct

maternal

pilgrimage

primate

unconscious

Vocabulary Builder

1. Read each sentence below and decide if the boldfaced vocabulary word is used correctly or incorrectly. Write a **C** on the line if the word is used correctly. Write an **I** if the word is used incorrectly.

2. If you don't know the meaning of a vocabulary word, find it in the selection and use context to figure it out. If using context doesn't help, use a dictionary.

_____ a. A **celebrity** is someone who has never been heard of before.

_____ b. An **endangered** species is one that is in danger of disappearing.

_____ c. An **instinct** is never natural but must always be taught.

_____ d. A **maternal** feeling is one that a father might feel.

_____ e. People make **pilgrimages** to places that are important to them in some way.

_____ f. The term *primate* refers to all animals with backbones.

_____ g. When you are **unconscious**, you can't hear what's going on around you.

3. Save your work. You will refer to it again in the Vocabulary Check.

Strategy Builder

Identifying Causes and Effects in a Newspaper Article

- **Newspaper articles** are nonfiction. They deal with facts—actual events, quotations from eyewitnesses and experts, and proven statistics. Newspaper articles present their information in a unique way. They state the most important facts first. Then they expand upon the facts by presenting background information and details.

- The **author's purpose** for writing a newspaper article is usually to inform readers about an event or a situation. For example, Stacey Singer wrote this newspaper article to inform readers about what happened when a little boy fell into a gorilla pen at a Chicago zoo.

- The article is filled with **cause-and-effect relationships** in which one event or situation causes the next. To find the causes and effects while you read, keep asking yourself "What happened?" and "Why did it happen?"

- Now read the following paragraph. See how many causes and effects you can identify.

> When Rusty's owners decided to move, they were nervous about whether their dog would adjust to his new home. Sure enough, after they moved Rusty ran away, probably because he missed his old home. The owners were heartbroken at the loss of their beloved pet. Several weeks went by and finally the owners gave up hope, resigning themselves to the idea of never seeing Rusty again. Then, one day about eight weeks after he left, Rusty came back. He was dirty and his fur was matted, but his owners were overjoyed that their dog had returned.

- If you wanted to show the causes and effects in this paragraph, you could use a **cause-and-effect chain**. It would look like this:

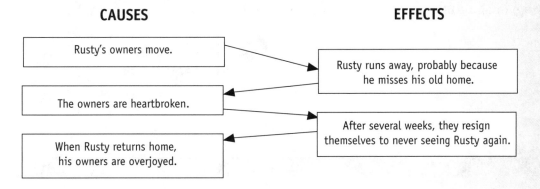

CAUSES

Rusty's owners move.

The owners are heartbroken.

When Rusty returns home, his owners are overjoyed.

EFFECTS

Rusty runs away, probably because he misses his old home.

After several weeks, they resign themselves to never seeing Rusty again.

Zoo's New Top Banana

Binti-Jua's rescue of boy thrills millions

by Stacey Singer, *Tribune* Staff Writer

As you read the first part of this newspaper article, apply the strategies that you just learned. To identify the causes and effects, keep asking yourself, "What happened?" and "Why did it happen?"

She's the talk of the world.

On Saturday, camera crews and reporters from England, Germany and Australia clamored to film her lounging at home with her baby. Dozens of people offered money to "adopt" her. And a Chicago grocer offered 25 pounds of free bananas.

The Chicago area's hottest new **celebrity** weighs 160 pounds, has black hair and long arms and is a vegetarian.

Binti-Jua, an 8-year-old western lowland gorilla at Brookfield Zoo, may be the most famous ape on the planet since rescuing an **unconscious** toddler who had fallen into her pen Friday.

As her photo beamed across international news wires and played on CNN, visitors to the zoo's Tropic World exhibit on Saturday expressed awe at the brief interaction between man and beast.

Some said they cried when they read the story. Others made a **pilgrimage** to the zoo just to see her.

"We saw it on TV, and the kids were just amazed," said Sandra Burl, 36, of Chicago, who had brought her niece and son to the zoo to see Binti. "I mean, she protected him."

Others could scarcely believe that Binti and the six other apes did not hurt the small boy who tumbled into their turf.

"I would have been terrified that they would hurt him," said Eliot Leby, 33, of Lake in the Hills. "I can see it happening."

But Binti's keeper, Craig Demitros, said western lowland gorillas are seldom angry or violent, despite the impression left by notorious films like "King Kong." Native to equatorial West Africa, they have become an **endangered** species because of habitat loss, he said.

Demitros attributed Binti's reaction to a strong **maternal instinct**, something the zoo has worked to instill since the San Francisco Zoo loaned Binti to Brookfield four years ago.

 **Stop here for the Strategy Break.**

Strategy Break

If you were to create a cause-and-effect chain for this article so far, it might look like this:

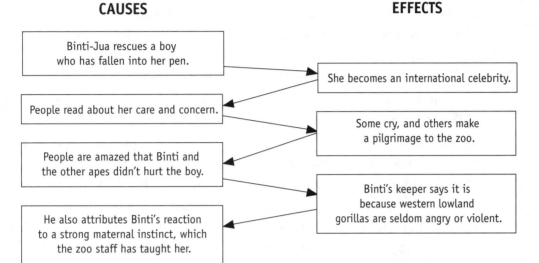

CAUSES

EFFECTS

Binti-Jua rescues a boy who has fallen into her pen.

People read about her care and concern.

People are amazed that Binti and the other apes didn't hurt the boy.

He also attributes Binti's reaction to a strong maternal instinct, which the zoo staff has taught her.

She becomes an international celebrity.

Some cry, and others make a pilgrimage to the zoo.

Binti's keeper says it is because western lowland gorillas are seldom angry or violent.

As you continue reading, keep looking for causes and effects. At the end of this article, you will use some of them to create a cause-and-effect chain of your own.

 Go on reading.

Binti-Jua's name means "daughter of sunlight" in Swahili, but as an infant she had little real mothering.

Born in the Columbus Zoo in Ohio on March 17, 1988, she was treated with indifference by her mother, Demitros said. Humans had to cradle and handfeed Binti with a bottle every two hours. As she grew, other female apes groomed and socialized her.

Once mature, Binti had to learn the basics of nurturing.

"If the mother is hand-reared, a lot of times they don't mother properly," Demitros said. "A lot of this behavior is learned."

And so Demitros and other keepers taught her to be a mom.

They put a stuffed animal in her care, teaching her to cradle it so that she would feel comfortable feeding a child, and teaching her baby-sitting behavior called retrieval.

"We would push the doll under her cage, and she would get it and then bring it back to the cage," Demitros said.

Retrieval is precisely what Binti did Friday afternoon, according to Jay Petersen, manager of Brookfield's **primate** collection.

Witnesses said the tow-haired 3-year-old crawled over a fence and planter at the highest point overlooking Tropic World's gorilla pen. He fell as far as 24 feet onto the concrete floor, landing on his buttocks and scraping his face.

Binti, with her own baby on her back, hurried over to the motionless child, scooped him up with one arm and took him to a safer place, the door where zookeepers entered.

Demitros was lunching nearby when he saw panicked visitors pouring out of the exhibit's emergency exits, and he rushed in.

"When I first came in, Binti was straddled over the kid," he said. "She probably carried him maybe 40 feet."

Brookfield spokeswoman Sondra Katzen said her phone has been ringing ever since the incident, with callers—locally and worldwide—asking about the boy, who will recover, and the gorilla.

The zoo has an "adoption" program in which sponsors can contribute at least $25 toward the annual care and feeding of an animal. Caller after caller has asked to join the Binti bandwagon, with one offering $100, she said.

Zookeepers wandering through the exhibit were peppered with cries of "Good job!" and pats on the back.

But a few have asked about the adequacy of the barriers between the animals and the public. Petersen said that perhaps 15 million people had already passed through without mishap. On Friday, the zoo brought in an independent, private firm to evaluate the exhibits. Everything was considered safe, officials said.

"We have looked at those barriers on and off through the years," Petersen said. "We don't want to put an 8-foot-high, chain-linked fence across."

Zoos are not just holding pens or display cases for the western lowland gorillas. They have become breeding centers as habitat destruction, population pressures and hunting have depleted the gorillas' numbers to about 35,000.

Binti has done her part to improve those numbers. In 1994, she gave birth to her own healthy girl, Koola, and has shown excellent mothering skills, officials said.

On Saturday, unruffled by her new celebrity, Binti lounged in the branches of one of the exhibit's leafless trees, pulling on a viney rope and occasionally grooming Koola.

Demitros said he was proud of the gorilla he and his team watch over.

"The way it has turned out," he said, "she has been a very good mother." ●

Strategy Follow-up

Work with a partner or a small group to complete this activity. On a separate sheet of paper, create a cause-and-effect chain that tells what happened during and after Binti's rescue of the boy. To help identify the causes and effects, keep asking each other, "What happened?" and "Why did it happen?"

Personal Checklist

Read each question and put a check (✓) in the correct box.

1. How well were you able to use the chart that you completed in Building Background to understand how Binti is like and unlike humans?
   - ☐ 3 (extremely well)
   - ☐ 2 (fairly well)
   - ☐ 1 (not well)

2. In the Vocabulary Builder, how many words did you correctly identify as being used correctly or incorrectly?
   - ☐ 3 (6–7 words)
   - ☐ 2 (3–5 words)
   - ☐ 1 (0–2 words)

3. How well were you able to help create a cause-and-effect chain in the Strategy Follow-up?
   - ☐ 3 (extremely well)
   - ☐ 2 (fairly well)
   - ☐ 1 (not well)

4. How well do you understand how and why the zoo staff encouraged Binti's maternal instincts?
   - ☐ 3 (extremely well)
   - ☐ 2 (fairly well)
   - ☐ 1 (not well)

5. How well do you understand how Binti's maternal instincts came into play when the boy fell into her pen?
   - ☐ 3 (extremely well)
   - ☐ 2 (fairly well)
   - ☐ 1 (not well)

Vocabulary Check

Look back at the work you did in the Vocabulary Builder. Then answer each question by circling the correct letter.

1. Which word would best describe the star of the latest blockbuster movie?
   - a. unconscious
   - b. endangered
   - c. celebrity

2. Which of these animals is considered a primate?
   - a. a bird
   - b. a dog
   - c. a monkey

3. Which of these events would probably *not* cause someone to become unconscious?
   - a. a fall from a great height
   - b. a good night's sleep
   - c. a car accident

4. Which word describes an animal or species that has become scarce?
   - a. endangered
   - b. maternal
   - c. unconscious

5. What is a pilgrimage?
   - a. a way to adopt wild animals
   - b. a kindly animal
   - c. a visit to an important or sacred place

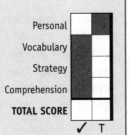

Add the numbers that you just checked to get your Personal Checklist score. Fill in your score here. Then turn to page 215 and transfer your score onto Graph 1.

Personal
Vocabulary
Strategy
Comprehension
TOTAL SCORE
✓ T

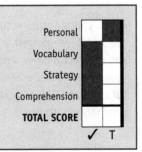

Check your answers with your teacher. Give yourself 1 point for each correct answer, and fill in your Vocabulary score here. Then turn to page 215 and transfer your score onto Graph 1.

Personal
Vocabulary
Strategy
Comprehension
TOTAL SCORE
✓ T

Strategy Check

Review the cause-and-effect chain that you completed for the Strategy Follow-up and the rest of the article. Then answer these questions:

1. What was the effect when the boy fell into Binti's pen?

   a. Binti straddled over the boy and wouldn't let anyone near him.

   b. Binti scooped up the boy and took him to the zookeepers' door.

   c. Binti started screeching and attacked the boy.

2. What caused Binti to react to the boy the way she did?

   a. She was using the skills that the zookeepers had taught her.

   b. She thought the boy was a doll and she was throwing him away.

   c. She was afraid of an unknown human inside the gorilla pen.

3. What caused Binti's keeper to rush into the gorilla pen?

   a. He saw gorillas coming out of the exits.

   b. He saw visitors coming out of the exits.

   c. He heard Binti screeching.

4. What effect did the fall have on the boy?

   a. He was badly shaken, but he walked away unharmed.

   b. He was knocked unconscious and was seriously injured.

   c. He died from his injuries.

5. What is one effect that Binti's actions had on the zoo?

   a. People have protested to shut down the zoo.

   b. The zoo has put up a chain-link fence.

   c. Caller after caller has contributed to the zoo's "adoption" program.

Comprehension Check

Review the article if necessary. Then answer these questions:

1. What does Binti-Jua's name mean?

   a. "dark daughter"

   b. "handfed daughter"

   c. "daughter of sunlight"

2. What had the zoo staff done to encourage Binti's maternal instincts?

   a. They gave her a stuffed animal to take care of.

   b. They gave her shots of hormones.

   c. They put young animals into her pen.

3. What behavior did the zoo staff teach Binti that probably led her to rescue the boy?

   a. feeding

   b. carrying

   c. retrieving

4. About how far did the toddler fall?

   a. about 5 feet

   b. about 24 feet

   c. about 40 feet

5. According to the manager of Brookfield's primate collection, how have zoos helped western lowland gorillas?

   a. by becoming holding pens and display cases for them

   b. by becoming places where the gorillas can safely reproduce

   c. by becoming centers for animal experimentation

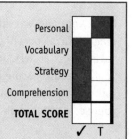

Check your answers with your teacher. Give yourself 1 point for each correct answer, and fill in your Strategy score here. Then turn to page 215 and transfer your score onto Graph 1.

Personal
Vocabulary
Strategy
Comprehension
TOTAL SCORE
✓ T

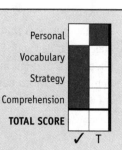

Check your answers with your teacher. Give yourself 1 point for each correct answer, and fill in your Comprehension score here. Then turn to page 215 and transfer your score onto Graph 1.

Personal
Vocabulary
Strategy
Comprehension
TOTAL SCORE
✓ T

Extending

Choose one or both of these activities:

LEARN ABOUT GORILLAS

According to this newspaper article, many people misunderstand gorillas. They think that gorillas are violent and frightening. Using some of the resources listed on this page or ones you find yourself, do some research on gorillas to find out how they behave in the wild. What do they eat? How do they treat their young? What type of society do they create for themselves when humans are not involved? Present your findings to the class in the form of a brief talk.

STAGE A MOCK INTERVIEW

Work with a partner to stage a mock interview with one of the zookeepers at the Brookfield Zoo. Together, plan the questions that one person will ask the other about how Binti was trained to be a good mother and the excitement of the day when the toddler fell in her pen. Also ask how the incident has changed the zoo. Rehearse your interview and then present it to the rest of the class.

Resources

Book

Fossey, Dian. *Gorillas in the Mist.* Mariner Books, 2000.

Web Sites

http://www.brookfieldzoo.org/content0.asp?pageid=187
This is the Tropic World page of the Brookfield Zoo Web site. Click on the "Western Lowland Gorillas" link for information on gorillas at the zoo.

http://www.dianfossey.org/home.html
This is the Web site of the Dian Fossey Gorilla Fund, which is dedicated to saving mountain gorillas from extinction.

Video/DVD

Search for the Great Apes. National Geographic Society, 1995.

LESSON **17** Animals on the Job

Building Background

Which animal is the most intelligent? Different people have different opinions on that question. Write about the animal that you think is the most intelligent by completing the following sentence and then listing your reasons.

I think that the most intelligent animal is the _____

Reason 1: _____

_____

Reason 2: _____

_____

Reason 3: _____

_____

olfactory
  receptors

opposable
  thumbs

positive
  reinforcement

quadriplegics

stimulus

traits

Vocabulary Builder

1. Many of the words that you will read in this article are explained in context. That means that the surrounding words and phrases contain examples or definitions that help explain the words.

2. Read the following sentences, which are taken from the article. Underline the context clues that help you understand each boldfaced word.

3. Then save your work. You will refer to it again in the Vocabulary Check.

   a. That's because dogs have millions of **olfactory receptors**, or smell nerves, in their nasal cavities.

   b. Like humans, monkeys have **opposable thumbs**—thumbs that face the hand's other fingers—so monkeys can pick up objects.

   c. Most trainers condition animals by using **positive reinforcement**, rewarding an animal for doing something correctly.

   d. Monkeys are perfect helpmates for **quadriplegics**, people paralyzed from the neck down who are unable to use their own hands (and legs).

   e. By using different methods of conditioning (training animals to act in a particular way in response to a **stimulus**, or signal), humans can teach animals to perform extraordinary tasks.

   f. Certain animals are "hired" for specific jobs based on their **traits**, or characteristics.

Strategy Builder

Outlining Main Ideas and Supporting Details

- You already know that an **informational article** is nonfiction writing that gives facts and details about a particular topic. The **topic** of an article is often mentioned in its **title**. For example, "Animals on the Job" is about animals—or more specifically, animals that are trained to help people do certain jobs.

- Many information articles are **descriptions** that are organized into **main ideas** and **supporting details**. These ideas and details help explain or support the topic. In the article you are about to read, the main ideas are stated in the boldfaced **headings**. The supporting details are given in the paragraphs below the headings.

- There are several ways to keep track of main ideas and details as you read an informational article. As you learned in Lesson 11, one way is to summarize them. Other ways are to put them on a concept map or a main idea table. Yet another way is to outline them. Some **outlines** use a system of Roman numerals (I, II, III, and so on), capital letters, Arabic numerals (1, 2, 3, and so on), and lowercase letters.

- Read the following paragraph from an article about German shepherd dogs. Then read how one student outlined the main ideas and details.

German Shepherds Make Good Work Dogs
German shepherds have many qualities that make them good work dogs. For one thing, they are the right size. They are quite large, which makes them strong. And with their big chests, they can get enough wind to run for a long time. They also have a thick coat of fur that protects them in bad weather and helps them stay clean. They are very alert and smart, so they are easy to train. And they are calm and patient with their owners.

I. German shepherds have many qualities that make them good work dogs.
   A. They are the right size.
      1. They're large, which makes them strong.
      2. Their big chests allow them to run for a long time.
   B. They have a thick coat of fur.
      1. It protects them in bad weather.
      2. It helps them stay clean.
   C. They are very alert and smart, so they're easy to train.
   D. They are calm and patient with their owners.

Animals on the Job

by Lynda Jones

As you read the first part of this article, apply some of the strategies that you just learned. Look for the main ideas and supporting details in this description, and think about how you might outline them.

Every morning Allie wakes up and accompanies her pal to the washroom. She turns on the light, soaps up a washcloth, and begins cleaning her friend's face. Is Allie an extremely devoted companion? Yes! Allie is a capuchin monkey who helps her disabled friend perform everyday tasks.

Monkeys like Allie are just one of the many kinds of animals that help improve—or even save—human lives. But not all animals are suited to do every job. Certain animals are "hired" for specific jobs based on their **traits**, or characteristics. By using different methods of conditioning (training animals to act in a particular way in response to a **stimulus**, or signal), humans can teach animals to perform extraordinary tasks.

Animal Sense

Throughout history, humans have relied on animals' traits to get certain jobs done. For example, compared with humans, dogs are "far superior at tracking down odors," says Marian Bailey, an animal behaviorist at Henderson State University in

Arkansas. That's because dogs have millions of **olfactory receptors**, or smell nerves, in their nasal cavities.

For that reason, hunters used dogs to track down prey even in ancient Egypt. Today, dogs may be employed to sniff out illegal substances in school lockers—or earthquake victims buried beneath the rubble of a collapsed building or highway.

Primates may not be good sniffers, but they can certainly lend a helping hand—or two. Monkeys are perfect helpmates for **quadriplegics**, people paralyzed from the neck down who are unable to use their own hands (and legs). Like humans, explains Bailey, monkeys have **opposable thumbs**—thumbs that face the hand's other fingers—so monkeys can pick up objects. Capuchins learn to open doors, clean up spills, and unscrew bottle tops. They can even get a sandwich out of the refrigerator and load your favorite tape into the VCR.

 Stop here for the Strategy Break.

Strategy Break

If you were to create an outline for this article so far, it might look something like this:

I. Animal sense
  A. Humans have always relied on animals to get certain jobs done.
    1. Dogs are far superior to humans at tracking down odors.
      a. Hunters used dogs to track down prey even in ancient Egypt.
      b. Today, dogs can sniff out illegal substances or buried earthquake victims.
    2. Monkeys are perfect helpmates for quadriplegics because of their opposable thumbs.
      a. Capuchins can open doors, clean spills, unscrew bottle tops, get sandwiches from the refrigerator, and put a tape into the VCR.

As you continue reading, keep paying attention to the main ideas and supporting details. At the end of this article, you will use some of them to create an outline of your own.

 Go on reading.

And speaking of VCRs, animals are even helping scientists make a videotape. Jenifer Hurley, an animal researcher at the Long Marine Lab in Santa Cruz, California, is training two sea lions to carry video cameras on their backs to record the natural behavior of whales.

Hurley could never dive to the depths at which whales swim, she says. But sea lions can. And whales behave naturally around sea lions because these mammals are part of the whales' natural environment—unlike humans or submarinelike research vessels.

On-the-Job Training
So how do you get an animal employee to do its job? The answer:

career-training. Trainers teach the animals to obey their instructions on command through a process called *conditioning*.

Most trainers condition animals by using **positive reinforcement**, rewarding an animal for doing something correctly, says animal behaviorist Bailey. For example, trainers teach their dogs how to sniff out drugs by hiding a narcotic-scented towel. "Dogs love to retrieve objects so the towel becomes a reward," says Morris Berkowitz, who heads up a canine drug-sniffing program in New York.

After repeating this game of hide-and-seek many times, the dog begins to "associate the odor with a reward," says Berkowitz. When he gives the command, or stimulus, the dog seeks out drugs. (It's kind of like learning to study hard for a test in order to get a good grade as a reward.)

At "Helping Hand—Monkey Helpers for the Disabled," capuchin monkeys are trained *twice* before being teamed with a disabled human. First, monkeys are placed with a foster family to become *socialized* to people. For five years, families help the monkeys adapt to a human environment, so the monkeys will trust and enjoy being around people.

Taking the monkeys in when they're four to six weeks old is important, says Bailey. "That's when monkeys normally become socialized to other monkeys," she says.

Second, trainers at Helping Hands custom-train the monkeys to perform specific tasks to assist a particular person. For example, a monkey may be trained to scratch an itch, or slip a floppy disc into a computer drive. Trainers reward the monkeys by using positive reinforcement, such as food, drink, praise, and affection. This phase of training can take a year.

Film School

Perhaps the animals that need the most motivation to learn are sea lions. They get bored easily, explains trainer Hurley, because they're smart. So she spends at least 20 minutes, three times a day with each sea lion. She plays games with them, teaches them new skills, and praises their efforts.

For example, Hurley started by training each sea lion to chase after a ball and touch it with its nose. First she waited for the sea lion to do it by chance. Then she praised the animal with positive reinforcement, such as food, petting, or a game. Eventually, the sea lions knew to chase after the ball to get a reward.

The next step was to get the sea lions to swim beside life-size plastic whale models, Hurley says. She and her team placed the models over a boat and the sea lions would follow them. "We began conditioning the animals to touch their noses to the whale's body," says Hurley, just like they did with the ball. "Eventually, the sea lions got the hang of it."

Now they're almost ready to chase after the real thing, Hurley says. If successful, she may send them to videotape other marine mammals, such as the enormous humpback and blue whales.

After doing all that work, you might wonder, do the animals get paid? Well, not in dollars and cents. But they do get loving caretakers, a good home, food, and drink—and human companions who are willing to play plenty of games. ●

Strategy Follow-up

On a separate sheet of paper, create an outline for the section of this article called "On-the-Job Training." When you are finished, compare your outline with those of other students. Do your outlines contain similar information? Why or why not? Revise your outline if necessary.

✓Personal Checklist

Read each question and put a check (✓) in the correct box.

1. How well do you understand the ideas presented in this article?
   - ☐ 3 (extremely well)
   - ☐ 2 (fairly well)
   - ☐ 1 (not well)

2. In Building Background, how well were you able to explain why your chosen animal is the most intelligent?
   - ☐ 3 (extremely well)
   - ☐ 2 (fairly well)
   - ☐ 1 (not well)

3. How well were you able to underline the context clues in the Vocabulary Builder?
   - ☐ 3 (extremely well)
   - ☐ 2 (fairly well)
   - ☐ 1 (not well)

4. In the Strategy Follow-up, how well were you able to create an outline for "On-the-Job Training"?
   - ☐ 3 (extremely well)
   - ☐ 2 (fairly well)
   - ☐ 1 (not well)

5. After reading this article, how well would you be able to explain how trainers encourage certain behaviors in animals?
   - ☐ 3 (extremely well)
   - ☐ 2 (fairly well)
   - ☐ 1 (not well)

Vocabulary Check

Look back at the work you did in the Vocabulary Builder. Then answer each question by circling the correct letter.

1. What is another word for *traits*?
   a. signals
   b. abilities
   c. characteristics

2. Which of these is an example of positive reinforcement?
   a. punishing a dog for running away
   b. rewarding a dog for doing something correctly
   c. withholding rewards when an animal disobeys you

3. Where are a dog's olfactory receptors located?
   a. in its ears
   b. in its nose
   c. on its tongue

4. Which word describes someone who doesn't have the use of his or her arms and legs?
   a. quadriplegic
   b. behaviorist
   c. trainer

5. What is another word for *stimulus*?
   a. punishment
   b. reinforcement
   c. signal

Add the numbers that you just checked to get your Personal Checklist score. Fill in your score here. Then turn to page 215 and transfer your score onto Graph 1.

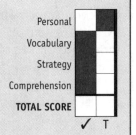

Personal
Vocabulary
Strategy
Comprehension
TOTAL SCORE
✓ T

Check your answers with your teacher. Give yourself 1 point for each correct answer, and fill in your Vocabulary score here. Then turn to page 215 and transfer your score onto Graph 1.

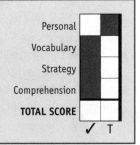

Personal
Vocabulary
Strategy
Comprehension
TOTAL SCORE
✓ T

Strategy Check

Review the outline that you created in the Strategy Follow-up. Then answer these questions:

1. What is the name of the process through which trainers teach animals to obey on command?
   a. conditioning
   b. career training
   c. on-the-job training

2. What do most trainers use to condition animals?
   a. positive reinforcement
   b. olfactory receptors
   c. videos of proper behavior

3. What do trainers use to teach dogs how to sniff out drugs?
   a. plastic bags filled with different substances
   b. a narcotics-scented towel
   c. a doll that resembles a drug dealer

4. How many times are capuchins trained before they are teamed with disabled humans?
   a. three times
   b. two times
   c. one time

5. How long do capuchins live with families in order to become socialized to people?
   a. three months
   b. two years
   c. five years

Comprehension Check

Review the article if necessary. Then answer these questions:

1. Why do people use animals to do tasks?
   a. People want animals to feel useful.
   b. People do not value animals much, so they use them to do tasks.
   c. Animals have skills that are superior to human skills in some areas.

2. Why do humans use dogs to track down odors?
   a. Dogs are not disgusted by bad smells.
   b. A dog's ability to smell is more developed than a human's.
   c. Dogs have special olfactory receptors in their mouths.

3. What is an animal researcher in California training sea lions to do?
   a. carry video cameras on their backs
   b. sniff out drugs
   c. search for whales

4. What is a capuchin?
   a. a kind of monkey
   b. a kind of dog
   c. a kind of sea lion

5. According to the article, which animals need the most motivation to learn, and why?
   a. dogs, because they are lazy
   b. sea lions, because they get bored easily
   c. monkeys, because they can't sit still for long

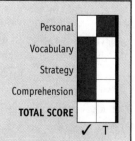

Check your answers with your teacher. Give yourself 1 point for each correct answer, and fill in your Strategy score here. Then turn to page 215 and transfer your score onto Graph 1.

Personal
Vocabulary
Strategy
Comprehension
TOTAL SCORE
✓ T

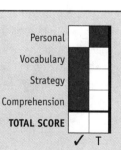

Check your answers with your teacher. Give yourself 1 point for each correct answer, and fill in your Comprehension score here. Then turn to page 215 and transfer your score onto Graph 1.

Personal
Vocabulary
Strategy
Comprehension
TOTAL SCORE
✓ T

Extending

Choose one or more of these activities:

RESEARCH ANIMAL-TRAINING REQUIREMENTS

Not everyone would make a good animal trainer. Work with a partner to write a list of personal qualities that an animal trainer needs. Consult your local telephone directory to see if there are any animal trainers in your city or town. If possible, invite a professional animal trainer to the classroom to tell more about his or her profession and its requirements.

RESEARCH CAPUCHIN MONKEYS

According to this article, capuchin monkeys are ideal helpers for the disabled. Aside from opposable thumbs, what qualities make capuchins so suited for the job? Use some of the resources listed on this page to find out why trainers have turned to this species to help the disabled. Record your findings in the form of an outline.

RESEARCH DOG-TRAINING

Find out more about training a dog to assist people with special needs. (Use the resources listed on this page if you need a place to start.) Choose a task, such as learning to search for something or learning to stop at a curb. Then make a list of the steps that you would need to take to train a dog to learn the task. Include the rewards and the number of trials you might expect before the dog is able to do the task properly and consistently.

Resources

Books

Bulanda, Susan. *Ready! The Training of the Search and Rescue Dog*. Doral, 1995.

Eames, Ed, and Toni Eames. *Partners in Independence: A Success Story of Dogs and the Disabled*. Hungry Minds, 1997.

Haldane, Suzanne. *Helping Hands: How Monkeys Assist People Who Are Disabled*. Dutton, 1991.

Whittemore, Hank with Caroline Hebard. *So That Others May Live: Caroline Hebard and Her Search-and-Rescue Dogs*. Bantam, 1995.

Web Sites

http://www.guidedogs.com/training.html
Read about training of guide dogs for the blind on this Web page.

http://www.helpinghandsmonkeys.org/
This is the Web site of Helping Hands, an organization dedicated to training capuchin monkeys as helpers for quadriplegics.

http://www.tampabaywired.com/family/article.asp?authorid=10&articleid=101
This Web article reports on high school kids involved in a program to train dogs as helpers for people with disabilities.

The Cobra's Venom

Building Background

What do you know about cobras? As you read this story, you will be given information about these deadly snakes. But now, before you read, answer as many of the questions below as you can, using things that you already know about cobras. Then as you read, look for the answers to any questions you left blank, and fill them in.

1. From what part of the world do cobras come? _____

   _____

2. What do cobras look like? _____

   _____

3. How can cobras be prevented from biting and/or poisoning someone? _____

   _____

   _____

4. What is the effect of a cobra bite on the human body? _____

   _____

   _____

   _____

herpetology

immunity

monitor

mutilated

paralyzed

venom

Vocabulary Builder

1. The words in the margin are found in "The Cobra's Venom." Before you begin reading, match each word on the left with its definition on the right. Write the number of the correct definition beside each word. If you need help with any of the words, use context or a dictionary.

2. Save your work. You will refer to it again in the Vocabulary Check.

   _____ venom   1) to watch or check

   _____ immunity   2) unable to move

   _____ herpetology   3) damaged

   _____ mutilated   4) the condition of being able to resist disease

   _____ paralyzed   5) poison produced by some animals

   _____ monitor   6) the study of reptiles and amphibians

Strategy Builder

Identifying Problems and Solutions in Stories

- Throughout this book, you've learned that a main element of every story is its **plot**, or sequence of events. In most stories, the plot revolves around a **problem** that the main characters try to solve. Sometimes they try more than one **solution**. By the end, they usually come up with the solution that works—**the end result**.

- Think back to the story "The Homesick Chicken." The following problem-solution frame shows the problem and what Barnabus Rex did to solve it:

What is the problem?
One of the research chickens pecked its way through
the security fence and crossed the road.
Why is it a problem?
Any abnormal behavior worries the scientists who work
with the chickens on this secret project.

Solutions	**Results**
1. Rex asks Professor Mintor about the chicken.	**1.** He begins gathering information that will help him.
2. Rex asks exactly what the chicken was doing when it was recovered.	**2.** He learns that it was pecking at the ground as if it were back home.
3. Rex asks if the chickens are identified in any way.	**3.** He learns that they are not tattooed until they're shipped out.
4. Using all the evidence he has gathered, Rex solves the riddle.	**4. END RESULT:** He explains that somebody from Beaverbrook implanted a tape recorder in the chicken's body and then planted the chicken at Tangaway. Using imprinting, they got the chicken to cross the road so they could get the tape recorder.

The Cobra's Venom

by Robert Elgin

In this story there are actually two different problems. As you begin reading, look for the first one. Notice the solutions the narrator tries, and the result of each solution.

The zoo's attendance figures for the few weeks of the season were a big disappointment. We had been rained out for two weekends, and if a zoo doesn't have top attendance during the weekends, it just isn't going to make it—period. I began to search for a solution—something big and spectacular. One rainy afternoon it came to me: cobra charming!

As far as I knew, no zoo in the country was featuring a cobra charming act, perhaps because it was so dangerous. Still, I had acquired a great deal of experience in handling poisonous snakes. At the zoo, I had been tube-feeding the larger part of our cobra collection every week for two years. I had also managed to build up an **immunity** to their **venom**. Convinced that I could not only handle the cobras but also draw large crowds to the zoo (even in the rain), I went ahead with the idea.

First I did some serious research. The business of cobra charming isn't nearly as daring as most people are led to believe. Most Oriental and African snake charmers sew the lips of their cobras together before the performance. Others break off the poisonous fangs. Some charmers practice a bit of surgery on the snake's venom glands, while others milk the snakes of their venom just before the act begins. All these techniques offer some degree of protection to the charmer, but breaking off fangs, operating on the venom glands, and sewing the lips shut always end in a fatal infection to the snake. My snakes were living creatures. I had no right to risk their lives. Milking the snakes was the most humane approach, but it was also the most risky for me. All in all, it seemed the only thing I could depend upon was my built-in immunity and a fast hand.

Once I had found the right-size baskets—if the basket in which the snake lies coiled is too high, the snake will be reluctant to emerge and do its hooded dance—I was ready to begin my first practice session. I sat in front of one of the baskets while the rest of the staff held their snake sticks at instant ready. A worker lifted the lid off the first round, flat basket. Huff, a six-foot Asiatic cobra, rose up from the bottom, hooded and hissing like a dragon. Immediately, he struck at the long flute I was waving in front of him. He then began to crawl from the basket onto the floor. My able assistants stuffed him back in the basket with their snake sticks. After a short wait, we tried again. The same thing happened, even though I was blowing the flute loudly and waving it furiously. Huff was not only *uncharmed*, he was uninterested.

Cobras have no external ears. The sound of the flute has no bearing upon the snake's performance. But I had assumed the reptiles did respond to the motion of the flute. Tom Weidner, our **herpetology** lecturer, explained Huff's disinterest. The flute was too long. The cobra saw only the stick-like flute and not me. In reality, said Weidner, the cobra is much more interested in the presence and motion of the hands and body of the snake charmer. We cut the flute down to just twelve inches, which of course meant bringing me just that much closer to the cobra. Still, I was ready to try again.

When we lifted the lid on the next cobra basket, I found myself eye-to-eye with big Puff, another Asiatic cobra. Puff struck at the flute, and I moved just in time to avoid being bitten on the hand. Right then I began to believe that some of the snake charmers of old India, at least the few honest ones who had not **mutilated** their reptiles, earned every penny that came their way.

With practice, I improved. The snakes accepted the baskets as their homes and would stand in place and dance well if my swaying motions kept them transfixed. As I had expected, the snake charming act was a success. The zoo began to get the weekend attendance figures it so badly needed. The local television station and newspapers gave us a lot of publicity. At last, things were looking up.

 Stop here for the Strategy Break.

Strategy Break

If you were to record the first problem, solutions, and end result on a problem-solution frame, they might look like this:

What is the problem?
The zoo's attendance figures for the first few weeks
of the season were a big disappointment.
Why is it a problem?
If a zoo doesn't have top attendance during
the weekends, it isn't going to make it.

Solutions to the first problem	Results of the first problem
1. The narrator decides on cobra charming to attract visitors.	1. He does some serious research to find out how to do it.
2. He finds the right-size baskets.	2. He has his first practice session.
3. He lets out Huff and blows and waves his flute.	3. Huff is uninterested.
4. He cuts the flute down to twelve inches and tries it on Puff.	4. With practice, the narrator improves.
5. The snakes accept the baskets and dance well if the narrator's swaying motions keep them transfixed.	5. **END RESULT:** The zoo begins to get the weekend attendance it so badly needs.

As you read the next part of this story, look for the second problem. Then look for what the characters do to solve it. At the end of the story, you will create a problem-solution frame for the second problem.

Go on reading to see what happens.

Then one day Jim Carr, a photographer, called us to do a feature story on the cobras. We scheduled a private performance so he could get some dramatic pictures to illustrate the article. I carried out the three baskets of cobras and placed them in the center of the zoo's lecture area. I sat down beside Huff's basket. I trilled out a few miserable bars of cobra dance music, then opened the basket. The fiery six-footer came up and out in his impressive way. Hood spread, hissing his hatred, Huff was intent on biting anything that came along.

I swayed from side to side, moving the flute back and forth in front of the reptile. His beady little eyes fixed on my hands. He followed gracefully, bending this way and that, in perfect time. But only for a moment. Huff was tired and lazy that day. He struck savagely at my fingers, missed, and then began to crawl from the basket. Disgusted, I grabbed him by the tail and the middle of his body and attempted to stuff him back in the basket for a second try. Before I could close the lid, he was out once more, crawling away to some quieter spot.

The only solution was to grab him by the back of the head so I could stuff him, tail first, into the basket and then pop his head in last. This way I could slam down the lid before he could get a start on me. Rather than get to my feet and cautiously use a snake hook to pin his head, as I

usually did, I grabbed Huff by the neck with just my hand.

Hissing with real anger, he whipped up and around in an attempt to bite me. I moved my hand just enough to make him miss, and as he fell, I stabbed out with my left hand and caught him again just behind the head.

This was my mistake. I'm not left-handed. While I had done the trick many times with my right hand, this time I was just a fraction of an inch too low. Huff turned his head, opened his big mouth, and hit me with everything he had.

Instantly, I tore him loose, but the fang remained sticking in my flesh. Blood streamed from the tiny wound, an indication that I had received a bad bite, probably into a vein. I wasn't too concerned, though. I had just received a booster shot of cobra venom the day before, and I was sure that the immunity I had built up would be sufficient to counteract the venom. I couldn't have been more mistaken.

Placing the cobra back in the basket, I apologized to the photographer. He understood, he said, but insisted that I see a doctor at once. Had he not insisted, I might not have gone to Dr. Redfield's office at all that afternoon. The doctor agreed with my thinking—most likely my immunity would counteract the venom. To be safe, however, he admitted me to the hospital for the night.

Cobra venom works rapidly in most cases. The victim feels the effects, quite terribly, within a few hours or even minutes. Few persons, if they receive a big injection of venom, live more than eight or ten hours unless they receive adequate treatment. But I felt wonderful—for twelve hours.

Then the lights went out.

My eyelids closed and I couldn't open them. My tongue became **paralyzed**. I lost control of my neck and leg muscles. The only parts of my body I could move were my hands and arms.

Then suddenly, I couldn't breathe. My chest muscles were paralyzed. I was helpless, gasping for breath like a fish out of water. The nurses placed a respirator tube in my mouth to do my breathing for me. I struggled for air; inwardly I *screamed* for air. Even with the respirator, I wasn't getting nearly enough oxygen. Sightless, speechless, and practically breathless, I had the terrible feeling that my own body was pressing in on me and becoming my coffin.

Yet I was aware of everything happening around me. And I could still use my hands. The doctors decided to send me to a university hospital in Iowa City where I'd have the constant attention of a number of specialists. Before they carried me to the waiting ambulance, I managed to scribble a word on the little slate the nurse had given me. HAAST, I wrote, hoping they'd understand. Bill Haast was the director of the Miami Serpentarium and had developed snakebite antitoxins for American soldiers serving in Vietnam. More importantly, Haast had antivenin serum in his blood.

Dr. Redfield studied the letters. "Yes, yes!" he said. "We'll get Haast for you!"

But would they get him in time?

At 10 A.M. the ambulance started for Iowa City, some 120 miles away. An hour into the trip, I began to drown.

Cobra venom affects the salivary glands, and now torrents of thick saliva poured down my throat into my paralyzed lungs. If my lungs filled up with this, even the respirator would be useless. The doctor who was accompanying me in the ambulance began to pump air into my lungs with a rubber bulb. At the same time, he tried to suction the saliva from my throat. Over and over again, he pumped and suctioned. Mile after mile as the ambulance sped toward the hospital, the doctor beside me refused to give up. I was still conscious. My heart was beating furiously as it struggled to keep me alive. I lay there, inside myself, listening to the pounding and wondering how much longer my heart could beat so hard and so fast.

The ambulance reached the hospital just before noon. The doctors performed a tracheotomy, slitting my throat in order to insert a breathing tube. Then they rushed me to the intensive care unit. I was in critical condition. Dozens of doctors and nurses, it seemed, began working on me. They taped wires in place all over me to **monitor** my heart. They inserted tubes everywhere and even placed a pacemaker in my heart as still another measure against the cobra's venom. And still, my body was pressing in upon me.

That afternoon came my first word of hope: Haast. Bill Haast is coming, they told me. He is coming from Miami.

Early that evening, Haast arrived. "You'll be fine, Bob," he said. "Just hang on a few more minutes while they get some of my blood into you."

His voice was quiet, sincere, and very reassuring.

He left for the blood lab. The technicians drew a pint of his blood and separated the plasma, or serum, portion from the red cells. Within thirty minutes of his arrival, Bill's human antivenin serum was slowly dripping into the vein in my arm. But had this last hope of survival come too late? The doctors waited, hoping for some indication that Bill's blood would save my life.

I disappointed them. I merely lay like a big, gray, long-nosed old mouse, hardly twitching. No improvement, the doctors were thinking.

But something *had* happened, something they couldn't see, something *inside* me. I could breathe. Suddenly I could breathe deeply on the respirator with complete freedom. It was beautiful; it was like music.

It was living. The respirator was still breathing for me, but now I was somehow getting a thousand times more oxygen.

While the doctors watched and waited, I drifted off into a wonderfully relaxed deep sleep. I went to sleep on them without even saying, "Excuse me." I slept like a lazy old log for hours.

Bill gave more plasma for another transfusion in the morning. This time I surprised everyone. My diaphragm muscles began moving. I was breathing on my own again. I opened my sad, droopy eyes and managed to mumble a feeble word of thanks.

"You're doing fine, Bob," Haast told me. "And don't worry about the thanks. Maybe someday you can do the same for me."

The Air Force jet was waiting. "When you're all better, come see me in Florida," he said. "In the meantime, be careful with those cobras."

He need not have warned me. My days of snake charming were over. ●

Strategy Follow-up

Now create a problem-solution frame for second problem in this story. Don't forget to label the end result. Use another sheet of paper if you need more room to write.

What is the second problem?

Why is it a problem?

Solutions to the second problem | **Results of the second problem**

1.   →   1.

2.   →   2.

3.   →   3.

4.   →   4.

5.   →   5. END RESULT:

✓Personal Checklist

Read each question and put a check (✓) in the correct box.

1. How well were you able to use the information in this story to answer the questions in Building Background?
   - ☐ 3 (extremely well)
   - ☐ 2 (fairly well)
   - ☐ 1 (not well)

2. In the Vocabulary Builder, how well were you able to match the vocabulary words with their definitions?
   - ☐ 3 (extremely well)
   - ☐ 2 (fairly well)
   - ☐ 1 (not well)

3. How well were you able to create a problem-solution frame for the second problem in this story?
   - ☐ 3 (extremely well)
   - ☐ 2 (fairly well)
   - ☐ 1 (not well)

4. How well do you understand why the narrator thought he would be fine after Huff bit him?
   - ☐ 3 (extremely well)
   - ☐ 2 (fairly well)
   - ☐ 1 (not well)

5. Now that you've read this story, how well would you be able to explain what happens during a snake charming?
   - ☐ 3 (extremely well)
   - ☐ 2 (fairly well)
   - ☐ 1 (not well)

Vocabulary Check

Look back at the work you did in the Vocabulary Builder. Then answer each question by circling the correct letter.

1. What happens when people become paralyzed?
   - a. They become unconscious.
   - b. They can't think straight.
   - c. They can't move.

2. Which word has almost the same meaning as *venom*?
   - a. immunity
   - b. poison
   - c. fang

3. What does a herpetologist study?
   - a. fish
   - b. apes
   - c. snakes

4. Which of these meanings of *monitor* matches the way the word is used in this selection?
   - a. tube used to display words or pictures
   - b. to watch or check
   - c. adviser or counselor

5. Which of these is an example of something that has been mutilated?
   - a. a fresh flower in a garden
   - b. a cake before it is sliced
   - c. a car that has had its tires slashed

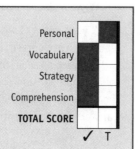

Add the numbers that you just checked to get your Personal Checklist score. Fill in your score here. Then turn to page 215 and transfer your score onto Graph 1.

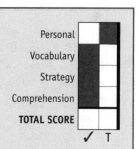

Check your answers with your teacher. Give yourself 1 point for each correct answer, and fill in your Vocabulary score here. Then turn to page 215 and transfer your score onto Graph 1.

Strategy Check

Look back at the problem-solution frame that you completed in the Strategy Follow-up. Use it to answer these questions:

1. What is the second problem in this story?
   a. While trying to charm Huff for a photographer, the narrator gets bitten.
   b. While trying to charm Puff for a group of visitors, the narrator gets bitten.
   c. While trying to charm Huff for a photographer, the photographer gets bitten.

2. Why is this a problem?
   a. After biting the photographer, Huff gets seriously ill.
   b. After biting the visitor, Puff gets seriously ill.
   c. Although fine for the first 12 hours, the narrator gets seriously ill.

3. When the narrator suddenly can't breathe at the first hospital, what is the result?
   a. The nurses put a respirator tube in his mouth.
   b. A doctor pumps air into his lungs.
   c. The doctors performed a tracheotomy.

4. What is the result when Dr. Haast gives the narrator a pint of his own blood?
   a. It is too late, and the narrator gets sicker.
   b. The narrator begins to breathe much more deeply.
   c. There is no improvement, and the narrator falls asleep.

5. What is the end result of the second problem?
   a. Dr. Haast becomes ill from giving so much blood.
   b. The narrator begins breathing on his own and is on his way to recovery.
   c. There is no improvement, and the narrator goes into a coma.

Comprehension Check

Review the story if necessary. Then answer these questions:

1. Why does the narrator decide to charm snakes?
   a. He wants to begin a new career.
   b. He wants to boost zoo attendance.
   c. He thinks that the cobras need exercise.

2. According to the herpetologist, what is the cobra concentrating on as it dances?
   a. the motion of the snake charmer's hands and body
   b. the sounds and rhythms of the flute music
   c. the waving flute itself

3. Why does the narrator get bitten?
   a. He grasps the snake with his right hand instead of his left.
   b. He catches the snake too far down its body.
   c. He lets go of the snake too quickly.

4. When do the effects of the venom hit the narrator?
   a. right after the bite
   b. after 12 hours
   c. after two days

5. How does Bill Haast save the narrator's life?
   a. He brings a bottle of antivenin serum with him.
   b. He tells the doctors the formula for the antivenin serum.
   c. He donates his own blood, which contains antivenin.

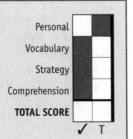

Check your answers with your teacher. Give yourself 1 point for each correct answer, and fill in your Strategy score here. Then turn to page 215 and transfer your score onto Graph 1.

Personal
Vocabulary
Strategy
Comprehension
TOTAL SCORE
✓ T

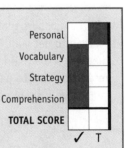

Check your answers with your teacher. Give yourself 1 point for each correct answer, and fill in your Comprehension score here. Then turn to page 215 and transfer your score onto Graph 1.

Personal
Vocabulary
Strategy
Comprehension
TOTAL SCORE
✓ T

Extending

Choose one or more of these activities:

FIND AN EXAMPLE OF "COBRA DANCE MUSIC"

The narrator in "The Cobra's Venom" explains that he played cobra dance music as he tried to charm the snakes. Find a recording of Asian flute music—the kind the narrator might have played while mesmerizing the cobra with his waving flute—and play it for the class. Discuss what makes this music an appropriate choice.

WRITE ABOUT A DIFFERENT SOLUTION TO THE ZOO'S PROBLEM

At the beginning of this story, the narrator states that the reason he took up snake charming was to boost attendance at the zoo. With a partner or a small group, brainstorm other ways in which the zoo could attract visitors. Make a list of at least five different promotions or attractions that would draw people to the zoo. Then choose one of the options and prepare a newspaper ad or poster to advertise it.

MAKE A CHART OF SNAKE FACTS AND FICTION

Many people have inaccurate information about snakes. For example, many people think that cobra bites are always fatal. Using the resources listed on this page or ones you find yourself, research several facts about cobras or other snakes. Then make a chart that lists real facts and common misperceptions, or fiction.

Resources

Books

Bargar, Sherie, and Linda Johnson. *Cobras*. Rourke, 1993.

Mara, W. P. *Venomous Snakes of the World*. TFH Publications, 1993.

Minton, Sherman A., Jr., and Madge Rutherford Minton. *Venomous Reptiles*. Macmillan, 1982.

Web Sites

http://www.nationalgeographic.com/kingcobra/index-n.html
Learn about king cobras on this National Geographic Web site.

http://www.umass.edu/umext/nrec/snake_pit/pages/myth.html
This Web site discusses common myths about snakes.

Videos/DVDs

Cobra: King of Snakes. Unapix, 1998.

Deadly Reptiles: Nightmares of Nature. National Geographic Society, 2003.

A Revolutionary Friendship

Building Background

Anyone who has ever celebrated the Fourth of July probably has heard the names of Thomas Jefferson and John Adams. These men were two of the most influential and powerful figures involved in the birth of the United States of America. Even though we know a great deal about the public life and achievements of Jefferson and Adams, we hardly ever think about their private lives and characters. In the selection you are about to read, the author tells about the private men behind the public figures.

On the lines below, list at least three questions that you have about either Thomas Jefferson, John Adams, or both. Then keep your questions in mind, and see if you can find their answers as you read "A Revolutionary Friendship."

_____

_____

_____

_____

_____

_____

_____

Vocabulary Builder

1. The words in the margin are all found in "A Revolutionary Friendship." Before you begin reading the selection, decide whether each word has a positive or negative **connotation**, or implied meaning. Then write each word on the appropriate clipboard.

2. As you read the selection, read the boldfaced vocabulary words in context and decide if you put them on the correct clipboards. Change your answers if necessary.

3. Save your work. You will refer to it again in the Vocabulary Check.

Strategy Builder

Comparing and Contrasting While You Read

- You may recall that nonfiction is usually organized in one of four patterns: description, sequence, cause-effect, or compare-contrast. The selection you are about to read follows the pattern of compare-contrast. When you **compare** two or more people, things, or ideas, you look at the ways in which they are alike. When you **contrast** them, you look at the ways in which they are different.

- Study the following **comparison chart**. See how quickly you can find three ways in which the states of Massachusetts and Virginia are alike and two ways in which they are different.

	Massachusetts	Virginia
Date admitted to the Union	1788	1788
Size	8,284 square miles	40,767 square miles
Estimated population (1998)	6,147,132	6,791,345
East or west of the Mississippi?	east	east
One of the original 13 colonies?	yes	yes

- This selection is also organized according to the pattern of **sequence**, or chronological order. It follows Jefferson and Adams over a period of many years. The writer uses **signal words** such as *the first time* and *in June and early July of 1776* to give readers a clear idea of when different events occurred.

admiration

aristocratic

calm

modesty

obnoxious

stubbornness

sturdy

unpopular

CLIPBOARD
Positive Connotations

CLIPBOARD
Negative Connotations

A Revolutionary Friendship

by Connie Nordhielm Wooldridge

As you begin reading this selection, apply the strategies that you just learned. Look for ways in which Thomas Jefferson and John Adams were both alike and different.

To the Second Continental Congress of 1775 came two men who were as different from each other as night is from day. Thirty-nine-year-old John Adams arrived from Massachusetts. He was short and round, he had **sturdy** Puritan ancestors, he loved his friends fiercely (and told them so), he disliked his enemies just as fiercely (and told *them* so), and that was that. Many people loved him; more did not.

Thomas Jefferson, seven years younger than Adams, arrived from Virginia. He was tall and **calm**, born into an **aristocratic** family, and when he expressed his opinions, he did it carefully. Almost everyone liked him, but they were never quite sure they really knew him.

Coming face to face for the first time, these two men realized that, in spite of all their differences, they shared one very important thing: a burning desire for independence from England. This shared desire made them become fast friends.

In June and early July of 1776 Adams and Jefferson were again present in Congress when an important question came up: should the colonies declare their independence from England *in writing*? "Yes!" thundered Adams as Jefferson sat back and watched in quiet **admiration**.

According to Jefferson, Adams argued the point with "a power of thought and expression that moved us from our seats." John Adams was the mighty "Colossus" on the floor of Congress that fateful summer.

When the point had been won, it was Adams's turn to sit back. He had spoken, and now it was up to Jefferson to write the declaration. Jefferson, with characteristic **modesty**, tried to give the task to Adams, but Adams, with characteristic **stubbornness**, refused to accept it. He gave Jefferson three reasons: "Reason first—You are a Virginian, and a Virginian ought to appear at the head of this business. Reason second—I am **obnoxious**, suspected, and **unpopular**. You are very much otherwise. Reason third—You can write ten times better than I can." Jefferson wrote, and the Revolution, which had really begun in the hearts of the colonists years earlier, spilled out onto the battlefields. The two friends watched much of the war from opposite sides of the Atlantic. Jefferson was involved in local Virginia politics, and Adams was ambassador to France. They wrote to each other, they shared bits of news, they hoped, and finally they rejoiced.

 Stop here for the Strategy Break.

Strategy Break

If you were to create a comparison chart for this selection so far, it might look like this:

	Adams	Jefferson
Age when they met	39	32
Where they lived	Massachusetts	Virginia
Appearance	short and round	tall
Personality	fierce, verbal, stubborn	calm, aristocratic, modest
Opinion regarding American independence	in favor	in favor
Tasks performed for Second Continental Congress	inspired with speeches	wrote Declaration of Independence
How they spent the war years	served as ambassador to France	involved in Virginia politics
Relationship to the other	friend	friend

As you continue reading, keep looking for ways in which Adams and Jefferson are alike and different. When you finish, you will complete a comparison chart for the second part of this selection.

 Go on reading.

Unfortunately, the friendship between Adams and Jefferson began to unravel after they had realized their dream of independence. Without this common goal, they began to find themselves on opposite sides of many issues. Before they knew it, two political parties had sprung up around them. Adams, who was elected president in 1796, began to mistrust Jefferson, his vice president. Rumors flew, unkind words found their way into print, and in 1800 President Adams was defeated in his bid for a second term by his former friend, Thomas Jefferson. Before leaving office, Adams appointed a host of men from his own party to important positions (an act that angered Jefferson), then quietly left town early on the morning of Jefferson's inauguration day.

There was a loud silence between these two men that remained unbroken for 12 years: not a word, not a letter was exchanged. During the silence, Adams retired to his home in Quincy, Massachusetts, where he tended his land, read, wrote, and thought about the events he had been a part of. Jefferson served two terms as president, then retired to Monticello, his beloved estate in Virginia. He also farmed and read and wrote and thought.

These two revolutionary figures might have ended their lives with silence still between them if it hadn't been for their mutual friend, a fellow signer of the Declaration of Independence, Dr. Benjamin Rush. Rush was determined to mend the friendship and began talking first to one, then to the other. Finally Adams blurted out, "I always loved Jefferson and still love him!"

"This is enough for me," Jefferson told Rush when he learned what Adams had said.

Rush then urged Adams to forgive any past wrongs. "If I ever received or suspected any injury from him," Adams replied, "I have forgotten it long and long ago."

On January 1, 1812, 76-year-old John Adams sent 68-year-old Thomas Jefferson a letter wishing him a happy new year. Jefferson wrote back, "A letter from you calls up recollections very dear to my mind. It carries me back to the times when . . . we were fellow laborers in the same cause. . . ."

The silence had been broken. The old friendship blossomed again with a rich tenderness it did not have in its earlier years. Though Adams and Jefferson were not destined to see each other again face to face, they carried on a conversation by mail for the rest of their lives.

Through their letters, they talked about the country they had helped bring into being. They shared joys and consoled each other when loved ones passed away. They were both great readers and delighted in discussing what they'd read. And over and over again they assured each other of their friendship.

"I am sure that I really know many, many things," wrote Jefferson, "and none more surely than that I love you with all my heart."

Adams replied, "While I breathe I shall be your friend."

When he was close to ninety, Adams predicted he would, of course, be the first of the two to die. He was wrong. He and his old friend Thomas Jefferson died on the very same day—July 4, 1826—the 50th birthday of the United States of America. ●

Strategy Follow-up

Now complete the comparison chart for the second part of this selection. If you need more room to write, use a separate sheet of paper.

	Adams	Jefferson
How they served the young United States		
Retired where?		
Reaction toward renewing their friendship		
Feeling toward the other at the end of their lives		
Date of death		

✓Personal Checklist

Read each question and put a check (✓) in the correct box.

1. How well do you understand the information presented in this selection?
   - ☐ 3 (extremely well)
   - ☐ 2 (fairly well)
   - ☐ 1 (not well)

2. After reading this selection, how well could you describe the relationship between Thomas Jefferson and John Adams?
   - ☐ 3 (extremely well)
   - ☐ 2 (fairly well)
   - ☐ 1 (not well)

3. In Building Background, how well were you able to list at least three questions about either Jefferson, Adams or both?
   - ☐ 3 (extremely well)
   - ☐ 2 (fairly well)
   - ☐ 1 (not well)

4. In the Vocabulary Builder, how well were you able to put the vocabulary words on the appropriate clipboards?
   - ☐ 3 (extremely well)
   - ☐ 2 (fairly well)
   - ☐ 1 (not well)

5. In the Strategy Follow-up, how well were you able to complete the comparison chart?
   - ☐ 3 (extremely well)
   - ☐ 2 (fairly well)
   - ☐ 1 (not well)

Vocabulary Check

Look back at the work you did in the Vocabulary Builder. Then answer each question by circling the correct letter.

1. What are people sometimes called when they dress and act as if they are part of an upper class?
   a. aristocratic
   b. sturdy
   c. calm

2. What did Jefferson feel in regard to Adams's ability to inspire people?
   a. modesty
   b. stubbornness
   c. admiration

3. If a television viewer says, "That announcer sure is obnoxious," how does the viewer feel about the announcer?
   a. positive
   b. negative
   c. indifferent

4. Which of these situations depicts a person acting with modesty?
   a. A student tells everyone that her own projects are always the best in the class.
   b. An actor receives an award but insists that much of the credit belongs to his coworkers.
   c. A singer advertises that he has the best voice in show business.

5. What is another word for *sturdy*?
   a. strong
   b. unpopular
   c. obnoxious

Add the numbers that you just checked to get your Personal Checklist score. Fill in your score here. Then turn to page 215 and transfer your score onto Graph 1.

Personal	
Vocabulary	
Strategy	
Comprehension	
TOTAL SCORE	

✓ T

Check your answers with your teacher. Give yourself 1 point for each correct answer, and fill in your Vocabulary score here. Then turn to page 215 and transfer your score onto Graph 1.

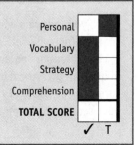

Personal	
Vocabulary	
Strategy	
Comprehension	
TOTAL SCORE	

✓ T

Strategy Check

Review the comparison chart that you completed in the Strategy Follow-up. Also review the rest of the selection. Then answer the following questions:

1. In what way were Adams and Jefferson different?
   a. in how they felt about each other at the end of their lives
   b. in their date of death
   c. in where they spent their retirement

2. In what way were they similar?
   a. in how they felt about each other at the end of their lives
   b. in their political views
   c. in the states they came from

3. How did Adams and Jefferson feel toward each other at the end of their lives?
   a. They were indifferent toward each other.
   b. They were angry with each other because of past injuries.
   c. They loved and admired each other.

4. Which of these events happened first?
   a. Adams and Jefferson met at the Second Continental Congress.
   b. Jefferson was elected President of the United States.
   c. Adams asked Jefferson to write the Declaration of Independence.

5. Which of these events happened last?
   a. Adams retired to his home in Quincy, Massachusetts.
   b. Dr. Benjamin Rush urged Adams and Jefferson to resume their friendship.
   c. The American Revolution was fought.

Comprehension Check

Review the selection if necessary. Then answer these questions:

1. When did Adams and Jefferson meet for the first time?
   a. in 1775, before the American Revolution
   b. in 1776, after Jefferson wrote the Declaration of Independence
   c. in 1777, during the American Revolution

2. What made the two men become fast friends?
   a. their similar personalities
   b. their desire for independence from England
   c. their similar backgrounds

3. What did John Adams do during the American Revolution?
   a. He fought in the army.
   b. He participated in the Virginia political scene.
   c. He served as ambassador to France.

4. How did the friendship between Adams and Jefferson change in the years immediately following the Revolution?
   a. The friendship suffered, and the men stopped speaking to each other.
   b. The friendship grew deeper and stronger.
   c. The friendship remained the same as it was before the war.

5. How did the men keep up their friendship in their old age?
   a. They wrote each other letters.
   b. They traveled great distances to visit each other.
   c. They moved close to each other and visited often.

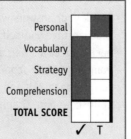

Check your answers with your teacher. Give yourself 1 point for each correct answer, and fill in your Strategy score here. Then turn to page 215 and transfer your score onto Graph 1.

Personal	
Vocabulary	
Strategy	
Comprehension	
TOTAL SCORE	✓ T

Check your answers with your teacher. Give yourself 1 point for each correct answer, and fill in your Comprehension score here. Then turn to page 215 and transfer your score onto Graph 1.

Personal	
Vocabulary	
Strategy	
Comprehension	
TOTAL SCORE	✓ T

Extending

Choose one or more of these activities:

WRITE A PERSONAL ESSAY ABOUT FRIENDSHIP

Adams and Jefferson became close friends during a time when they shared the goal of gaining independence. Life pulled them apart, but they finally were reunited and became closer than before. Consider their friendship, as well as the experiences that you have had in making and keeping friends. Then write a short personal essay about friendship. In your essay, you may want to answer questions such as these: What draws friends together in the first place? What makes a good friend? What should friends be willing to do for each other? How can friends avoid hurting each other? What can destroy a friendship? How can a friendship be maintained for many years?

FIND OUT ABOUT JEFFERSON'S OR ADAMS'S PRESIDENCY

What kind of presidents were Jefferson and Adams? How many terms did each man serve, and what important contributions did he make to this country and its people? Using the resources listed on this page or ones you find yourself, find out about the presidency of John Adams or Thomas Jefferson. If you'd like, divide the class into two groups, and work together to find and present your information.

LEARN ABOUT ABIGAIL ADAMS

John Adams's wife, Abigail Adams, was a strong supporter of women's rights at a time when such views were not widely accepted. She influenced her husband in a number of different ways throughout his life. Research the life of Abigail Adams, and present your findings in the form of a brief report.

Resources

Books

Cappon, Lester J., ed. *The Adams-Jefferson Letters: The Complete Correspondence Between Thomas Jefferson and Abigail and John Adams.* University of North Carolina Press, 1988.

Crisman, Ruth. *Thomas Jefferson: Man with a Vision.* Scholastic Biography. Scholastic, 1992.

Ellis, Joseph J. *Passionate Sage: The Character and Legacy of John Adams.* Norton, 2001.

Miller, Douglas T. *Thomas Jefferson and the Creation of America.* Makers of America. Facts on File, 1997.

Stefoff, Rebecca. *John Adams, 2nd President of the United States.* Presidents of the United States. Garrett Educational Corporation, 1988.

Web Sites

http://abigailadams.org/Abigail/abigail.html
This is the Web site of the Abigail Adams Historical Society. Click on "Abigail" for biographies and portraits of Abigail Adams.

http://www.whitehouse.gov/history/presidents/
This White House Web site offers brief biographies of the U.S. presidents.

Audio Recording

Ellis, Joseph J. *Passionate Sage.* Blackstone Audio Books, 1995.

Blessing from America

Building Background

The selection you are about to read is a chapter from the biography of a popular writer named Amy Tan. In 1985, Tan wrote the story "Rules of the Game" for a writing workshop. That story later became a part of Tan's book *The Joy Luck Club* (1989), which was on the *New York Times* bestseller list longer than any other book in 1989. It also won the L.A. Times Book Award and the National Book Award in 1989. Tan's books *The Kitchen God's Wife* and *The Hundred Secret Senses* also have appeared on the *New York Times* bestseller list, and all three books have been translated into 20 different languages. Tan also has written children's books, most notably *The Chinese Siamese Cat*.

biased

complication

immigrate

integrated

neurosurgeon

rebellion

segregated

Vocabulary Builder

1. Read each sentence below and decide if it is true or false. Write a **T** on the line if the sentence is true. Write an **F** if the sentence is false.

2. If you don't know the meaning of the boldfaced vocabulary word in a sentence, find the word in the selection and use context to figure it out. If using context doesn't help, use a dictionary.

3. Then save your work. You will refer to it again in the Vocabulary Check.

_____ a. A **biased** person has an open mind.

_____ b. If you encounter a **complication**, it probably will be difficult to figure a way out.

_____ c. When you **immigrate**, you move to a new country.

_____ d. An **integrated** neighborhood has residents of more than one culture or race.

_____ e. If you have a problem with your foot, you should visit a **neurosurgeon**.

_____ f. An example of a **rebellion** is the American Revolution.

_____ g. A club that is **segregated** will take anyone as a member.

Strategy Builder

How to Read a Biography

- A **biography** is the story of a real person's life, as written by someone else. The selection you are about to read is a chapter from a biography of author Amy Tan. It describes events from before Amy was born until she was 14 years old.

- Like all biographies, Amy's story is written in the **third-person point of view**. That means that the author describes Amy and her life using words such as *she, her, hers, they,* and *theirs.*

- The events in most biographies are organized in chronological order, or **sequence**. There are times, however, when events are told out of sequence. In such cases, the author uses a **flashback** to tell about an important event (or events) that happened earlier in a person's life or before the person was born. Then the author goes back and relates the events that led up to that important event.

- When you read a biography that contains a flashback, it is more important than ever to use **signal words** to help keep the sequence of events straight. Some signal words—such as *then, next,* and *a short time later*—help you link one smaller event to the next in a person's life. However, signal words such as *when she was eight years old* or *in the mid-1940s* help you see the sequence of the major events.

- Even though the flashback events in this selection are told out of sequence, you still can record the major events in this portion of Amy's biography on a **time line**. The Strategy Break and Strategy Follow-up will show you how to do it.

Blessing from America

by Barbara Kramer

As you begin reading this selection, remember that it contains a flashback. Use the signal words to help you keep track of the correct order of events.

Amy Tan's Chinese name is An-mei. It means "blessing from America." It was a fitting choice for the only daughter of parents who had immigrated to the United States from China only a few years earlier.

Amy was born in Oakland, California, on February 19, 1952. Her parents, John and Daisy Tan, had come to the United States from China in the late 1940s to escape the Communist takeover of their country. They left behind a homeland that had been torn apart by decades of war. . . .

Amy Tan's parents met in China in the mid-1940s. They fell in love, but there was a **complication**—she was already married. Chinese women had few rights at that time. Marriages were arranged for them by their families. Daisy Tan, whose maiden name was Tu Ching, was forced into a marriage to a man who was an abusive husband. She eventually left him, which was a crime in China, and for that she spent three months in prison.

John Tan had been educated in Beijing as an electrical engineer. Since he had been schooled by Christian missionaries, he could speak English, and during World War II he worked for the United States Information Service. That wartime experience made it easier for him to **immigrate** to the United States in 1947.

John Tan planned to get settled in the United States and work things out so that Daisy Tan could join him after she got out of jail. However, it was hard for him to begin life in a new country. He was haunted by the difficulties Daisy Tan was facing in China. "He felt responsible for her suffering," Amy Tan later explained. "He felt that if he placed his hopes in God, she would be saved and allowed to join him."

His prayers were answered. Daisy Tan succeed in getting a divorce after twelve years of marriage. Then she escaped on the last boat out of Shanghai in 1949 before the Communists took control of China.

With the Communist takeover, the once friendly relationship between the United States and China came to an end. The United States refused to recognize the People's Republic of China. Instead, they supported Chiang Kai-shek's Nationalist government on Taiwan. The new immigrants were completely cut off from their relatives and friends who remained in China. They did not know if they would ever see each other again.

John and Daisy Tan were married shortly after her arrival in the United States. John Tan had been offered a scholarship to study engineering in the United States, but he turned it down and enrolled at Berkeley Baptist Divinity School to become a minister. It was his way of thanking God for his wife's safety.

The Tans had three children—their daughter, Amy, and two sons, Peter and John, Jr. Peter was born in 1950; Amy in 1952; and John, Jr., in 1954.

Daisy Tan worked nights as a vocational nurse while raising her family. Vocational nurses, or licensed practical nurses, as they are called in some states, work under the direction of physicians or registered nurses.

 Stop here for the Strategy Break.

Strategy Break

If you were to stop and arrange the main events in this selection so far, your time line might look like the one below. Notice how the time line is in chronological order, even though the selection isn't.

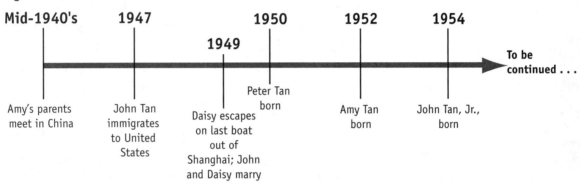

As you continue reading, keep paying attention to the major events and the words that signal when they happened. At the end of this selection, you will complete the time line on your own.

Go on reading.

In America, Amy's parents tried to keep their Chinese traditions. When Amy was young, her mother spoke to her "half in English, half in Mandarin." Mandarin is the language spoken in most of China. After Amy started school, her mother still spoke to her in Chinese, but Amy would answer in English. It was an early act of **rebellion** for a daughter who wanted to be like her American friends.

John and Daisy Tan knew that America offered their children many opportunities. They set high goals for their daughter. When Amy was five, they bought a piano so that she could begin piano lessons. When she was six, she was part of an education study done in Oakland, California. The psychologist who conducted the study concluded that Amy "was smart enough to become a physician." To her parents, that meant that she would grow up to be a doctor. Since they thought the brain was the most important part of the body, they decided she would be a **neurosurgeon**. "From the age of 6, I was led to believe that I would grow up to be a neurosurgeon by trade and a concert pianist by hobby," Tan once told an interviewer.

The family moved often—each time John Tan found a better position as a minister. They lived in Oakland, Fresno, and Berkeley, California, and in various suburbs of San Francisco, before finally settling in Santa Clara, California. Although they never left the Bay Area, each move meant a change in schools. "I moved every year, so I was constantly adjusting," Tan said.

Many immigrants from China settled in **segregated** communities like Chinatown in San Francisco. However, the Tans lived in **integrated** neighborhoods. From third grade on, Amy was the only Chinese-American girl in her class. She was always aware that she was not like the other students. "I remember trying to belong and feeling isolated. I felt ashamed of being different and ashamed of feeling that way," Tan said. She worried about what kind of treats her mother would bring to school for her birthdays. She was afraid it might be something Chinese that would embarrass her in front of the other students.

Amy entered her first writing contest when she was eight years old. She liked to read, and most of her reading material came from the local library. Unfortunately, the library was old. When Amy was in third grade, the building was found to be unsafe for library patrons. It had to be shut down.

A campaign was started to raise funds for a new building. Part of the campaign was to have children write essays about what the library meant to them. Amy entered the contest.

She patterned her essay after one of her father's sermons. She felt his sermons were honest, and he always used simple language. She began her essay, "My name is Amy Tan."

Another thing she remembered about her father's sermons was that he always asked for money at the end. She did that too. She clinched her plea by saying that she was donating seventeen cents to the library fund. It "was all the money I had in the world," Tan later said.

Although Amy was only eight years old, she already seemed to sense the importance of writing with emotion. She told how much she loved to read and how she enjoyed trips to the library with her father. Then she expressed her disappointment that the library had to be closed. "I missed it like a good friend," she wrote.

Students from the elementary schools and junior and senior high schools in the area entered the contest. There were 148 entries altogether representing three different age groups. Six winners, a girl and a boy from each group, were selected. Amy won in the elementary school division. Her essay was published in the Santa Rosa *Press-Democrat*, along with the essays of two other winners.

In spite of that early literary success, Tan says that she was steered away from pursuing English and writing by both her teachers and her parents. They encouraged her in subjects like science and mathematics—subjects in which she did well on standardized tests. According to Tan, Asian-American students traditionally do better on the science and mathematics portions of those tests. She believes that it is because the tests are culturally **biased**. In an essay Tan later wrote, called "Mother Tongue," she explained, "Math is precise; there is only one correct answer. Whereas, for me at least, the answers on English tests were always a judgment call, a matter of opinion and personal experience."

Although Amy was a good student, she sometimes struggled to make sense out of her studies. She tried to identify with the pilgrims and pioneers in her history books, but they had nothing to do with her own past. American history "was just a barrage of facts that had no relevance to me," she said.

The United States has been called a melting pot, which means that various races and cultures have been blended to produce a so-called American culture. Amy was learning that this was not entirely true. In the process of trying to be accepted, she found, she was "deliberately choosing the American things—hot dogs and apple pie—and ignoring the Chinese offerings."

Amy's attempts to be like her American friends caused tension between her mother and herself. Generations of teenagers have complained that their parents do not understand them. They point out the difference in their ages and the way times have changed since their parents were young. For Amy and Daisy Tan, those problems were multiplied. They not only had generational differences, there were cultural differences as well.

Tan says what she believes hurt her mother most was that Amy did not feel more responsibility toward her family. "She couldn't understand why I would want to be with my friends more than with her or with my family."

When Amy was fourteen, she became infatuated with a boy named Robert who was not Chinese. Much to Amy's dismay, her mother invited Robert's family to their house for dinner on Christmas Eve. Tan later wrote about that episode in an essay for

Seventeen magazine. She said that instead of turkey, her mother served raw fish. "The kitchen was littered with appalling mounds of raw food," Tan wrote. During dinner, Amy's family used chopsticks and reached across the table to help themselves to the platters of food, while Robert's family waited for the food to be passed to them. Amy's ultimate embarrassment came when her father ended the meal with a loud belch. "It's a polite Chinese custom to show you are satisfied," he explained, but Amy could only think about how her family must have looked to Robert.

After their guests left, Amy's mother gave her an early Christmas present.

It was a beige miniskirt, which was in fashion at the time. Then Daisy Tan said, "You want to be the same as American girls on the outside. But inside you must always be Chinese. You must be proud you are different. Your only shame is to have shame."

It would be many years before Amy Tan fully understood her mother's words, yet that evening she did learn one thing: her mother did know how embarrassed Amy was, and she understood Amy's feelings. Looking back on that time, Tan realized how her mother had decided what to serve for that dinner—"she had chosen all my favorite foods," Tan wrote. ●

Strategy Follow-up

On another sheet of paper, complete the time line for this chapter of Amy Tan's biography. Begin by copying the time line from the Strategy Break, and then fill in the major events and dates that are described in the second part of this selection. The first date has been supplied for you.

1957

✓Personal Checklist

Read each question and put a check (✓) in the correct box.

1. How well were you able to use the information in Building Background to help you understand why Amy won a writing contest when she was eight years old?
   - ☐ 3 (extremely well)
   - ☐ 2 (fairly well)
   - ☐ 1 (not well)

2. In the Vocabulary Builder, how well were you able to identify whether each sentence was true or false?
   - ☐ 3 (extremely well)
   - ☐ 2 (fairly well)
   - ☐ 1 (not well)

3. How well were you able to complete the time line in the Strategy Follow-up?
   - ☐ 3 (extremely well)
   - ☐ 2 (fairly well)
   - ☐ 1 (not well)

4. How well do you understand why Amy's parents named her An-mei?
   - ☐ 3 (extremely well)
   - ☐ 2 (fairly well)
   - ☐ 1 (not well)

5. How well do you understand why Amy was embarrassed in front of Robert's family one Christmas Eve?
   - ☐ 3 (extremely well)
   - ☐ 2 (fairly well)
   - ☐ 1 (not well)

Vocabulary Check

Look back at the work you did in the Vocabulary Builder. Then answer each question by circling the correct letter.

1. Which word best describes a complication?
   - a. embarrassment
   - b. rebellion
   - c. difficulty

2. What is another word for *rebellion*?
   - a. revolt
   - b. payment
   - c. anger

3. If a neurosurgeon performs surgery on the brain and the nervous system, to what body part does the word part *neuro* refer?
   - a. heart
   - b. lungs
   - c. nerves

4. If someone has her mind made up about an issue before she hears all the facts, how would you describe her?
   - a. fair-minded
   - b. biased
   - c. intelligent

5. Which word is an antonym of *segregated*?
   - a. integrated
   - b. immigrated
   - c. biased

Add the numbers that you just checked to get your Personal Checklist score. Fill in your score here. Then turn to page 215 and transfer your score onto Graph 1.

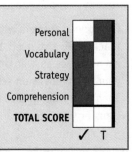

Check your answers with your teacher. Give yourself 1 point for each correct answer, and fill in your Vocabulary score here. Then turn to page 215 and transfer your score onto Graph 1.

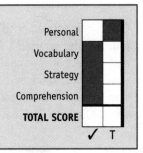

Strategy Check

Review the time line that you completed for the Strategy Follow-up. Also review the rest of the selection. Then answer these questions:

1. In what year did Amy begin piano lessons?

    a. 1957

    b. 1960

    c. 1966

2. How old was Amy when her parents decided she would become a neurosurgeon?

    a. five years old

    b. six years old

    c. fourteen years old

3. Approximately how many years apart were Amy and each of her brothers born?

    a. six years

    b. four years

    c. two years

4. In what year did Amy write an award-winning essay?

    a. 1957

    b. 1960

    c. 1966

5. Which of the following is *not* an example of signal words?

    a. when Amy was five

    b. after their guests left

    c. looking back on that time

Comprehension Check

Review the selection if necessary. Then answer the following questions:

1. Why did Daisy Tan marry a man who abused her?

    a. He fooled her into believing that he was kind and gentle.

    b. She loved him before the marriage but then changed her mind.

    c. Her marriage was arranged by her family, and she had no choice.

2. Why did John Tan become a minister?

    a. He wanted to thank God for Daisy's safety.

    b. He had no other options available at the time.

    c. He had always planned on entering the ministry.

3. How did Amy say she felt every time she entered a new school?

    a. angry at her parents and brothers

    b. ashamed of being different

    c. afraid of her teachers

4. What was the purpose of Amy's prize-winning essay?

    a. to explain how difficult it is to be different

    b. to raise funds for a new library building

    c. to teach people about the history of Chinese Americans

5. What did Daisy Tan mean when she told Amy, "Your only shame is to have shame"?

    a. Amy should realize that the Chinese culture is better than American culture.

    b. Amy should realize that the American culture is better than Chinese culture.

    c. Amy should be proud of her Chinese heritage, not embarrassed about it.

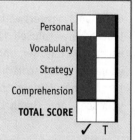

Check your answers with your teacher. Give yourself 1 point for each correct answer, and fill in your Strategy score here. Then turn to page 215 and transfer your score onto Graph 1.

Personal
Vocabulary
Strategy
Comprehension
TOTAL SCORE

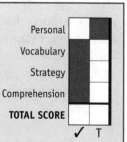

Check your answers with your teacher. Give yourself 1 point for each correct answer, and fill in your Comprehension score here. Then turn to page 215 and transfer your score onto Graph 1.

Personal
Vocabulary
Strategy
Comprehension
TOTAL SCORE

Extending

Choose one or more of these activities:

READ THE REST OF AMY TAN'S BIOGRAPHY

The selection you just read is a chapter from the book *Amy Tan: Author of* The Joy Luck Club by Barbara Kramer. (For information on the book, see the resource section on this page.) Locate and read the entire book, and then make a time line of some of the significant events described in the biography.

READ, VIEW, OR LISTEN TO MORE OF AMY TAN'S WORK

Amy Tan's work has been produced in a variety of ways. (See the resource section on this page for a partial listing.) Her most famous book, *The Joy Luck Club*, was made into a movie, which is now on video. Tan herself recorded audiocassettes of many of her books and stories. And her books are available in almost every library. Read, view, or listen to more of Amy Tan's work. Then write a short review in which you summarize the story and give your opinion of it. If any of your classmates chose this activity too, you might share your opinions in a panel discussion.

RESEARCH ANOTHER LIFE STORY

Research other real-life stories by asking adults you know well—perhaps parents, grandparents, or close family friends—about the most memorable events in their lives and the obstacles they overcame along the way. Then create a time line of the main events in their lives.

Resources

Books

Kramer, Barbara. *Amy Tan: Author of* The Joy Luck Club. People to Know. Enslow Publishers, 1996.

Tan, Amy. *The Hundred Secret Senses.* Ivy Books, 1996.

———. *The Joy Luck Club.* Prentice, 1994.

———. *The Kitchen God's Wife.* Ivy Books, 1992.

Web Site

http://www.luminarium.org/contemporary/amytan/index.html
This Web site provides links to interviews with Amy Tan, reviews of her work, and other related information.

Audio Recordings

Amy Tan. *Amy Tan Two-Pack* (abridged). Dove Books Audio, 1998.

———. *The Hundred Secret Senses* (abridged). Dove Books Audio, 1995.

Video/DVD

The Joy Luck Club. Walt Disney Home Video, 2002.

Learning New Words

VOCABULARY

From Lesson 20
- integrated
- segregated

Antonyms

An antonym is a word that means the opposite of another word. For example, in "Blessing from America," the author uses the antonyms *segregated* and *integrated* to describe different kinds of neighborhoods. *Segregated* refers to neighborhoods whose residents are all from similar backgrounds. *Integrated* refers to neighborhoods whose residents are from a variety of backgrounds.

Draw a line from each word in Column 1 to its antonym in Column 2.

Column 1	Column 2
freezing	excited
joyful	mournful
calm	rare
blessing	boiling
common	curse

Combining Forms

A combining form is a word part that is added to another word or combining form to make a new word. For example, *psycho-* is a combining form. If you add it to the word *therapy,* you create the word *psychotherapy,* which means "mental therapy."

From Lesson 17
- quadriplegics

quadri-

The combining form *quadri-* (also spelled *quadr-*) means "four" or "having four _____." In Lesson 17 you learned that *quadriplegics* have paralysis of all four limbs.

Draw a line from each word in Column 1 to its definition in Column 2. Use a dictionary if necessary.

Column 1	Column 2
quadrangle	square dance for four couples
quadriceps	four-sided space or court
quadrille	record by using four channels
quadrennial	occurring every four years
quadraphonic	thigh muscle with four heads

neuro-

The combining form *neuro-* forms words related to nerves, nerve tissue, or the nervous system—including the brain. For example, when Amy Tan was six, her parents decided that she would become a neurosurgeon. A *neurosurgeon* is someone who performs surgery on the brain or other parts of the nervous system.

Complete each sentence with one of the words below. Use a dictionary if necessary.

neuron   neurosis   neurology   neuromuscular   neurotransmitter

1. The study of the nervous system and its diseases is called
   _____.

2. A _____ ailment is a problem having to do with both the nerves and the muscles.

3. A _____ is one of the impulse-conducting cells of which the brain, spinal cord, and nerves are composed.

4. A mental disorder in which a person suffers from depression, anxiety, or compulsive behavior is known as a _____.

5. A _____ is a chemical substance that carries or stops impulses from traveling between nerve cells.

VOCABULARY

From Lesson 20
• neurosurgeon

Graphing Your Progress

The graphs on page 215 will help you track your progress as you work through this book. Follow these directions to fill in the graphs:

Graph 1

1. Start by looking across the top of the graph for the number of the lesson you just finished.

2. In the first column for that lesson, write your Personal Checklist score in both the top and bottom boxes. (Notice the places where *13* is filled in on the sample.)

3. In the second column for that lesson, fill in your scores for the Vocabulary, Strategy, and Comprehension Checks.

4. Add the three scores, and write their total in the box above the letter *T*. (The *T* stands for "Total." The ✓ stands for "Personal Checklist.")

5. Compare your scores. Does your Personal Checklist score match or come close to your total scores for that lesson? Why or why not?

Graph 2

1. Again, start by looking across the top of the graph for the number of the lesson you just finished.

2. In the first column for that lesson, shade the number of squares that match your Personal Checklist score.

3. In the second column for that lesson, shade the number of squares that match your total score.

4. As you fill in this graph, you will be able to check your progress across the book. You'll be able to see your strengths and areas of improvement. You'll also be able to see areas where you might need a little extra help. You and your teacher can discuss ways to work on those areas.

Graph 1

For each lesson, enter the scores from your Personal Checklist and your Vocabulary, Strategy, and Comprehension Checks. Total your scores and then compare them. Does your Personal Checklist score match or come close to your total scores for that lesson? Why or why not?

Go down to Graph 2 and shade your scores for the lesson you just completed.

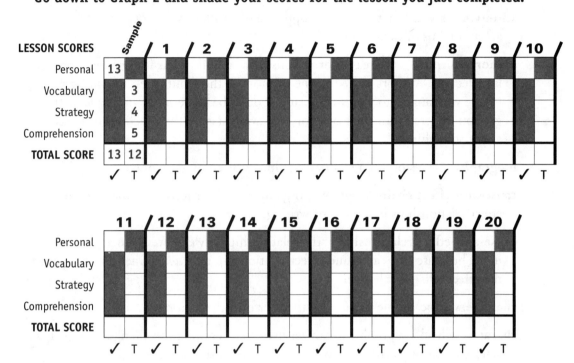

Graph 2

Now record your overall progress. In the first column for the lesson you just completed, shade the number of squares that match your Personal Checklist score. In the second column for that lesson, shade the number of squares that match your total score. As you fill in this graph, you will be able to check your progress across the book.

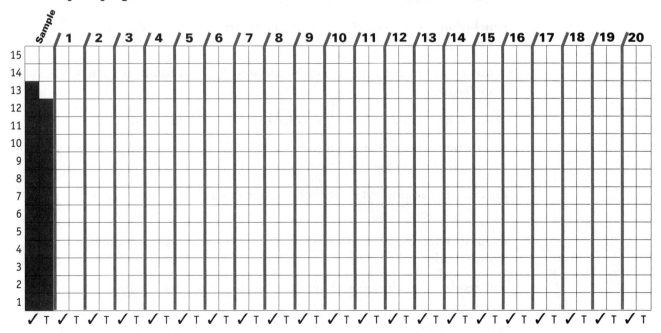

Glossary of Terms

This glossary includes definitions for important terms introduced in this book.

antonym   a word that means the opposite of another word. *Quickly* and *slowly* are antonyms of each other.

author's purpose   the reason or reasons that an author has for writing a particular selection. Authors write for one or more of these purposes: to *entertain* (make you laugh), to *inform* (explain or describe something), to *persuade* (try to get you to agree with their opinion), to *express* (share their feelings or ideas about something).

biography   the story of a real person's life, written by someone else.

cause-and-effect chain   a graphic organizer used for recording the cause-and-effect relationships in a piece of writing.

cause-and-effect relationship   the relationship between events in a piece of writing. The cause in a cause-and-effect relationship tells *why* something happened; the effect tells *what* happened.

characters   the people or animals that perform the action in a story.

character wheel   a graphic organizer used for recording the changes that a character goes through from the beginning to the end of a story.

comparing   looking at how two or more things are alike.

comparison chart   a graphic organizer used for showing how two or more people, places, things, or events are alike and different.

compound word   a word that is made up of two words put together. *Breakdown* and *snowdrifts* are examples of compound words.

concept map   a graphic organizer used for recording the main ideas and supporting details in a piece of writing.

conclusion   a decision that is reached after thinking about certain facts or information.

context   information that comes before and after a word or situation to help you understand it.

contrasting   looking at how two or more things are different.

description   in nonfiction, the organizational pattern that explains what something is, what it does, or how and why it works.

dialect   the unique style of speech used by groups of people in particular places and/or times.

dynamic characters   characters that change in some way from the beginning of a story to the end.

end result   the solution a character or characters try that finally solves the problem in a story.

essay   a brief piece of writing that expresses a writer's opinions or views about a particular topic.

event   a happening. The plot of any story contains one or more events during which the characters try to solve their problems.

exaggeration   an intentional overstatement of facts or events so that their meanings are made stronger. Exaggeration is not meant to fool the reader but to create humorous results.

fact   a statement that can be proved.

fiction   stories about made-up characters or events. Forms of fiction include short stories, science fiction, mystery, and folktales.

first-person point of view   the perspective, or viewpoint, of one of the characters in a story. That character uses words such as *I, me, my,* and *mine* to tell the story.

flashback   an event that is told out of sequence and describes something that happened in the past.

graphic organizer   a chart, graph, or drawing used to show how the main ideas in a piece of writing are organized and related.

headings   the short titles given throughout a piece of nonfiction. The headings often state the main ideas of a selection.

informational article   a piece of writing that gives facts and details about a particular subject, or topic.

interview   a piece of writing that records the questions and answers given during a conversation.

journal   a book or notebook in which a person records his or her thoughts and feelings about a particular event or situation.

main idea   the most important idea of a paragraph, section, or whole piece of writing.

main idea table   a graphic organizer used for recording the main ideas and supporting details in a piece of writing.

multiple-meaning word   a word that has more than one meaning. The word *sledge* is a multiple-meaning word whose meanings include "large, heavy hammer" and "heavy sleigh or sled."

mystery   a story that contains a kind of puzzle that the characters must solve.

narrator   the person or character who is telling a story.

nonfiction   writing that gives facts and information about real people, events, and topics. Informational articles, newspaper articles, and biographies are some forms of nonfiction.

opinion   a statement, or belief, that cannot be proved as fact.

organizational pattern   in nonfiction, the pattern in which the text is written and organized. Common organizational patterns include description, cause-effect, sequence, compare-contrast, and problem-solution.

outline   a framework for organizing the main ideas and supporting details in a piece of writing. Some outlines are organized according to a system of Roman numerals (I, II, III, and so on), capital letters, Arabic numerals (1, 2, 3, and so on), and lowercase letters.

plot   the sequence of events in a piece of writing.

point of view   the perspective, or viewpoint, from which a story is told.

prediction   a kind of guess that is based on the context clues given in a story.

prefix   a word part added to the beginning of a word to make a new word. Adding a prefix usually changes the word's meaning and function. For example, the suffix *un-* means "not" or "the opposite of." So adding *un-* to *true* changes *true* to its opposite meaning.

problem   difficulty or question that a character must solve or answer.

problem-solution frame   a graphic organizer used for recording the problem, solutions, and end result in a piece of writing.

root word   a word to which prefixes and suffixes are added to make other words.

science fiction   fiction that is often based on real or possible scientific developments. Much science fiction is set in outer space, in some future time.

sequence   the order of events in a piece of writing. The sequence shows what happens or what to do first, second, and so on.

sequence chain   a graphic organizer used for recording the sequence of events in a piece of writing. Sequence chains are used mostly for shorter periods of time, and time lines are used mostly for longer periods of time.

setting   the time and place in which a story happens.

short story   a work of fiction that usually can be read in one sitting.

signal words   words and phrases that tell when something happens or when to do something. Examples of signal words are *first, next, finally, after lunch, two years later,* and *in 1820.*

solution   the things that characters or people do to solve a problem.

specialized vocabulary   words that are related to a particular subject, or topic. Specialized vocabulary words in the selection "The First Gliders" include *drag, gravity,* and *lift.*

static characters   characters that stay the same from the beginning of a story to the end.

story map   a graphic organizer used for recording the main parts of a story: its title, setting, character, problem, events, and solution.

suffix   a word part that is added to the end of a word. Adding a suffix usually changes the word's meaning and function. For example, the suffix *-less* means "without," so the word *painless* changes from the noun *pain* to an adjective meaning "without pain."

summary   a short description. A summary describes what has happened so far in a piece of fiction, or what the main ideas are in a piece of nonfiction.

supporting details   details that describe or explain the main idea of a paragraph, section, or whole piece of text.

synonym   a word that has the same meaning as another word. *Fast* and *quick* are synonyms of each other.

third-person point of view   the perspective, or viewpoint, of a narrator who is not a character in a story. That narrator uses words such as *she, her, he, his, they,* and *their* to tell the story.

time line   a graphic organizer used for recording the sequence of events in a piece of writing. Time lines are used mostly for longer periods of time, and sequence chains are used mostly for shorter periods of time.

title   the name of a piece of writing.

tone   the attitude that a story conveys.

topic   the subject of a piece of writing. The topic is what the selection is all about.

Acknowledgments

Acknowledgment is gratefully made to the following publishers, authors, and agents for permission to reprint these works. Every effort has been made to determine copyright owners. In the case of any omissions, the Publisher will be pleased to make suitable acknowledgments in future editions.

"Across the Frozen Sea" by Jessie V. Robinette, from COBBLESTONE's November 1990 issue: *To the North Pole,* © 1990 Cobblestone Publishing, 30 Grove Street, Suite C, Peterborough, NH 03458. All Rights Reserved. Reprinted by permission of Carus Publishing Company.

"Animals on the Job" by Lynda Jones. From *Science World,* September 6, 1996, issue. Copyright © 1996 by Scholastic Inc. Reprinted by permission of Scholastic Inc.

"Blessing from America" by Barbara Kramer, adapted from *People to Know: Amy Tan, Author of The Joy Luck Club.* Published by Enslow Publishing, Inc., Berkeley Heights, New Jersey. Copyright © 1996 by Barbara Kramer. Reprinted by permission of the publisher.

"The Cobra's Venom," reprinted from *Man in a Cage,* © 1972 by Robert Elgin, by permission of Collier Associates, PO Box 20149, West Palm Beach, FL 33416.

"The Craft of Writing." Adapted and reprinted with permission from *How I Came to Be a Writer* by Phyllis Reynolds Naylor. Copyright © 1978 by Phyllis Reynolds Naylor. Published by Atheneum Publishers, Inc.

"Elegy for Woodward" by Richard Bedard, from *Weatherwise,* April/May 1997, Vol. 50, No. 2, pp. 19–23. Reprinted with permission of the Helen Dwight Reid Educational Foundation. Published by Heldref Publications, 1319 Eighteenth St., NW, Washington, DC 20036-1802. Copyright © 1997.

"The First Gliders" from *Soaring: A First Book* by Phyllis J. Perry. Copyright © 1997 by Phyllis J. Perry. Reprinted by permission of the publisher.

"Follow Your Dreams" by Louise Tolle Huffman, from COBBLESTONE's November 1990 issue: *To the North Pole,* © 1990 Cobblestone Publishing, 30 Grove Street, Suite C, Peterborough, NH 03458. All Rights Reserved. Reprinted by permission of Carus Publishing Company.

"The Homesick Chicken" by Edward D. Hoch. Copyright © 1976 by Davis Publications, Inc. Reprinted by permission of the author.

"The Impossible Race" reprinted by permission of *Cricket* magazine, June 1996, Vol. 23, No.10, © 1996 by Gary L. Blackwood.

"The Long Carry" reprinted by permission of William Durbin and *Boys Life,* September 1998, published by Boy Scouts of America.

"A Revolutionary Friendship" by Connie Nordhielm Wooldridge as appeared in *Cricket,* July 1994, Vol. 21, No. 11. Reprinted by permission of the author.

"Solo Flight" by Allen Ury. From *More Scary Stories When You're Home Alone* by Allen Ury © 1996. Used with permission of Lowell House.

"Sons and Daughters" from *Tales of Gold Mountain: Stories of the Chinese in the New World*. Text copyright © 1989 by Paul Yee. First published in Canada by Groundwood Books/Douglas & McIntyre. Reprinted by permission of the publisher.

"The Storm" from *Tales from the Plum Grove Hills* by Jesse Stuart. Copyright © 1946 E. P. Dutton & Co.; copyright © 1997 The Jesse Stuart Foundation. Used by permission of the Jesse Stuart Foundation, P.O. Box 391, Ashland, KY 41114.

Excerpt from *Walking Through the Dark* by Phyllis Reynolds Naylor. Copyright © 1976 by Phyllis Reynolds Naylor. Published by Atheneum Publishers, Inc.

"When Freedom Came" from *Long Journey Home: Stories from Black History* by Julius Lester. Copyright © 1972 by Julius Lester. Used by permission of Doubleday, a division of Random House, Inc.

"Zoo's New Top Banana" by Stacey Singer, as appeared in *The Chicago Tribune*, Sunday, August 18, 1996. Reprinted by permission of *The Chicago Tribune*.